THE REMINISCENCES OF

Admiral Bruce DeMars
U.S. Navy (Retired)

INTERVIEWED BY
Paul Stillwell

U.S. Naval Institute • Annapolis, Maryland

Copyright © 2012

Preface

The list of flag officers who have served as Director, Naval Nuclear Propulsion, comprises a small, exclusive group. Only six individuals have held the billet, going back to Admiral Hyman G. Rickover, who began laying the foundations in the late 1940s for the U.S. Navy's fleet of nuclear-powered ships. One of his early successors was Admiral Bruce DeMars, who took over in 1988, six years after Rickover left active duty.

In the memoir that follows, Admiral DeMars traces much of his success back to his growing up in Chicago, which he describes as "the city of the possible." Time after time, he cites the Chicago outlook, which can be summed up as "Work hard, tell the truth, obey the rules that must be followed, and ignore the others." Obviously, some judgment is required to tell the difference. Indeed, his appointment to the Naval Academy in 1953 came about through a bit of political chicanery that broke the rules. It came from a Chicago congressman who didn't represent the district in which DeMars lived. But he owed a favor, and someone else owed a favor, and indirectly the payoff came in the form of a spot at the Naval Academy.

DeMars soon discovered what sort of Navy he was getting into. When he showed up in Annapolis for his physical, his blood pressure initially tested too high for him to be admitted. A kindly hospital corpsman suggested that DeMars take a nap. The corpsman waited until the prospective midshipman was asleep, then took another reading, which was satisfactory. DeMars thought to himself, "If you've got sailors like that, this is a great organization." DeMars's Naval Academy yearbook entry described him as one who engaged in good-natured teasing. During our interviews I enjoyed his down-to-earth manner and frequent injections of humor.

In his initial commissioned service, the new ensign served in amphibious warfare ships and decided there must be another option. He volunteered for submarine duty and eventually rose to the pinnacle of that arm of the Navy, serving for three years in the mid-1980s as Deputy Chief of Naval Operations (Submarine Warfare). In the meantime, he qualified as a submariner in the diesel boat *Capitaine* (SS-336). After the ritual hazing when interviewed by Admiral Rickover, DeMars was selected for the nuclear power program and began moving up. His first assignment in the program was the USS *George*

Washington (SSBN-598), the first U.S. nuclear-powered ballistic missile submarine. He joined a handpicked crew, and his professional development grew considerably.

Fitted in with instructor assignments in Nuclear Power School and Submarine School, he served in three attack submarines that had special operations against the Soviet Navy as their principal charter, the *Snook* (SSN-592), *Sturgeon* (SSN-637), and *Cavalla* (SSN-684). His first skipper in the *Snook* was Commander James Watkins, future Chief of Naval Operations. DeMars observed and made notes, building up a seabag of professional skills in how to operate covertly against the Soviets: trailing their submarines, observing missile launches, taking photographs through the periscope, and collecting electronic signatures for intelligence purposes—all without being detected. He modeled his later actions on Watkins's aggressiveness.

In the *Sturgeon*, DeMars was executive officer to Commander William Bohannon, another aggressive skipper. DeMars's memories of that tour include his relations with the enlisted crew, empowering them to become involved in the special operations process. As skipper of the *Cavalla*, DeMars continued to emulate his mentors in conducting successful operations against the Soviets.

Along with his operational capabilities, DeMars also used his expertise as a nuclear engineer, heading the Atlantic Fleet's Nuclear Propulsion Examining Board. Following the Rickover model, he and his team visited dozens of ships to test for training of personnel and proper operation of nuclear power plants, with particular emphasis on safety and reliability. Other steps in his career progression included Pentagon tours in the submarine directorate and his only flag assignment outside of submarines. In the early 1980s, he was Commander Naval Base Guam with additional duties as Commander U.S. Naval Forces Marianas and CinCPac Representative Guam/Trust Territory of the Pacific Islands. His recollections tell of being "El Supremo" in that area on behalf of the United States and experiencing a life-style much different from his tours in submarines.

DeMars likes to describe himself as "a different kind of admiral:" one who never attended postgraduate school and never served as aide to a flag officer or civilian official. He told himself and others that his main goal was to command an attack submarine on special operations, and if he didn't like what came after that, he could leave the Navy and do something else. As it happened, he continued to be promoted and to have jobs that he liked. Eventually he became the DCNO for submarines and in that role was one of the major warfare "barons" in the Pentagon. Among his challenges was to get approval for the funds necessary to operate and modernize the submarine force. He also wound up with a collateral duty that proved controversial, as he describes in some detail. In 1986 he was president of a Navy selection board that chose officers for promotion to the rank of captain. The Secretary of the Navy, John Lehman, was not pleased with the results, and a brouhaha ensued. DeMars stood his ground and eventually prevailed.

The admiral's final active duty billet, from 1988 to 1996 was as director of the nuclear power program, Admiral Rickover's former job. In that role, as when he was in OpNav earlier, he continued to push for funding for nuclear power plants. He led an organization that had 19 different departments reporting directly to him about the nuclear navy. During that time the Soviet Union dissolved, the Cold War ended, and DeMars had to adjust to reduced funding as the nation looked for a "peace dividend." In that circumstance, he had to keep the industrial base going and to look toward ever-more capable, and affordable, submarines. Among his duties were those of riding new nuclear ships on initial sea trials and interviewing candidates for the nuclear power program.

The genesis for this oral history came from Vice Admiral Robert Dunn, who has recently stepped down as president of the Naval Historical Foundation. He suggested the project to Admiral DeMars, and then the capable staff of NHF—Captain Todd Creekman and Dr. David Winkler—carried through with the administration of it. John Maloney, who worked for Admiral DeMars in the Naval Reactors office as a civilian, did the initial excellent transcription of the interview tapes. I have done some editing and annotating of the initial transcript, and Admiral DeMars has made additional changes and blessed the final product. The Naval Historical Foundation donated the oral history to the Naval Institute collection so that it can be made widely available. Janis Jorgensen of the Naval Institute has overseen the printing and binding of the volume.

Paul Stillwell
U.S. Naval Institute/Naval Historical Foundation
November 2012

ADMIRAL BRUCE DEMARS
UNITED STATES NAVY (RETIRED)

Personal Data:

Born: 3 June 1935 in Chicago, Illinois

Parents: Leon and Isabelle DeMars

Married: Margaret Ann Milburn, 7 June 1957

Children: Bruce F. DeMars, born 2 March 1958
Margaret A. DeMars Troup, born 17 May 1960

Qualifications: Bachelor of Science (Naval Science), U.S. Naval Academy, 1957
Graduate of Armed Forces Staff College, 1967

Dates of rank: Midshipman, 29 June 1953
Ensign, 7 June 1957
Lieutenant (junior grade), 7 December 1958
Lieutenant, 1 June 1961
Lieutenant Commander, 1 March 1966
Commander, 1 July 1970
Captain, 1 July 1976
Designated Rear Admiral while serving in billets commensurate with that grade, August 1981
Rear Admiral, 1 October 1982
Vice Admiral, 5 December 1985
Admiral, 1 November 1988

Assignments and Duties:

Jun 1953 – Jun 1957	U.S. Naval Academy, Annapolis, Maryland
Jun 1957 – Sep 1957	Naval Amphibious Base, Coronado, California, student
Sep 1957 – Nov 1957	USS *Telfair* (APA-210), deck division officer
Nov 1957 – May 1958	USS *Okanogan* (APA-220), deck division officer
May 1958 – Jan 1959	Naval Submarine School, New London, Connecticut, student
Jan 1959 – Mar 1960	USS *Capitaine* (SS-336), supply officer/weapons officer
Mar 1960 – Sep 1960	Naval Nuclear Power School, Mare Island, Vallejo, California, student
Sep 1960 – Apr 1961	Atomic Energy Commission, Naval Reactor Operations Office, Schenectady, New York, student
Apr 1961 – Sep 1962	USS *George Washington* (SSBN-598) (Blue), main propulsion assistant and damage control assistant

Sep 1962 – Oct 1964	Naval Nuclear Power School, Mare Island, Vallejo, California, instructor
Oct 1964 – Dec 1966	USS *Snook* (SSN-592), navigator/operations officer
Dec 1966 – Jun 1967	Armed Forces Staff College, Norfolk, Virginia, student
Jun 1967 – Jul 1969	USS *Sturgeon* (SSN-637), executive officer
Jul 1969 – Jun 1971	Naval Submarine School, Groton, Connecticut, director, executive division, officers' training department
Jun 1971 – Oct 1971	Division of Naval Reactors, U.S. Atomic Energy Commission, Washington, D.C., student
Oct 1971 – Dec 1971	Staff, Commander Submarine Force, U.S. Atlantic Fleet, duty under instruction
Dec 1971 – Feb 1973	*Cavalla* (SSN-684), prospective commanding officer
Feb 1973 – Jan 1975	USS *Cavalla* (SSN-684), commanding officer
Jan 1975 – Jul 1975	Staff, Commander Submarine Squadron Ten, deputy commander for training
Jul 1975 – Jun 1978	CinCLantFlt Nuclear Propulsion Examining Board, senior member
Jun 1978 – May 1979	Commander Submarine Development Squadron 12
May 1979 – Aug 1981	Office of the Chief of Naval Operations, Deputy Director, Attack Submarine Division
Aug 1981 – Jun 1983	Commander Naval Base Guam with additional duties as Commander U.S. Naval Forces Marianas and CinCPac Representative Guam/Trust Territory of the Pacific Islands
Jul 1983 – Nov 1985	Office of the Chief of Naval Operations, Deputy Chief, Submarine Warfare (OP-02B)
Nov 1985 – Oct 1988	Office of the Chief of Naval Operations, Assistant Chief of Naval Operations, Undersea Warfare (OP-02)
Oct 1988 – Sep 1996	Director, Naval Nuclear Propulsion
1 October 1996	Retired from active duty

Medals and Awards:

Distinguished Service Medal with one gold star in lieu of subsequent award
Legion of Merit with three gold stars in lieu of subsequent awards
Meritorious Service Medal with one gold star in lieu of second award
Navy Commendation Medal with one gold star in lieu of second award
Navy Achievement Medal
Navy Unit Commendation
Meritorious Unit Commendation with two bronze stars
Navy "E" Ribbon
Navy Expeditionary Medal
National Defense Service Medal with two bronze stars
Vietnam Service Medal with one bronze star
Navy Overseas Service Medal

Deed of Gift

The U.S. Naval Institute is hereby authorized to make available to individuals, libraries, and other repositories of its choosing the tapes and/or transcripts of four oral history interviews concerning the life and naval career of the undersigned. The interviews were recorded on 3 May 2012, 10 May 2012, 17 May 2012, and 24 May 2012 in collaboration with Paul Stillwell for the U.S. Naval Institute and the Naval Historical Foundation. The Naval Institute and the Naval Historical Foundation may also, at their discretion, use the material in electronic/digital format, including posting on the Internet.

The undersigned does hereby release and assign to the U.S. Naval Institute the rights and title to these interviews, with the exception that the undersigned retains the right to use the material for his own purposes, as he sees fit. The copyright in both the oral and transcribed versions shall be the property of the U.S. Naval Institute. The tape recordings of the interviews are and will remain the property of the U.S. Naval Institute.

Signed and sealed this 9TH day of Nov 2012.

Bruce DeMars
Admiral, U.S. Navy (Retired)

Interview Number 1 with Admiral Bruce DeMars, U.S. Navy (Retired)
Place: Admiral DeMars's home in Alexandria, Virginia
Date: Thursday, 3 May 2012

Paul Stillwell: Good morning, Admiral. It's a pleasure to get this series started with you. Could you please begin in the conventional way—when and where you were born, and something about your parents?

Admiral DeMars: Sure, Paul. I'm really a dyed-in-the-wool Chicagoan, was born in Chicago. My dad was a mailman, and my mother worked second shift downtown at the Time-Life Building, so I came from a working family. Their names were Isabelle and Leon. My dad went in the Navy after Pearl Harbor, was a postal clerk on a destroyer in the Pacific. We didn't see him for three years. And so that's how I initially got interested in the Navy.

Chicago, of course, is a very ethnic city, and I grew up knowing what Lithuanians, Poles, Swedes, Germans, Serbs—what they all were. I won't tell you the nicknames we used in those days for those ethnicities, because they're not appropriate now. Went to grammar school, Emmet Grammar School, my brother and I. Had about 3,000 Jewish kids there, so on the Jewish high holidays my brother and I were there all by ourselves. But I came to know the whole Jewish culture very well and still very fond of it to this day.

I met my future wife, Margaret Ann Milburn, in high school when I was a junior and she was a sophomore. We had a long courtship after that. I played on the football team for four years. The high school was predominantly Czechoslovakian and Jewish.

Paul Stillwell: What was the name of it?

Admiral DeMars: Farragut High School, which may have been a forerunner of my future career.* I played football, center and linebacker, played both ways, for four years. We never won a game [chuckle]. But the school always won the band competition, the choral competition, the battle of the books, on and on, because it was a very cerebral place, but it wasn't much of an athletic powerhouse.

Paul Stillwell: How far south did you live? I remember Comiskey Park was at 35th Street.†

Admiral DeMars: Yes, we were at 2300 South and a little farther west, between Crawford and Kedzie, Crawford or Pulaski, depending upon your ethnicity is what you called it. My brother and I always had jobs. We used to carry 200 newspapers seven days a week. The nice thing about it was that we didn't have to collect, and so we made 30 bucks a month doing that, which was not bad money in those days.

Paul Stillwell: What was your brother's name?

Admiral DeMars: Chuck, Charles.

Paul Stillwell: Is he still living?

Admiral DeMars: Yes. And I have another younger brother. Chuck is 18 months younger than me, and my other brother, Lee, is 12 years younger than me.

Paul Stillwell: Any other siblings?

Admiral DeMars: No, that was it. Just three boys.

---

* David G. Farragut (1801-1870) was the senior Union naval leader in the Civil War; in 1862 he became the first officer in the U.S. Navy to hold the rank of rear admiral. He was particularly noted for his victory in the Battle of Mobile Bay in August 1864. He served in the Navy from the time he was a midshipman in 1810 until his death.
† Comiskey Park, which has since been demolished, was the home of the Chicago White Sox of baseball's American League and the Chicago Cardinals of the National Football League.

Paul Stillwell: Did the Depression have any effect on your family?*

Admiral DeMars: Oh, absolutely. Absolutely. My mother was from downstate Illinois, a coal-mining town. She and her sister went to what is now Illinois State University, then called the Normal School, to be a teacher. It was a one-year curriculum, and you got a teaching certificate. The times got hard, so she and her sister decided to come to Chicago, and they had an apartment. They met my dad there and went on from there.

Paul Stillwell: The university is in the town of Normal.

Admiral DeMars: That's where Illinois State is, which is like 30,000 people now. I mean, it's a gigundous university now. My dad was from Chippewa Falls, Wisconsin, way up north.

So it was a normal upbringing as a kid, always working, always doing this and that, always busy. In those days, of course, you made you own enjoyment and entertainment. But we never had a lot of money. We were clearly, in retrospect, lower middle class [chuckle]. But it didn't bother us in those days. As I'm sure you recall, kids weren't as class conscious as they are today. We knew there were kids that were better off than us in high school, but it didn't matter. Everybody got along, and so on. So, yes, the Depression did impact us but not so it made an awful lot of difference.

Paul Stillwell: Did your mother continue to work after she got married?

Admiral DeMars: Yes, oh yes. Absolutely. I mean, we sort of had to because we wanted a little higher standard of living than a mail carrier brought home. So my mother always worked, second shift. She'd go to work at 4:00 in the afternoon and come home about midnight. My dad had to get up about 4:00 in the morning in order to get out and

---

* Following the crash of the New York Stock Exchange in late October 1929, the United States was plunged into the Great Depression, from which it did not recover until the nation geared up for World War II at the beginning of the 1940s. The Depression was marked by high unemployment and many business failures.

deliver his mail. Mailmen were different in those days. They wore full uniforms, and they delivered twice a day during the week and once on Saturdays. It was a whole different business. He went away to the war, came back three years later, resumed his same mail route again. They gave it back to him. And on and on.

Paul Stillwell: So you did not wind up being latchkey kids, because the shifts were staggered.

Admiral DeMars: Yes, the shifts were staggered. But my brother and I sort of grew up at the Boys Club. In those days you could do your homework in school if you were really sharp and quick. I mean, nobody took books home and studied at home. [Chuckle] Why would you do that? So we would go to the Boys Club every night and play some kind of sports there—basketball, wrestling, volleyball, on and on—and then travel around the city playing against other teams. We'd bicycle there and bicycle back; it was about 12 blocks, big city blocks. So we did kind of raise ourselves. My dad cooked the meals because my mother wasn't home, except on the weekends my mother made the meals.

So it was a different kind of upbringing. So I smile when I see these things about mothers working and all that nowadays. There were a lot of people who did that back in those days because you just needed the money.

Paul Stillwell: What values did you get from your parents?

Admiral DeMars: I think it was hard work. Be honest, be truthful, but mostly be industrious, be a hard worker. My dad loved to read, and I think he passed that love of reading on to me. He would read just about everything and anything. When he was in the Navy, we lived with my grandmother on the West Side of Chicago and my Aunt Chris lived with us; she was in her late teens then. We were, like, four and six or something, six and eight. And she would read every night, books like *How Green Was My Valley* and that sort of stuff to us.*

Paul Stillwell: That's a pretty long book.

Admiral DeMars: Yes, a very long book. Well, my dad was away for three years, so we had lots of time. [Laughter] And so one of the things that I developed early on in life was the love of reading. I love to read. To this day I just read voraciously, and so that was a good start.

Paul Stillwell: Did you keep up well with the outside world? Because this was a period of great turmoil, obviously.

Admiral DeMars: Ah, yes, but not excessively so. I mean, you just kind of took it in your stride. Yes, the war was going on. I remember where I was when the President died, FDR, and I remember where I was when the war was over in Europe and the war was over in Japan, because we wanted my dad to come home.† But it was such a continuous turmoil that you just sort of got on with your life.

Paul Stillwell: Did you listen to the radio quite a bit?

Admiral DeMars: Oh yes, absolutely. News, entertainment—that was our upbringing. Later on, of course, we had a little TV set and watched things like the Friday night fights and those sorts of things.

Paul Stillwell: The fights were sponsored by Gillette.

---

* Richard Llewellyn's 1939 novel *How Green Was My Valley* told the story of a Welsh mining town. The story was made into a 1941 movie that starred Walter Pidgeon and Maureen O'Hara. It won the Academy Award as best movie of the year.
† Franklin D. Roosevelt was President of the United States from 4 March 1933 until his death on 12 April 1945. World War II ended in Europe in May 1945 and in the Pacific in August 1945.

Admiral DeMars: Yes, by Gillette.

One of my jobs did lead me to the Naval Academy. When I was in high school, I had a job that I guess you'd call a second assistant janitor at a savings and loan on the South Side of Chicago. I worked full time during the summer and part time during the school year. I was mopping floors and all that sort of stuff. It was Second Federal Savings and Loan on 26th and Pulaski. It was run by the Sierocinski family. John A. Sierocinski was a little guy you didn't see much of; he was the president. E. John Sierocinski was his son, and he ran the place.

One day, after I'd been working there for a couple of years, E. John called me in and said, "Bruce, when you graduate from high school what do you want to do?"

I told him, "I want to go to the Naval Academy."

He was clearly crestfallen. I mean, this was a Republican businessman. "You want to go to the Naval—why do you want to do that?"

I said, "Well, my dad was in the Navy." I had two uncles that had been in the Navy and were in the Pacific also; they used to send us back coconuts and rating badges. And I said, "It looks like..."

He said, "Okay, go back to work." [Laughter] I went back to work and wondered, "What the devil was that all about?"

Three months later he called me in and said, "You have an appointment to the Naval Academy." I was overwhelmed. I don't know exactly what I said. And he said, "Here's a card. This is the address you have to use." It was 46 North Lake Road, Riverside, Illinois, which is a very posh suburb. My brother and I used to caddy out at the Riverside Country Club.

I said, "Well, thank you, Mr. Sierocinski. I'm overwhelmed. Anything else I have to do?"

He said, "Yes. The congressman from Riverside owes the editor of the *Southwest News* [which was the free shopping news that my brother and I delivered also], and the editor of the *Southwest News* owes me a favor, and you're the favor. But he would be very embarrassed if his constituents knew that he had appointed somebody from outside his district. So this is your address."

"Yes, sir."

Paul Stillwell: But that was not unknown for appointments back then.

Admiral DeMars: Well, I guess not. I don't know. I only had one experience. This was before SATs were common, but he said, "You have to go down to the post office building and take these two civil service exams."* And they were tough exams. One was in mathematics, and the other was in social studies.

Paul Stillwell: Did you get any specific preparation or use old tests?

Admiral DeMars: No, no. I just went in cold. And he said, "There's going to be others down there from the congressman's district because he said this is competitive, and whoever scores the highest is going to go, so don't disabuse them of that." And I didn't. And there were fellows down there that thought this was competitive. [Chuckle] So I got my appointment to the Naval Academy sort of under false pretences. I guess you'd call it fraudulent enlistment. But it all worked out. I stayed in uniform for 43 years, so it was time well spent.

Paul Stillwell: How good a student were you in high school?

Admiral DeMars: I was very good. I was on the honor roll, national honor roll, all the time. Stood high in my class; I forget how high. I was the vice president of the class. It was a good high school, but it was a public high school, so when I got to the Naval Academy I had a hard time, because I just didn't know how to study. I never did any homework [chuckle], didn't know how to study, and I really had to catch up.

Paul Stillwell: How good an athlete were you on the football team?

Admiral DeMars: Oh, I was very good. I was captain of the football team the last year.

---

* At various times, the SAT, administered by the College Board, has been known as the Scholastic Aptitude Test and the Scholastic Assessment Test. Now known only as SAT, it is widely used in measuring the ability of high school students to do college work.

But when I got to the academy I found out that I was slow, and not very big. So I went out for the football team there; I lasted three days and, ah, that was it. So I went out for lightweight football, which I had to lose 20 pounds to do, which meant I didn't have any energy. So none of that panned out very well.

Paul Stillwell: This was when Eddie Erdelatz and Rip Miller were there.*

Admiral DeMars: Right, right. The old-timers were there.

Paul Stillwell: How much a factor did religion play in your family while you were growing up?

Admiral DeMars: My dad took my brother and me to church every Sunday, the Fowler-Clifton Methodist Church. So we were raised in the church. That was my mother's day to sleep in, so she didn't go to church with us. But yes, it played a fairly considerable role, I think. I always brag—you got a prize if you read the entire Bible, so I read the entire Bible. Obviously, I didn't get much out of it, because I was rushing through it, but I did read it.

Paul Stillwell: What was the prize?

Admiral DeMars: [Laughter] I forget now. Ten bucks or something like that, which was enormous. But I always thought that Chicago was sort of the city of the possible. And I didn't realize that till later in my career. But certain things were possible and you could do things. That sort of molded my approach in the Navy. I mean, yes, you've got to have a lot of rules, and you have a lot of regulations. Some are more important than others. Some you really should follow; some—ah, who cares? So it was the Chicago background that I think stood me well in life since then.

---

* Edward J. Erdelatz was the Naval Academy's head football coach for the 1950 through 1958 seasons. The team's overall record in those years was 50-26-8, a percentage of .643. Edgar E. "Rip" Miller served from 1931 to 1933 as the Naval Academy's head football coach. For many years thereafter he worked as a coach and assistant athletic director.

Paul Stillwell: Did you go to professional sports games at Comiskey Park or Chicago Stadium?

Admiral DeMars: [Laughter] Yes, we did. My brother and I played on Pee Wee football teams that were sponsored by various local things, and my brother got to play once in Comiskey Park against another little team. We went to watch him. But also, about twice a year, my brother and I would cut school with a couple of other friends, and we'd go down to Comiskey Park—which was just get on a streetcar and go, a 15-minute ride. There was a side door they left open for people to come and go, because this was like 9:30 in the morning, well before the game. We'd go up and we'd climb over the fence to the upper deck, sit along the first-base line, and the groundskeepers would be out there titivating the field.

A little later the PR people would come out and be taking pictures of the players, and on and on. Then the game would start about 12:30 or something like that. The Andy Frain ushers were too lazy to come up and chase us, so you'd be there with your box lunch and watch the whole game, then go home. The hard thing was the next morning—my mother, of course, having worked second shift was pretty tired in the morning—we'd say, "Mom, would you sign this note for school?"

She'd say, "You went to the baseball game again, didn't you?"

"Mom, just sign the note, would you please?" We didn't do it too often, maybe twice a semester. She'd sign the notes, and away we went. So yes, we did go to Comiskey Park. [Chuckle]

Paul Stillwell: Well, the football Cardinals played there too.

Admiral DeMars: Yes, the football Cardinals played there. That was our team, Charlie Trippi, Johnny Lujack, and Pat Harder.[*]

---

[*] In 1947 the Chicago Cardinals won the National Football League championship with a "Million Dollar Backfield" composed of Paul Christman, Charley Trippi, Pat Harder, and Elmer Angsman. Johnny Lujack won the 1947 Heisman Trophy with Notre Dame and later played for the Chicago Bears.

Paul Stillwell: What did you do for recreation while you weren't either studying or in school or doing these jobs.

Admiral DeMars: We would hop on our bikes, my brother and I, when we weren't going to the Boys Club, which was in the evenings. But during the weekends or when we had some time we'd jump on our bikes and we'd pedal to one of the city parks and play tennis. We played tennis, and then we caddied during the summer, which was quite lucrative. You could carry at the Riverside Country Club, which we took a streetcar to get to. You carried a double in the morning, two large bags; a double in the afternoon; and a twilight nine double. And you could make out of that, with tip and everything, 25 bucks, which was big money in those days. So we would do that Saturday and Sunday. But it was hard work, because these were big leather bags. But it was fun, and you were young, and it was good money. So we did that and we played tennis.

We played a sort of sandlot football, which meant you had a helmet and shoulder pads and wore Levis and that. They were pickup games. Tackle football. So we kept busy.

Paul Stillwell: I'm guessing you spent more time with your next younger brother than with the youngest.

Admiral DeMars: Yes, the youngest didn't come along until, as I said, 12 years later. They're both fundamentally different. The closest one became an insurance executive. The youngest one became a policeman in Chicago and spent 30 years and ended up a detective; he's retired now from that.

Paul Stillwell: How much dating did you do in high school with your future wife? I'm sure it was more sedate than things they have now [chuckle].

Admiral DeMars: Oh, we went out a lot. I mean, she was my one and only. She was the first girl I really got serious about, and stayed serious about it, and vice versa. So we dated heavily for two years, and then went away four years to the Naval Academy. I'd come home, and we'd date heavily while I was home. Then she came out maybe once a year to the Naval Academy to some special event or that. We got married graduation day.

Paul Stillwell: And Bruce came along nine months later.

Admiral DeMars: Yes, exactly. Exactly. So it was a torrid relationship.

How I got into the Naval Academy. Of course, I got the appointment; that was all fine. Then I went up to Great Lakes to take my physical, and I failed on high blood pressure.* So I went to see our family doctor, who had a son who'd graduated from West Point and got killed in Korea. It was very tragic. Wonderful family doctor. So he gave me some, I think, nitroglycerine pills. He said, "Put one of these under your tongue and hope for the best, and stop using too much salt." In those days, if you went back for re-exam you had to pay 300 bucks, and they wouldn't refund it if you failed. If you passed, you got it refunded. So 300 bucks was a lot of money. So I went on the train to Baltimore, got a bus from Baltimore down to the Naval Academy, and arrived late in the day, just beat and tired. Everybody that was lame and halt, such as me, lived in the visiting team barracks, and then the next day you had a re-exam.

So I went in and sat down, and this second-class corpsman came up.† I had red hair in those days, and he said, "Red, you look tired."

I said, "You know, Chicago to Baltimore."

So he put the cuff on and went sss-sss-sss—"Yeah, you really do look tired. There's that ward over there. Why don't you lay down in there? Get a little rest and then we'll do this again." So I lay down, and I fell sound asleep. About three hours later I felt this cuff being put on my arm. Sss-sss-sss. The corpsman said, "Okay, Red, you passed." I thought: "This is a good organization. [Laughter] If you've got sailors like that, this is a great organization." I've felt that way ever since. That's how I got in.

---

* Naval Training Station, Great Lakes, Illinois, about 30 miles north of downtown Chicago on the shore of Lake Michigan.
† A hospital corpsman is an enlisted man or woman in the Navy's medical department. Second class was the pay grade designation of the petty officer.

Paul Stillwell: Did you have any direct contact with the congressman?

Admiral DeMars: No. I never even knew him, never met him. That wasn't unusual in Chicago. It's just the way things were run.

Paul Stillwell: You talked about the various ethnicities. What was your genealogical background?

Admiral DeMars: Well, French Canadian, English on my dad's side, and Scottish on my mother's side, predominantly Scottish, nothing else there [chuckle]. And Margaret's is Czechoslovakian and English. Her dad was English, came over from Whitehaven at age 18. So it was a typical Chicago mixture.

Paul Stillwell: Were the schools integrated at that point?

Admiral DeMars: Slightly. Slightly. As I said, I was on the football team, and we had this black kid come and go out for football, and he was a halfback. We thought, "God, this is going to be great. We're going to have a great, fast halfback." He was slower than hell. [Laughter] So we had probably in my class four or five black kids out of 120 or so. Not very integrated.

Paul Stillwell: How did you stand in the class?

Admiral DeMars: I don't remember, but it was top 10% or something like that. As I said, I was on the National Honor Society every semester. Just cranked it out.

We went back to our 50th reunion from high school, and the people that put it together gave us all a nice little brochure that had a picture of each one of our teachers and a little CV on them, where they'd gone to school and that. I was absolutely amazed. Teachers were older in those days, obviously, but every one of them had a master's degree in their subject from either Northwestern or the University of Chicago. Master's degree from those two schools! Now, obviously, if you did that you probably got extra money or something. But they were wonderful teachers, great teachers. But it was different. When I got to the Naval Academy, as I said, it was tough sledding the first year. I thought I was going to fail out.

Paul Stillwell: Did any of the high school teachers prove particularly inspiring to you?

Admiral DeMars: A number of them did. Mr. Gammersfelter who taught physics. Another fellow, whose name I can't remember, taught chemistry. And my homeroom teacher—can't remember the name right now [chuckle]—that's why I took Spanish; she was the Spanish teacher. But most of them were good teachers. Football team, we had one coach. We used to play Lane Tech, maybe 6,000 boys, and we had 1,800 kids, 900 boys. They'd have almost more coaches than we had players. We had one coach, who also taught hygiene or something. But they were all good. They were very professional teachers. The school was very orderly; there were no fights or anything of that nature. It was a very-well-run operation.

Paul Stillwell: Once you passed the blood pressure test, what happened then?

Admiral DeMars: Well, we started at the Naval Academy, which quite frankly I found quite tolerable. You know, everybody talks about hazing, and this and that, but I found it a very tolerable environment. The food was good. You had a lot of sports, athletics, and while I couldn't make it in the varsity teams because I was short and slow, I did play a lot of intramural sports. Every semester had that.

It was run differently in those days, as I'm sure you realize from your other interviews. The midshipmen didn't lead the brigade. They led them at parades, that's all. The officers ran the place. And it really was sort of cops and robbers. If you got away with something, you got away with it. But the thing you really knew was: "Don't lie. If you got caught, tell the truth and take your punishment." That was the thing that I walked away from the Naval Academy realizing. There are a lot of rules, and some of them are good and some of them are—ah, who made up this rule? But if you get caught, tell the truth. And responsibility and showing up on time and all that sort of stuff. But I enjoyed the four years at the Naval Academy. I thought it was a good education. Well, I ran the world's largest operating—because the Soviets didn't operate—nuclear power program based only on a Naval Academy education. I never went to PG school. So it had to be pretty good.

Paul Stillwell: Any highlights of the plebe summer that stand out in your mind?*

Admiral DeMars: No, not at all. Just kind of went through it. Now, we were in a company that was reasonably benign. I mean, the first class were good, not a lot of hazing. They got down on a couple people who should have been gotten down on. But our first class pulled us in the first day and said, "Okay, we're all on a first-name basis here, and we're here to help you get through this place." It was different in our company, and particularly with our first classmen. Ed Oscarson and Noel T. Wood were the two first-class, wonderful guys.† So no, nothing stuck out for plebe summer. I just went through it.

Paul Stillwell: It sounds as if you adapted to the regimentation fairly easily.

Admiral DeMars: Yes. Yes. Most people did. One thing that stuck with me. One of the fellows that was in the sick-and-lame barracks with me was there for psychological reasons. They said he was too independent. And I thought, "Jeez, I thought you needed those kind of guys in the Navy." And they didn't take him. They said a psychiatrist talked to him, and they didn't take him. I don't know how you make that call on a kid who's 18 years old, so I thought that was screwed up even at my young age. But he went off about other things. I'm sure he's probably CEO of a big company or something [chuckle].

But I thought the Naval Academy was a fine education, a fine place. I liked the way it was run. You got to go to football games. We didn't have a lot of money in those

---

* A midshipman in his or her first year is called a plebe; second year, youngster or third classman; third year, second classman; fourth year, first classman.
† Midshipman Edward R. Oscarson, USN, and Midshipman Noel T. Wood, USN, class of 1954.

days, so the intercollegiate athletic things, the wrestling matches and the boxing matches and the gymnastics, were always packed, always packed, no matter who we were going up against. I don't think it's that way nowadays. Basketball games were just sold out. Mids were just there because we didn't have anything else to do. [Laughter] It was a nice environment.

Paul Stillwell: What do you recall about getting into the academics?

Admiral DeMars: It was very hard for me. The first year I stood about 500. I graduated, I don't know, 100, 150, something like that.* So I really learned. On-the-job training. I had to work really hard and study very hard. But I slowly taught myself how to study. Plus, the Naval Academy is largely memorization. If you can memorize—and I have a reasonably good memory—you'll get through.

Paul Stillwell: More then than now, by just the way the system is set up.

Admiral DeMars: Yes. It's different, because they have majors now, and the midshipmen always seem much smarter than I was when I was there [chuckle]. They present themselves quite well. Much more worldly than we were 60 years ago.

Paul Stillwell: What sort of mix was there of instructors—civilians and service people?

Admiral DeMars: It was about the same as it is now, about 50-50. And we had some of the famous ones, such as Potter, the author that wrote the Nimitz book.† The instructor that stands out most in my mind taught navigation. He was a lieutenant from Penn State. He was NROTC.‡ And I thought, "Oh, that's not bad; NROTC has good guys too [chuckle]. He's the one I remember prominently, simply because he was just so good.

---

* The Naval Academy register indicates that Midshipman DeMars stood number 146 of the 948 graduates in the class of 1957.
† E. B. Potter, *Nimitz* (Annapolis: Naval Institute Press, 1976). Fleet Admiral Chester W. Nimitz, USN, served as Commander in Chief Pacific Fleet and Pacific Ocean Areas, 1941-45.
‡ NROTC – Naval Reserve Officers' Training Corps.

He was so personable, and good teacher.

Paul Stillwell: What was his name?

Admiral DeMars: I can't remember it. Can't remember.

So it was just the sort of thing that you faced every day and got through it. The cruises were great. They'd make up two battleships, five cruisers, and 20 destroyers, and you'd load on. They'd take a bunch of sailors off, and they'd put on a bunch of midshipmen and take us to Europe. So this was something to go off and do that for a guy from Chicago who the farthest east he'd ever been was Annapolis. On the first cruise I was on a battleship.

Paul Stillwell: Which one?

Admiral DeMars: *Missouri*.* And we'd holystone the decks.† You took the place of an enlisted man the first cruise. They off-loaded 600 sailors and put on 600 mids. Of course, it was a big ship. I don't know, 3,000 people or so. We went to Lisbon and Cherbourg as liberty ports. We practiced with the big guns on the way over, and then we came back and fired down at Guantanamo Bay.‡ I was the number-one gunpowder hoist operator in the number-two turret. I ran the electric powder hoist that would go way down. They'd put the silk bags of powder in, I'd bring them up, open the shuttle, put them into the gun room, they'd load them in, and boom. And then we fired three rounds from each gun. It cost a lot of money, but I guess they had a lot of money in those days for that sort of thing. So it was quite exciting.

Paul Stillwell: I've gathered that the sensation, really, inside the turret is much more muted than outside.

---

* The battleship *Missouri* (BB-63) was the site of the Japanese signing of surrender documents in Tokyo Bay on 2 September 1945.
† Holystoning refers to the practice of cleaning a ship's wooden decks by scraping them with bricks pushed back and forth across the planks by means of wooden handles. It is a laborious operation.
‡ Guantánamo Bay, on the south coast of Cuba, near the eastern end of the island, for many years provided a fleet anchorage and training area for U.S. Navy ships.

Admiral DeMars: Oh, yes, yes. You just feel kind of a whumpf. It wasn't overwhelming. Outside it *was* overwhelming. But that was quite a big deal for a young 19-year-old kid.

Paul Stillwell: What do you remember about relating with the enlisted crew members during your first cruise?

Admiral DeMars: It was not good. They didn't like us and we learned not to like them. We got our comeuppance when they had a boxing smoker. We had some pretty good boxers because they were the Naval Academy intramural champs and NCAA champs, so we put together quite a nice team.[*] The ship had burly young boatswain's mates and Marines and that. We beat the crap out of them, and the mids loved it. Now, that didn't do any good for continued bad relations, but it gave the mids a good feeling.

Paul Stillwell: But that also gave you exposure to how the enlisted men lived and worked.

Admiral DeMars: Yes. Oh, absolutely, and started to convince me that this was a thing you had to be careful of. But I learned more about that on the two APAs I was on.[†] That was a real education.

For the first-class cruise I was on a destroyer, the *Turner*.[‡] I remember that because the captain's name was Turner.[§] And that was smaller, much better relations. Of course, you were operating as a junior officer on that. Not really, but the relationships were different. But the crew was different also. I mean, they were much easier to get along with, to talk to, because it was a destroyer. And we went to two good liberty ports on that one and had a good time.

---

[*] NCAA – National Collegiate Athletic Association.
[†] After being commissioned in 1957, Ensign DeMars served on board two attack transports (APAs).
[‡] USS *Turner* (DD-834) was a *Gearing*-class destroyer commissioned 12 June 1945. She was reclassified DDR-834 in 1949 and modernized to serve the role of radar picket destroyer.
[§] Commander Charles Wesley Turner II, USN, commanded the ship from 4 January 1955 to 22 April 1957.

Paul Stillwell: Which ports were those?

Admiral DeMars: That one went to Lisbon and Oslo. And Oslo was great, obviously a beautiful place. Lisbon we went up the coast to Figueira da Foz, which was a great big gambling center up there. We went in these James Bond casinos, that sort of thing. Heady stuff for a young man.

One of the other fond memories of the Naval Academy was the rifle range. We learned how to shoot—I wasn't very good. We went up in those Yellow Perils, the N3N floatplanes.[*] I don't like heights, and that convinced me I didn't like heights. I wanted to become an aviator, but my right eye went 20/30. It was 20/15 in the left, 20/30 in the right, so that disqualified me for that, but it wasn't a big deal for me because the surface Navy in those days was quite prestigious. I'm not so sure it is nowadays for any number of different reasons, most of their own doing. But in those days I was ready to become a surface warfare officer, line officer.

Paul Stillwell: Second-class summer is usually devoted to exposure to the Marines and aviation.

Admiral DeMars: Right, Marines and aviation. And we went on a carrier. I remember standing up on buzzard's row there on the carrier, and this F4U Corsair came down.[†] Those were the gull-winged ones, beautiful looking airplanes. Caught the wire, broke in half right behind the cockpit, went over the side. You could see the guy getting out of his gear, and he hit the water. A helicopter took off and recovered him. I thought, "Eh, I'm glad my eye is bad." [Laughter] So we did that, and we went down to Little Creek and scrambled around with the Marines. That convinced me I'd never want to be a Marine. God, do this for a living, people shooting at you.

So it was a good exposure. They don't do a lot of that anymore for any number of

---

[*] "Yellow Peril" was the nickname for the yellow-painted N3N trainer, a biplane equipped with a centerline pontoon.
[†] The Vought F4U Corsair was in production longer than any other U.S. fighter plane of World War II. It first entered fleet squadrons in 1942. The last Corsair was produced in 1953. The F4U-1 was 33 feet, 4 inches long; wingspan of 41 feet; gross weight of 14,000 pounds; and top speed of 417 miles per hour.

different reasons. They don't have enough ships to do it. And some people do their midshipman cruises in Washington now. God. They go and they work with OLA and learn who knows what.[*] Terrible.

Anyway, it was a good education and it taught you your business. It was the boat school, you know. It was a trade school.

Paul Stillwell: And it included mandatory social training as well. What do you recall of that?

Admiral DeMars: Not much, because there wasn't much of it. We had what were called tea fights.[†]

Paul Stillwell: Yes. [Chuckle]

Admiral DeMars: You really didn't have to throw yourself into it. And, of course, I had Margaret, so I wasn't on the lookout for anything. I pretty much avoided most of that as much as I could.

Paul Stillwell: How much opportunity for liberty in Annapolis?

Admiral DeMars: Not much. We got Saturdays off, and you had to be back at, I don't know, 10:00-10:30, something like that. And then Sunday you had to be back at 6.00. So we'd go out in town and catch a movie. My mother used to send me five bucks a month, which was a lot of money in those days, so I was the richest guy among my roommates. We'd go out and go get a grilled cheese sandwich at the Little Campus restaurant there on Maryland Avenue, and then go out and see a movie, and that was the big day, and then come back. Went over the wall once just to say I'd done it; that was a big deal.

---

[*] OLA – the Navy's Office of Legislative Affairs.
[†] This was the nickname for mandatory tea dances.

First-class year, three of us bought a car. It was a 1935 Chrysler or something like that, big old behemoth. Of course, you couldn't have cars in those days. You couldn't even *drive* cars in those days. We kept it parked out in town, and when the weekend would come one of the girlfriends of whoever was dragging would drive it, and we'd go over across the river into Maryland and go to someplace where you could get some beer, and we'd drink. Big deal.

At least once, maybe twice, Margaret was there, and she was the only one, so she was going to drive it. She didn't know how to drive a stick shift. So I sat next to her and I worked the clutch and the gearshift [laughter] and she handled the accelerator and the brake and steered. We got across safe; nothing happened.

Paul Stillwell: That's a lot of togetherness.

Admiral DeMars: Yes, it is, it is. A lot of coordination. So we did crazy things like that. And you knew if you were caught you were caught, and you'd march around with a rifle. But if you got caught, don't lie.

So it was an interesting place. I look back on it fondly.

I never went back. The first time I went back was for my 20th reunion. Well, I was mostly on the West Coast and at sea, and other priorities in life, obviously. But it wasn't because I didn't like the place.

Paul Stillwell: Any classmates whom you particularly got close to?

Admiral DeMars: Oh, yes, my roommates. Hugo Marxer, who retired as a captain in the Navy and went off to work for INPO, the Institute of Nuclear Power Operations.[*] He and Jim Wilber were my roommates for a while.[†] Jim Wilber's dead now; he became a Supply Corps officer. He retired as a captain. And then for another couple of years I

---

[*] Midshipman Hugo E. Marxer, USN.
[†] Midshipman James R. Wilber, USN.

roomed with Willie Whitmire, who was center on the football team, and Frank Fendler—the two of us roomed together.[*] And good friends. I'm pretty close.

We have a fairly close class. We play golf once a month during the summer around here. Some guy—it's his job to find a course and get a special deal for us. We have a Christmas party. We have a picnic every year. So very close. For our 50th reunion gift I was the fundraiser. We raised three and a half million dollars to endow the chair in naval heritage in the history department. It is quite a prestigious chair there now, so we felt very proud about that. So it's a good class. I'm close with a lot of my classmates. I'm sort of the go-to guy if they want to raise money or decide on something. I was the chairman of the Washington chapter, which is sort of the business group, for about four years, and then I passed it on to somebody else. So I've stayed reasonably active with my class.

Paul Stillwell: There was a fundraising drive at that time for a new football stadium that Gene Fluckey headed.[†]

Admiral DeMars: Yes. Yes, yes. Amazingly enough, I only knew this in retrospect; we weren't aware it was going on at the time [chuckle]. We didn't have any money, so they never asked us. But he raised three million bucks to build that stadium, which is an amazing amount to get such a nice stadium. I was on the stadium memorial committee to help oversee the redo of it, when we put in all the memorial arches and rearranged the plaques and everything, and that was interesting. Jim Holloway was the head of that committee.[‡]

Now I'm the chairman of the Naval Academy memorials committee. There are about 18 of us, and we span all genders, races, classes, but it's a good group. It's our job to evaluate requests to do certain things from a memorial standpoint at the Naval

---

[*] Midshipman William R. Whitmire, USN, who retired as a captain. Midshipman Francis J. Fendler Jr., USN; he resigned from the Navy in 1961 after completing his obligated service.
[†] Navy-Marine Corps Memorial Stadium opened in September 1959. Captain Eugene B. Fluckey, USN, who was chairman of the electrical engineering department, had the collateral duty of heading the fleet-wide fundraising effort to raise money for construction.
[‡] Admiral James L. Holloway III, USN (Ret.), had served as Chief of Naval Operations, 1974 to 1978.

Academy, and either say yes or no. The real reason it's there is so they don't get mad at the superintendent for saying yes or no; they get mad at me [laughter] so the people will continue to give money. But we try to be very balanced in it. I mean, some of the ideas are just squirrelly, and others are not totally squirrelly, but maybe if you change this or do this or that. The Naval Academy on this side of the river is only 300 acres, and so there's not a lot of room there to do anything dramatic.

Paul Stillwell: And a lot of memorials are there already.

Admiral DeMars: Yes, there's a lot already. Fortunately there's a very nice instruction that has been drawn up that says what they'd like done and not done, but most of these people that send things in have never read the instruction, obviously.

Our biggest caper was with the Royal and Ancient Order of Hibernians. They believe that John Barry, not John Paul Jones, is the father of the U.S. Navy.[*] There are good arguments on both sides, but it is what it is. So they wanted to put in this big thing that looked like two Cadillacs stuck one on top of the other, with his original commission on one side and his bio on the other and everything, right across from Buchanan House.[†]

We obviously turned that down on a whole bunch of grounds. So they asked: Could they have a second hearing? We said, "Sure, why not?" So we met with them, and I said, "Well, we're going to just have a subcommittee for this." So I picked Mike Hagee, former Commandant of the Marine Corps, and Bob Natter, former four-star CinCLantFlt, and me.[‡] Three easy guys to get along with. So we sat down with them in the basement of Ogle Hall.[§] About 15 of them came in. Only five sat at the table. And looking across at them, I thought I was at an IRA meeting.[**] [Laughter] You know, shallow-cheeked, dark-haired, stern-looking guys. But they were very disciplined. Each

---

[*] John Paul Jones (1747-1792) was the young country's first great naval officer and a hero of the Revolutionary War. John Barry (1745-1803), born in Ireland, also served in the Continental Navy during the Revolution. In 1797 he received the first commission as an officer in the U.S. Navy.
[†] Buchanan House in the residence of the Naval Academy Superintendent.
[‡] General Michael W. Hagee, USMC, served as Commandant of the Marine Corps on 13 January 2003 to 13 November 2006. Admiral Robert J. Natter, USN, served as Commander in Chief Atlantic Fleet from 23 June 2000 to 24 October 2002.
[§] Ogle Hall is the alumni house for the Naval Academy.
[**] IRA – Irish Republican Army.

had about five minutes to talk about a different aspect of it. One guy seemed reasonably malleable and that, and we said, "Okay, we'll get back to you with our answer." So I went up to him afterward and I said, "You know where most Irishmen came from?"

He looked at me and said, "No. Where?"

I said, "They were Scotsmen that could swim." [Laughter]

He came right back and said, "You know what a well-balanced Irishman is? That's one with a chip on both shoulders." [Laughter] So he was a good guy.

The solution came from Bob Hofford.[*] You know him, I think.

Paul Stillwell: No.

Admiral DeMars: He just is retiring from working at the Naval Academy. He's class of '61. He's been a longtime worker there. Retired as a captain, naval aviator, really a go-to guy for the foundation. He's been very helpful for me in everything I did there—raising money for my class or this memorials committee, and on and on and on.

Bob came with this idea that we've got this gate way down at the waterfront, Annapolis side, and it's gate people can just come in. You don't have to show IDs or anything because you don't get inside the secure area. You can go to the field house there, the store, and on and on. He said, "Why don't we name it the Barry Gate?"

I said, "That's a brilliant idea." So we went back to them and proposed that. They leaped on it. I'm a hero to the Hibernians now. But the superintendent was getting letters from every Irish governor, mayor, congressman, across the country. "Why are you against the Hibernians?" you know, blah blah blah. So that solved that, and it went away. So I think that was our biggest success. The Hibernians ended up being happy, the Naval Academy's happy, and we got it off our backs so we're happy too.

So I still do a lot of things for the Naval Academy.

Paul Stillwell: I remember one time my son's in-laws came to visit Annapolis, and we were giving them a tour. We went through that elaborate procedure in that area to get in, and his father-in-law said, "Just how many terrorists has this prevented from getting in?"

---

[*] Captain Robert F. Hofford, USN (Ret.).

I said, "All of them." [Laughter]

Admiral DeMars: What are you protecting? Protecting mids? I mean, give me a break. So, anyway, I do do a lot. And I have fond memories of the Naval Academy.

Paul Stillwell: Your *Lucky Bag* entry said that you indulged in good-natured teasing.[*] What sorts of things did that involve?

Admiral DeMars: I don't know. I've always had kind of an acerbic nature, I guess. I find humor in just about everything [chuckle]. I'm a student of human nature. I just like to sit and watch people, watch crowds go by, and what people are doing. And I never hesitated to speak up; I still don't. So I had a good time there, and it was recognized.

Paul Stillwell: Some midshipmen take things too seriously. Obviously you weren't one of them.

Admiral DeMars: No, I wasn't one of them. I was not one of them. As I said, I enjoyed my life there.

When we went to ship selection, in those days you picked numbers out of a fishbowl. It was like the Selective Service, like the draft. I pulled out number—I think it was 810. About 850 were graduating. So oh, God. Everything was gone. The only things left were some aircraft carriers and some amphibs. I said, "Well, I'm going to get married, so I'll pick a nice homeport. I picked USS *Telfair* out of San Diego. And then you did the same thing for when you could get married, and I was very lucky there. So we got married; I think it was about 7:00 o'clock graduation day. So that showed I had luck in good things.

Paul Stillwell: Let me go back to the Eighth Company briefly. What do you remember about Captain Holt as the company officer?[†]

---

[*] *Lucky Bag* is the name of the yearbook for each Naval Academy graduating class.
[†] Captain Edward J. Holt Jr., USMC.

Admiral DeMars: He was a good man. We liked him. He was a dyed-in-the-wool Marine. Very nice guy. When we were first class he had us over in small groups to his little apartment quarters, which were the ones up on the hill there, and his wife put on a spaghetti dinner for us. And so I thought that was nice. I liked him. He wasn't overly harsh. We had good company officers there, I think. A number of them were very fine. So good memories of that.

Paul Stillwell: You were in the leadership group during the fall set, first-class year. What did that involve?

Admiral DeMars: Absolutely nothing. Carrying a sword during parades was all that that entailed. I was the deputy company commander, I think, a two-star, which was not a big deal. And the whole thing was not a big deal, because it just wasn't run that way. It was run differently than it is today.

I object a little bit to the way it's run today. I think they demand too much time from the midshipmen, particularly the good ones are way up at the top worrying about all this scheduling and this and that, and trying to run the brigade. It's not what they're there for. They're there for an education. That is prime. They say, "Well, we're teaching them how to be leaders." You don't learn how to be a leader at the Naval Academy. You learn some character traits, but you learn how to be a leader once you get out in the fleet. That's where you learn how to be a leader. We had leadership courses there, and they were kind of case studies. The case of the unwashed seaman—how do you handle that, on and on and on.

Of course, I'm a Rickover sort of guy.[*] I think you're there for an education. Do the rest of it other places.

Paul Stillwell: Interestingly, the *Lucky Bag* said you were better at the liberal arts and humanities.

---

[*] Hyman G. Rickover was considered the father of the nuclear Navy. He ran the U.S. Navy's nuclear-power program for many years, from 1948 until he eventually left active duty in 1982 with the rank of four-star admiral on the retired list. Rickover Hall at the Naval Academy is named in his honor, as is the nuclear-powered attack submarine *Hyman G. Rickover* (SSN-709), which was commissioned 21 July 1984.

Admiral DeMars: I was. I was. I just said, once again, it was the reading. I enjoyed that. I think I stood first in leadership, whatever that meant [chuckle]. Because we had to take exams and this and that, but it was mostly a BS course. Yes, I did well. I like to read, and I liked those parts. I survived the other ones, but I wasn't real topnotch in them.

Paul Stillwell: Well, in this love of reading, going back to high school and before, what sort of things did you read for pleasure?

Admiral DeMars: Everything, but I did like history. I read history and biography.

Paul Stillwell: Fiction?

Admiral DeMars: A little bit. I enjoyed—this was a little later—Cold-War spy novels I loved, but when John le Carré retired that kind of went away.[*] When the Soviets became Russians it went away. But I enjoyed spies, and detective sort of things, Dashiell Hammett sort of stuff.[†] But I still to this day am today wading through—I passed two things on to my son I'm very proud of. One is a love of reading, and the other is a love of golf. But he, for Christmas, gave me this book on *American Prometheus*, the story of Robert Oppenheimer.[‡] God, it was a paperback, but it was about that thick so I waded through all of that.

Paul Stillwell: Two or three inches.

Admiral DeMars: Oh! But I got back at him. I sent it back to him to read after I finished it. Now I'm reading the new bio on George Washington by Ron Chernow.[§] It's about

---

[*] Le Carré's best-known work is *Tinker Tailor Soldier Spy*, a 1974 novel about a mole within the British intelligence service.
[†] Dashiell Hammett (1894-1961) was a novelist who specialized in detective stories. His own experiences as a detective added to the realism of his works, the best known of which are *The Maltese Falcon* (1930) and *The Thin Man* (1934).
[‡] J. Robert Oppenheimer (1904-1967) was an American theoretical phyicist who had a major role in the development of the U.S. atomic bomb during World War II. Kai Bird and Martin J. Sherwin, *American Prometheus: the Triumph and Tragedy of J. Robert Oppenheimer* (New York: Alfred A. Knopf, 2005).
[§] Ron Chernow, *Washington: a Life* (New York: Penguin Press, 2010).

that thick. It's a wonderful bio of Washington because it goes more into his individual personality and character and that. So I've always enjoyed reading, and it was back at the Naval Academy also.

Well, when I graduated we didn't have a lot of money. Margaret and I bought a '53 Chevy for 300 bucks. It was a four-year-old car then. But you had an account there, and you got paid. I think you got paid what a seaman got, and then they took out for your food and your uniforms and everything else, so you didn't make a lot of money. When it came down to the end, you were allowed to spend from that account whatever you wanted at the midshipman store. So I went down there and I bought a set of golf clubs, and I bought ten shirts. We had to wear stiff collars, boiled collars that attached to your shirt, and cuffs that attached to your shirt. So you had a shirt that didn't have a collar or cuffs and you hooked these things on, and you sent them off to the laundry separately. Midshipmen hated those. So I bought ten white shirts and a set of golf clubs. So when they went and passed out the checks at the end of your account time, I still have the check down below somewhere in my archives—it says "only ten cents." [Laughter] Now, I wasn't planning that, and I'm sure if I'd run over they would have told me, but I only had ten cents left in my account. You didn't make a lot of money then.

Paul Stillwell: Well, and weren't the girls expected to pay their expenses when they came in town for dates?

Admiral DeMars: Oh, yes. Absolutely. I mean, they had to get there, and then they lived in some drag house out there.* We had a very nice lady. She was a telephone operator at the Naval Academy exchange, and Margaret always stayed in her house. It was right up the street from the main gate.

Paul Stillwell: In your company, one class behind, was Chuck Larson.† What do you recall of him as a midshipman?

---

* "Drag" was Naval Academy slang for dating girls.
† Midshipman Charles R. Larson, USN, who eventually became a four-star admiral.

Admiral DeMars: Not a lot. He was personable, and a good guy. We're friends to this day because he became a submariner, obviously, and so our careers were sort of very close throughout, except he was a lot smarter and a lot more politically attuned than I was ever going to be. He's a good man.

Paul Stillwell: Did you have any contact with Captain Shinn as the commandant, or Admiral Smedberg?[*]

Admiral DeMars: In those days midshipmen—if you were smart, you avoided officers like a plague. What was there to be gained by talking to an officer? And the only time you ever saw the admiral was when you did "eyes right" during a parade. "Eyes right!"—oh, that's that little guy. The first guy that was there was the one that had done the Panmunjom thing.

Paul Stillwell: Turner Joy.[†]

Admiral DeMars: Turner Joy, and then he died after that, early on, because he was so worn down from all of that. But no, we didn't go out of our way to cotton up to officers. Just, they were bad news. That's all changed now, it's amazing, for the better I think. But we just avoided it like the plague. [Chuckle]

Paul Stillwell: What do you recall of the graduation? Did you parents come out for that?

Admiral DeMars: Yes, they did. They came out, Margaret's parents came out, a couple of my uncles from Chicago came out, and so did both of my brothers. And so it was very nice. We rented a house out in Sherwood Forest. It was very nice, accommodated

---

[*] Captain Allen M. Shinn, USN, served from 1956 to 1958 as the Naval Academy's commandant of midshipmen. Rear Admiral William R. Smedberg III, USN, was superintendent of the Naval Academy from March 1956 to June 1958. His oral history is in the Naval Institute collection.

[†] Vice Admiral C. Turner Joy, USN, was superintendent of the Naval Academy from August 1952 to August 1954. Before that he had headed the U.S. team negotiating in Panmunjom, Korea, in an attempt to end the Korean War. He wrote a book about the experience, C. Turner Joy, *How Communists Negotiate* (New York, Macmillan, 1955).

everybody. So it was good. It was a nice, bright, sunny day. Nice ceremony.

Paul Stillwell: And the wedding that evening.

Admiral DeMars: And the wedding that evening. Then we shoved off and came back, and we had a big reception in Chicago for all the family that came to celebrate the wedding. Then we headed for San Diego via Lewiston, Idaho, where my one roommate lived, and then to Portland, Oregon, where my other roommate lived. So we stopped and saw them and then headed down the West Coast. It was quite idyllic. But it was a nice upbringing. The whole thing has been nice.

We held swords in Lewiston, Idaho, for my roommate's wedding, Jim Wilber. He was married there. And I swear across the street there were Indians watching, with pigtails and all of that. That was the kind of town Lewiston was in those days. It was really a frontier sort of town.

Paul Stillwell: So you were really a curiosity.

Admiral DeMars: We were a curiosity. We all had on our high-necked whites, with swords. "What's this? They're attacking us again!" [Laughter] So that was fun.

Then we went to Portland and my other roommate, Hugh Marxer; he loved to fish. He took us fishing on the Salmon River. We went trout fishing up on Mount Hood. So that was very pleasant. Nice time.

Paul Stillwell: Then you had to go to work.

Admiral DeMars: Then I had to go to work and report in.

Paul Stillwell: What were your initial experiences from the *Telfair*?

Admiral DeMars: Well, not bad, but not good. I do remember three or four of us were having beer at our apartment. We lived in Coronado because one of my roommates,

Willie Whitmire, was from Coronado and that's all he talked about. So we drove to San Diego, got right on the ferry—in those days they didn't have that bridge over there—and rented this little apartment in Coronado.

Paul Stillwell: You had some initial training there at the amphib base in Coronado, didn't you, before you went to the ship?

Admiral DeMars: Ah, yes, yes, that's right. So we lived there and did that. Yes, small-boat handling and stuff like that.

We were all together drinking beer, and the next day we were going to report in, so we were all kind of sharing—what's going to happen? What's this going to be all about? That was when Sputnik had been launched, and that came on the TV and that started us thinking a little differently.*

As I was walking down the pier towards USS *Telfair*, I was only an ensign, but I noticed it didn't have any boats.† You know, this was an APA, supposed to have LCVPs on it to land Marines.‡ Didn't have any boats. So I walked up the gangway, the brow, and saluted, and this young sailor said, "Gee, I'm surprised they're getting any new officers; we're going out of commission in three months." My God. You know, in just a little glimmer I was beginning to see how screwed up the Bureau of Naval Personnel was. But I said okay.

So I checked in, and I was made first division officer, with a bunch of boatswain's mates to run. And that was fun. I enjoyed them. They were good guys. And the XO said, "Don't worry about it; we'll get you another APA."§ Well, they did—in Long Beach. So I'd been in the Navy three months, and I was getting a permanent change of station to another ship.

Margaret said, "Is this going to always be like this?"

---

* On 4 October 1957, the Soviet Union launched Sputnik I, the first artificial earth satellite. It caused great uproar in the United States, which had expected to be first in space.
† USS *Telfair* (APA-210), a *Haskell*-class attack transport, was commissioned 31 October 1944. She displaced 8,100 tons standard, 14,837 fully loaded. She was 455 feet long, 62 feet in the beam, had a maximum draft of 24 feet, and a top speed of 18 knots. She was armed with one 5-inch gun, smaller antiaircraft guns, and carried a variety of landing craft for amphibious warfare operations.
‡ LCVP – landing craft, vehicle and personnel.
§ XO – executive officer.

"Well, not always, but...." I couldn't believe it. I couldn't believe it.

But it was a good ship. I learned some nice things on there. My leading petty officer was a first-class boatswain's mate, a good man. One day I was talking with him, and he said he was really worried. The next week he had to go to court for his son, who was in high school and done something bad, and so they were going to cloud up and rain all over him. I said, "Would you like me to go with you?"

He said, "Would you?"

I said, "Sure. Get a couple of other sailors, tall guys that look good in their uniforms—I don't want any fat guys. We'll all wear our blues, we'll all get buffed up, and we'll go. And if I can I'll say a few words for you."

He said, "Oh, would you?"

I said, "Sure. It doesn't cost anything." So we did. We went out to the courthouse, and we went in. I had made some arrangement ahead of time, talked to the bailiff or something, and said if the judge would please call on me I'd be happy to be a character witness. Didn't know the kid from Adam. Seemed like a decent kid. It wasn't a very serious charge, but enough to go to court. So I stood up and said what a wonderful family it was and how hardworking his dad is, etc., etc., etc., how difficult it is for families and that. And he dismissed the case. [Laughter] Probably my first lesson: Don't hesitate to stand up for your people. So I was king in that division for the next two months, and then I left.

Paul Stillwell: Loyalty down produces loyalty up.

Admiral DeMars: Absolutely. And just talking to people, just getting what's on their mind and why are they worried, what can you do about it if anything. Yes, I thought that was a little audacious but not far beyond my audacity quotient.

So we changed the homeport up to Long Beach. Got a nicer apartment there, a cheaper apartment actually. This was a real APA; they had boats.* I was one of 22

---

* In November 1957, Ensign DeMars reported to the USS *Okanogan* (APA-220), a *Haskell*-class attack transport that was commissioned 3 December 1944. Her characteristics were essentially the same as those of the *Telfair*.

ensigns on board. And I learned another lesson there. The crew was sort of the same as the *Telfair*'s: hardworking, good guys, mostly boatswain's mates. But the officers were a different group. The CO was an aviator on his deep-draft command.* His family was in Washington, so he was there by himself.

The XO had been the CO of the *Blackfin* during the '50s. A couple of famous guys—Bill Leisk, who became my CO later, and Lando Zech—were on there.† When they were on board, the captain surfaced the boat, went into Vladivostok harbor, and was steaming around at night. Searchlights came on and boom, boom, boats came out after he took off, got out of there, came back. He sent a radio message saying what went on. When he stepped ashore at Pearl Harbor, he was relieved immediately. He had a strange finger; it was broken. So he would point. But he was a defrocked submariner. They took his dolphins away.

Paul Stillwell: Because of the Vladivostok incident?

Admiral DeMars: Oh, yes, yes, yes. It used to be a great story in the submarine force, still is. People get older and forget them. But he never mentioned submarines to me at all, even after I applied.

So he was the XO. So you kind of push them aside. They didn't have anything to do with the ship operating; they were just kind of there. Three people made that ship operate. One was the ops officer, who was an LDO commander, very capable guy.‡ Good leader, smart, knew how to get things done. The second was the warrant boatswain, who ran all the deck stuff. He looked like Gregory Peck in *Moby Dick*.§ He was tall, thin, stooped, but he made the deck run. And the engineer was an LDO ensign. It was clear to me, as an ensign, that without those three guys the ship would never get under way, let alone carry out its mission. That was a big lesson for a young ensign.

---

* CO – commanding officer.
† Lieutenant William H. Leisk Jr., USN; Lieutenant Lando W. Zech Jr., USN, later a vice admiral.
‡ LDO – limited duty officer, a former enlisted man whose duties related to his enlisted specialty.
§ Actor Gregory Peck portrayed the obsessive 19th century whaling ship master, Captain Ahab, in the 1956 film version of the Herman Melville novel *Moby Dick*.

Paul Stillwell: Do you remember the names of these gents?

Admiral DeMars: No, I don't. No, I don't. But they were, it was clear, amazing guys.

Paul Stillwell: Was there a perception then that the amphibs were populated by second-class citizens?

Admiral DeMars: Not really. At least, not down at my level as an ensign, but clearly they were. [Laughter]

My son was born there in Long Beach.* Then I put Margaret and my brand-new son on an airplane and sent them back to Chicago to stay with her folks. The ship headed for WestPac independently at something like 12 knots, steaming along.† We picked up Korean Marines and we made practice landings on the east coast of Korea below the DMZ there.‡ So I was in a small boat running about eight LCVPs, and we'd go out and circle. Then we'd come in, and Marines would come down and get on and we'd do it. I thought, "Gee, this is a hell of a lot of fun, but no career."

So the first time that I could volunteer for was submarines, I volunteered for submarines never having been on one in my life. I don't think I saw one. Maybe I saw one, but not close.

Paul Stillwell: Why submarines?

Admiral DeMars: It's the first thing I could volunteer for. I had to get off this thing. What else could you volunteer for? I mean, that was it. I could wait it out, but BuPers had screwed me at least twice now, so I didn't have any hope for them.§ And with 22 ensigns on board they could spare me. So I got off in the Philippines and island-hopped

---

* Bruce F. DeMars was born 2 March 1958.
† WestPac – Western Pacific.
‡ DMZ – demilitarized zone.
§ BuPers – Bureau of Naval Personnel.

back on a big Constellation, and that was the beginning of the submarine business.* But it was a worthwhile time on there. I learned a lot, and would continue to mature.

Paul Stillwell: In the *Okanogan* did you have landing operations in any overseas ports or beaches?

Admiral DeMars: Oh, yes, yes, the east coast of Korea. We landed there four or five times. And it was sort of humorous to a degree. I mean, the Koreans are a lot smaller than us, and they had U.S. Marine gear, so they were just dragging. We were always worried when they were coming down the cargo nets, were they going to fall down or come down? But they were tough, very tough.

One time I was kind of standing out on deck and they had a long chow line there. We used to set the tables on the benches so they had to eat standing up. That was the way you did it on APAs, at least with Korean Marines [chuckle]. And so I was standing there watching this long chow line there. This one young Marine turned around, and he was jabbering with the guy behind him and the line opened up about three or four paces. This little sergeant came along, saw that, went over and tapped the guy on the shoulder. The guy turned around and he knocked him out, coldcocked. The guy just fell down. I thought, "God, these guys are tough." And they were tough, they were tough. But they had all this oversized gear. I mean, they were lugging big guns and bazookas and all of these things made for much bigger people. I got to really respect the Koreans there, and subsequently more so.

Paul Stillwell: Did you have U.S. Marines on board also?

Admiral DeMars: No, no. Just Koreans. There were a couple liaison officers, I guess, but they were just Korean Marines. So the food was terrible.

Paul Stillwell: What did you have for liberty ports in the Far East?

---

* The Lockheed Constellation was a four-engine propeller aircraft that was flown by commercial airlines at the time and also had a number of military variants.

Admiral DeMars: I don't remember any, to tell you the truth. I think we went to Naha, Okinawa. But nothing stuck out. I mean, I wasn't on there that long. I was on there like a year at the most, and some of it was workup and then we were over there, and then I left to go to sub school.

Paul Stillwell: What was your job in that ship?

Admiral DeMars: I was first division again, deck gang. It was not much to do, really, except make sure you don't get any rust in your space, and observe the passing scene.

Paul Stillwell: Did you stand deck watches?

Admiral DeMars: No. I stood CIC, I qualified as CIC officer.* Just wasn't on there long enough. And I sort of finessed it. In order to apply for sub school, you had to be at sea for a year, and qualify either as a deck officer or an engineering officer of the watch. Well, I was almost qualified as a deck officer, so they sort of gave me the qualification. But we never did anything but steam at 12 knots. We went across from Long Beach to— we picked them up in Okinawa or something—by ourselves at 12 knots. You talk about bored. God.

Paul Stillwell: Were you a boat officer for any of the landings?

Admiral DeMars: Yes, yes. For all of them. I ran my own little division of eight LCVPs, so that was fun. You had a radio and a coxswain, you went out and you circled, and then they called you in to load the Marines on. "Away all boats, away all boats!" It was all choreographed and an interesting thing to watch, particularly if you've read a lot of history of those sort of things.

---

* CIC – combat information center.

Paul Stillwell: There's a novel called *Away All Boats* about a World War II APA.*

Admiral DeMars: Yes, that's right. That's right. I read it. So it was an interesting time, and I knew it wasn't going to be the rest of my life, so that was good.

Paul Stillwell: What was your introduction to Submarine School?

Admiral DeMars: Well, it was sort of humorous. Submarine School was listed as being in New London, Connecticut, so we drove over there from Chicago, my wife and our new son, in our '53 Chevrolet. We came up to New London, turned right, and started looking for Submarine School. Well, of course, it's in Groton across the river. But we were looking all around. I finally stopped at a gas station and said, "Where's the submarine base?"

"Oh, that's across the river," or such. Oh, okay. So we went across the river down there. They didn't have the big Highway 12 built yet, so we went along the water, which was just a little two-lane highway. I mean, it's sort of hilly on one side, not a lot of homes, and on the other side's the water. I thought, God, this is really a secret place. [Laughter]

So we got in there and we checked in. We had very nice housing on the base, right essentially on the golf course. There were little two bedrooms upstairs, very small, and downstairs housing. But very nice. Margaret liked it.

The curriculum, I thought, was very functional, very basic. They taught you about the nuts and bolts of becoming a submariner. They had diving trainers you operated on. At least twice you went under way on diesel submarines and made dives and that, and surfaced, and drills, and that sort of thing.

They had the escape tower. That was the only problem I had there. You had to make a buoyant ascent from 100 feet. Now, they don't have it anymore. Now you do it in a swimming pool or something. But it's a little claustrophobic. That didn't bother me. But you had this lock way down at the bottom, and they'd put, like, six guys in there and

---

* Kenneth Dodson, *Away All Boats* (Boston: Little, Brown and Company, 1954). It was subsequently made into a 1956 feature film starring Jeff Chandler.

an instructor, and then they'd press it up with pressure to equalize pressure. You opened this big submarine door out, and then you'd go out there and you inflate your lifejacket and you start up. Now, they tell you you have to blow out or your lungs are going to explode, so you have to—whoooo. And they said, "Now, it's going to feel like you're running out of air, but you're not." Well, I felt like I was running out of air, so I stopped blowing out about halfway up and this diver pulled me in under this thing and hit me in the gut and says, "God damn it, Red, blow out! That's what we told you to do." And so he said, "Now, are you going to do it?"

"Yes, I'm going to do it."

He said, "Well, you're going to have to do it again, but do it." I had to go back down and do it again. I did it right the second time.

Paul Stillwell: Did you have a Momsen lung?

Admiral DeMars: No, no, no. That came later. And that was—oh, that guy Momsen should have been given a Congressional Medal of Honor.[*] Because the Momsen lung, of course, they put a hood over your head with a Plexiglas shield you could look out of, and then that hood was connected up to your lifejacket, which equalized the pressure. So you just breathed normally. No, we just went up. It was a buoyant ascent. So you were going to get up there, but you had to blow out. So I did that. That was the only thing I remember that was tough.

But it was an interesting time. We had damage control trainers. They had a whole course in how to be a submarine supply officer, because we didn't have Supply Corps officers in the submarines in those days. The first submarine you were on, that was always your job, which is what happened to me on *Capitaine*.

So it was good. The camaraderie was good. Everybody got along well.

---

[*] Invented by submariner Charles B. Momsen, the Momsen lung was a breathing apparatus to be used when ascending from a damaged submarine to the surface. It did not have its own air supply but used the air already in a man's lungs.

Paul Stillwell: How competitive was it within the class?

Admiral DeMars: No, not competitive. Everybody worked hard and tried to learn because they knew this was useful training. You were going to go off and do it on a ship, so that motivated most people. But I don't think anybody was trying to stand number one or anything.

One fellow was having a lot of problems; he was a lieutenant, and it was clear to most of us he wasn't going to make it. We had a commander there, Commander Tex Proctor, who was a real grommet.* He was loud, he was a Texan, he was always hanging around the bar up at the O-club.† On the second time under way, Proctor had ridden this young lieutenant hard. So they ran one drill and this lieutenant, who was going to be kicked out anyway, was on the bridge, and he shut the hatch and came down, and we were submerging. Then they passed the word, "An instructor was left topside." This kid turned around and said, "Which one?" [Laughter] Proctor was riding the submarine. "Which one?" Well, that was it; when we went back in he was gone. But everyone got a kick out of that.

Proctor was really something. We were going to have a skit before we graduated, up at the officers' club, and so they were up rehearsing and practicing, and Proctor was up there trying to make a run on somebody's wife or that. And there was this other lieutenant up there; I can't remember his name. He ended up going into nuclear power. But he was kind of an obstreperous guy. He was a qualified submariner. And so he walked up to Proctor, and Proctor was boozing and trying to hit on the women, and the lieutenant said, "Hey, Tex, you know what we do where I'm from when a Texan dies?"

Proctor knew he'd been had, but he didn't know how to get out of it. He said, "No, what?"

He said, "We give him an enema and bury him in a matchbox." [Laughter] Of course, all the students just erupted with laughter on that one. And that kind of calmed Proctor down for about two days.

---

* Commander Erman Oran Proctor, USN.
† O-club – officers' club.

But it was a fun time. I mean, there was a lot of socialness, and everybody got along well. We made good friends and we're still friends to this day.

Paul Stillwell: What was the school boat?

Admiral DeMars: Well, there were two of them. I can't remember their names. And they rotated, because we had a lot of diesel boats in those days.

Paul Stillwell: Did you practice making approaches?

Admiral DeMars: Oh yes, yes. We made approaches, mostly in the attack center trainers. They had—I don't know if you've ever seen it—a very interesting periscope where, if you went up topside the periscope came up and then they had a bunch of ships that moved around. So from down below if you put the scope up it looked like you were looking at a convoy. And so you'd make approaches and get in there. And if you got trapped by a destroyer, they would drop a big heavy weight up on top so it sounded like a depth charge. You got graded on that. And then you did some practice of that at sea, which must have driven the commanding officers nuts making sure that this young lieutenant didn't sink his ship on anything.

You made landings and you ran drills. It was very good training. It was six months, and when you left there you felt ready to go aboard your submarine.[*]

Paul Stillwell: Well, also a lot of memorization as at the Naval Academy, wasn't it?

Admiral DeMars: Right. Yep. Once again, if you could memorize you could get through it in good shape.

Paul Stillwell: What do you remember about learning about the diesels?

---

[*] Ensign DeMars attended Submarine School from November 1957 to May 1958.

Admiral DeMars: Ah, it wasn't that complicated or hard. We had to learn how to light them off and run them, and on and on. And the cubicle where you put the motors on the generators. It was a very simple machine, the diesel-electric submarine, a very straightforward, simple machine. Torpedo tubes, you had to learn all the interlocks, and on and on. You had to learn how to tune the radio transmitter. I mean, a lot of stuff, really practical sort of things, because when you got to your submarine you had to learn all that and be able to operate. So this was the intro to that.

Paul Stillwell: I talked to Admiral Crowe, and he said one thing he noticed in the great skippers was the ability to visualize spatial relationships in their heads so they could work out the geometry of an attack.*

Admiral DeMars: Yes. Yes. I agree 100%. When I was XO and then commanding officer, we used to have wardroom meetings, and I would always start off each one with some mental arithmetic of angle on the bow, distance, speed across the line of sight, to cause people to have to think in their minds of this very thing. Because in the modern day when the machines are doing most of the thinking for you, you have to visualize that in your own mind. And some people just don't come by it naturally. You have to teach them why it's important and how it's important.

Paul Stillwell: I presume you learned how to dive the boat and keep her in trim.

Admiral DeMars: Oh, yes. All of that was very important. And you did a lot of that on the diving trainers too. That was very helpful, those old diving trainers. So you were very well prepared when you left there to go aboard your first submarine.

Paul Stillwell: What was family life like there for you?

---

* See the Naval Historical Foundation oral history of Admiral William J. Crowe Jr., USN (Ret.). Crowe's final active duty billet was as Chairman of the Joint Chiefs of Staff from October 1985 to September 1989.

Admiral DeMars: Very good. Very good. I mean, it was a very social thing. You got home about 4:30 in the afternoon and didn't work on Saturdays [chuckle] or Sundays. It was very nice. And next to the golf course. You played a lot of golf. That'll come up later during my first Rickover interview. But it was very pleasant, very pleasant.

Paul Stillwell: Was the choice of duty after that based on class standing?

Admiral DeMars: Yes, yes it was. I had reasonable class standing, and we wanted to go back to San Diego because we liked that. I picked the USS *Capitaine*, which in retrospect was a great choice because of the commanding officer, Bill Leisk.* He was a very unique individual. He had been commissioned by the V-12 program, where you went off to college for two to three months or so, and then you were it.† His dad had run the liberty launches, ran the ferryboat between Santa Catalina Island and Long Beach, and so he grew up on the water. He was a fisherman, and on and on and on. But he was a real character. I mean, he was just an amazing, amazing man.

Paul Stillwell: What stories could you tell to illustrate that amazingness?

Admiral DeMars: Well, a number of them. I don't know where to start. Once we went out and were night steaming off the Coronado Islands, which are southwest of San Diego. They belong to Mexico. So we were out there, staying out of their territorial waters, and I had the midwatch. And about 2:00 in the morning the CO came up on deck and he said, "Bruce, turn off the diesels, go on the battery, turn off all the running lights."

"Yes, sir." Did that.

---

* USS *Capitaine* (SS-336) was a *Gato*-class submarine commissioned 26 January 1945. She had a displacement of 1,525 tons on the surface and 2,410 tons submerged. She was 312 feet long, 27 feet in the beam, and had a draft of 15 feet. Her top speed was 20 knots surfaced and 9 knots submerged. She was initially armed with ten 21-inch torpedo tubes and a 5-inch deck gun. She was decommissioned in February 1950 and recommissioned in February 1957. Ensign DeMars reported aboard in January 1959. The commanding officer was Lieutenant Commander William H. Leisk Jr., USN.
† During World War II, V-12 was a Naval Reserve officer training program in which individuals received naval instruction at the same time they worked toward bachelor's degrees. The program, which was held at civilian colleges and universities, took about two years. See James G. Schneider, *The Navy V-12 Program: Leadership for a Lifetime* (Boston: Houghton Mifflin, 1987).

He said, "We're going to go in and get some lobster." [Laughter] So we went into Mexican territorial waters on the battery with all the lights off, him down in the bow directing me, looking for—"There's one, okay. Come on, Bruce, make a good landing here." Boom, boom, he'd pull these lobster pots up on deck. He came up with enough lobster so the crew and the wardroom could have lobster with their eggs the next morning. He did stuff like that. Amazing guy.

The *Capitaine* was an unreconstructed World War II submarine. It had a cigarette deck back aft. No snorkel. Once we snorkeled through the bridge access hatch. We had to get from here to there, so he flooded the boat down quite a bit and lit off the diesels and took a suction through the bridge access hatch back through the tunnel doors and that to the diesels. My only thought was, "Somebody makes a mistake and we're all going to go to the bottom."

Once we were coming into port after a week out there, and there was this big carrier bobbing along waiting obviously to pick up a pilot, and we had the right of way. So the captain was bombing in, and all of a sudden the signal light came over from the carrier. One of our quartermasters was really a signalman. Roach was his name; of course, his nickname was Cocky—Cocky Roach. And he was just a blur on the light. He always amazed people there. How does a submarine have such a good signalman? So the signal came over from the carrier: "Please fall in behind."

Leisk was on the bridge, and he was swearing—ah, goddamn carriers, you know. So we fell in behind, and we were bobbing along, I don't know, about eight knots or something. And so after about five minutes the captain said, "Cocky, send them 'By your leave, sir,'" which is, of course, the naval term if you want to pass a senior. Usually it's when you're walking. You say, "By your leave, sir." And so he said, "Send that."

So Cocky: Brrrrrrrr. Long silence, about ten minutes. And then came back from the carrier, "Go ahead." [Laughter]

Paul Stillwell: They just thought about it for a little longer.

Admiral DeMars: He did stuff like that, though, all the time. He just—boom, boom, boom.

He had me make the first underway departure when I got aboard, had me make the first landing when we came back in. And I set about to qualify.

Oh, another thing we did. Twice we went up to the Puget Sound area and took reserves out on the weekends, from Seattle and Portland. And we had kind of a warped upper bridge access hatch. You pulled it shut, and you really had to cinch it down, or it would leak.

Paul Stillwell: Was there a problem with the gasket?

Admiral DeMars: No, it was actually warped. I mean, the gasket was there but it was warped just a little bit, and you really had to cinch it down. Well, we wouldn't tell the reserves who were making the dives about that hatch. They'd come down, they'd pull it shut, and, God, water was spewing in. Yaah! So we got a big kick out of that.

We bought our first house there, up on Clairemont Mesa. Pulled all the money together.

It's supposed to take 12 months; I qualified in ten months.[*] It all went very well. And in order to qualify in submarines in those days—I don't know what it is nowadays—you had an in-port exam by a commanding officer; then you had an underway exam by a commanding officer. Then the division commander kind of talked to you. Well, we had a division commander, Captain Wright, who had been the XO on *Cochino* when they lost it.[†] And they had lost several sailors when they were trying to transfer to another boat.

Paul Stillwell: The XO was badly burned.

---

[*] To qualify as a submariner and earn his dolphins, an officer or enlisted man must go through a formal process to demonstrate a thorough knowledge of the submarine's equipment and operating procedures.
[†] USS *Cochino* (SS-345) was lost off Norway on 26 August 1949 as the result of battery explosions and fires. For details see the Naval Institute oral history of Rear Admiral Roy S. Benson, USN (Ret.), and William J. Lederer, *The Last Voyage* (New York: Henry Holt and Company, 1950). Lieutenant Commander Richard M. Wright, USN, was the *Cochino*'s executive officer at the time of the fire.

Admiral DeMars: Yes, he was. This was the *Cochino*'s XO, now our division commander.* So I did my in-port test, and that was not bad. They had me walk through the boat and explain a few things and this and that.

Then I went under way on the *Raton*, which was an SSR that had a big radar mast on it.† A friend of mine from the Eighth Company, Pete Blair, was on there.‡ He was an Olympic wrestling champ, he was the intercollegiate heavyweight wrestling champ for, like, two years running at the Naval Academy. Wonderful guy. Powerful, big, strong guy. So he was a good friend of mine. So we were eating lunch, and the captain of the *Raton* said, "Okay, Bruce, we'll run you through a few things." And he said, "We got a crypto message in today, and they're having trouble breaking it. Pete, take Bruce down and tell him to see if he can figure out why we can't break this message."

So I went down and—again, from what I learned at Submarine School—the first thing you check is that the key lists you're using are the right date.§ So I checked that and I said, "Pete, this is the wrong date."

Blair said, "Oh, crap. The captain's going to be all over me. That's the third time that's happened."

I said, "Well, Pete, you've got to be more careful."

"I know, I know. Can we just sit down here for a while? Then we'll go up, and we'll have some kind of an excuse as to why we couldn't break it."

I said, "How about dirty rotors?" [Laughter] You know, that's a thing that frequently happened.

He said, "Oh, that would be great, Bruce." We sat down there for about 20 minutes, half an hour, then finally went up and Pete said, "Bruce broke the message, Captain. He did a great job."

"What was the problem?"

"Oh, the rotors were dirty."

---

* In 1959 Captain Wright became Commander Submarine Division 51. His oral history is in the collection of the Joyner Library, East Carolina University.
† USS *Raton* (SSR-270), which had been converted to a radar picket submarine.
‡ Lieutenant Peter S. Blair, USN, Naval Academy class of 1955.
§ Key lists provide the daily settings for the machines used in decrypting messages.

Paul Stillwell: Was this the old Adonis system?*

Admiral DeMars: Yes, yes. So that was a humorous story with my under way. The rest of the under way obviously went well.

So I was all done. I had passed the in-port exam and the underway exam. So I went up to see Captain Wright, the division commander. And he said—and you could tell he had been burned, you know, the side of his face—said, "What I'd like to do, Bruce, is go under way with you."

I didn't say I'd already had my under way. I just said, "Fine. Yes, sir."

"On your own boat. On *Capitaine*."

So about a week later he came down, and we went out and he told the captain, "Go out and anchor off of Coronado there." We went out and anchored off Coronado. Then he sat down in the wardroom with me and the captain and he said, "Okay, Bruce, what I'd like you to do here, all by yourself, is go, put the diesels,"—the diesels were shutdown; we were just on battery power—"go back, light off a diesel engine, go up forward, pull up the anchor, steer the ship around, get it under way, rig for dive, all compartments, submerge the ship, and get it on a level at 110 feet."

Paul Stillwell: Was this single-handed for you?

Admiral DeMars: Single-handed. I said, "Yes, sir." [Chuckle] It was more of a physical challenge. Oh, the crew loved it. I mean, I was running my ass off. First of all, I had to go through the entire ship and rig for dive. That wasn't hard because you've got a table you use—check this, boom, boom, boom. Then I started the diesel, and that wasn't hard; I knew how to do that. And then put the propulsion on the diesels and went up forward, pulled up the anchor, got that, went back and, boom. And then diving, I had to really think my way through that—how do you do that? Well, first of all I secured the diesel engine, went on the battery, then came up and shut the bridge hatch and secured all

---

* Adonis was the name of an off-line electro-mechanical crypto system in which a basket held a series of rotor whose settings could be adjusted. The machine was not hooked into the radio communication system for automatic encryption and decryption. The machine converted plain text to five-number code groups and vice versa. The results of encryption were then put into the radio system manually.

that. And then opened the vents and on and on, blew negative, went through the whole thing, which took about three hours. And the crew loved it, just watching. I got through all of that, and Captain Wright was pleased. He said, "That's good, Bruce. Very well done. You're now qualified in submarines."

Terror went through all the other unqualled officers in that division. They were all rushing to see when Captain Wright was going to get transferred. [Laughter] "Should I delay my qualification?" But it was memorable.

Paul Stillwell: And it had to be very satisfying for you.

Admiral DeMars: Oh, yes. I felt good. It meant that you really had learned your boat.

Paul Stillwell: Did you have any initiation or drinking your dolphins?

Admiral DeMars: Nah, we didn't do that in those days. We didn't do that in those days. No pounding them in or anything. I had to give a wetting-down party; that was the tradition, and I did, in our new house up at Clairemont Mesa. So that was the major thing there.

Paul Stillwell: Well, and that had to be another satisfying thing, to have your own home for the first time.

Admiral DeMars: Oh, yes. And we'd saved up. Of course, you started getting sub pay as soon as you reported in submarines. Saved that up.

After I'd been on board the ship now for not quite a year, I got orders to go back for an interview with Rickover. So I told Captain Leisk, "I don't want to leave. My God, I'm a big dog now, I just got qualified in submarines. Got a new house. Got a son here, a family."

The captain was a good man. He said, "I'll talk to the division commander," who was a different guy then; Wright had moved on.

So the division commander said, "I'll talk to the squadron commander." The squadron commander said, "I'll call back and see."

The word came back down: "Tell DeMars to get his ass to Washington." [Laughter]

So I was ordered to the first Rickover interview. I'd only been on the boat like 18 months, just beginning to enjoy life. Went back for the first Rickover interview. It was in Main Navy, downtown.*

Paul Stillwell: Constitution Avenue.

Admiral DeMars: Constitution Avenue. Old, beat-up old buildings. Linoleum on the deck.

You had two preliminary interviews with Rickover's staffers. Panoff was one of them, and the Supply Corps officer who was there, who was the toughest one.† Panoff was one, and—it'll come to me later.

So I went in and sat down. I had barely compressed the cushion of the chair. Rickover was the first admiral I'd even spoken to in my life, or maybe the first one I'd ever been this close to in my life. He was a three-star then. He said, "Why didn't you stand as well at Submarine School as you did at the Naval Academy?"

The other interviewers had warned me, "Tell the truth, tell the truth."

I said, "Well, Admiral, I was married. We lived close to the golf course, and I played too much golf."

"Get *out* of here!" I was probably in there 30 seconds; he threw me out.

So I went off, and I sat in this little cubicle for two hours. Finally somebody came in—you can't tell who's who because they all wear civilian clothes—and he gave me two books, one on math and the other on physics. He said, "You're going to come

---

* Main Navy was the popular name for the old Navy Department building at 17th Street and Constitution Avenue in Washington, D.C. The building remained in use from its opening in 1918 until the early 1970s, when President Richard Nixon directed that it be demolished. The adjacent Munitions Building was long occupied by the War Department. In 1943, with the opening of the Pentagon, the Army moved out and transferred the Munitions Building to the Navy.

† Robert Panoff was a civilian engineer who had met Rickover while both were with the Bureau of Ships during World War II. Panoff specialized in submarine design issues.

back in four months and take an exam."

I said, "Look, I'm standing one in three watches under way, one in four watches in port; I don't have time for this."

He said, "Just do what we're telling you, jaygee."*

So I went back home. I'd come off the bridge on the *Capitaine*, wet, cold, sitting in my little stateroom there trying to study physics and math. Anyway, I went back four months later, took about a six-hour exam, never knew how I did at that. Then I went back in for my second interview after this three- or four-month study program, I can't remember exactly what.

Rickover said, "Do you smoke cigars?"

Now, in the back of my mind I thought: "This is going better already, this is going better."

I said, "Yes, sir. I don't buy them, but if somebody gives me one I smoke it."

So he picked up this box, opened it up, pulled out this cigar, and flipped it right across the desk to me. I caught it, and he said, "Go off, smoke that cigar, and write me a report on it."

"Yes, sir."

When I got up and left, I thought: "I think I've got it made now; how can you screw up smoking a cigar?" I could hear guys coughing in other cubicles because they were actually inhaling. You know, if you smoke cigars you don't inhale. So I fired this baby off, and it was drier than a dog turd, so I didn't really smoke it.

So I wrote the report. I wrote, "From: Lieutenant (j.g.) B. DeMars; To: VADM H. G. Rickover; Subj: Cigars. This was once probably a very fine cigar, but I recommend you upgrade the storage facilities. Very respectfully, B. DeMars."

So I called in this guy who I thought was a yeoman. I said, "Would you type this up? It's something Admiral Rickover asked me."

He said, "Oh, we don't have to type it."

I said, "Type it up." And they'd never had people talk to them like that there.

I said, "Goddamn it, type it up."

---

* Jaygee – lieutenant (junior grade).

"Oh, yes sir, yes sir." So he went, brrrrr. Because I wanted it to look formal. So he brought it back in, I proofread it, I signed it, I gave it to him, and he went back in. Two hours later somebody came in and said, "Okay, you've been accepted."

Never knew how I did on the exam. The exam and the four-month study were clearly my penance for playing too much golf or something. And I ended up being the head of Naval Reactors years later, but I got thrown out twice by Rickover. [Laughter]

Paul Stillwell: I gather that you didn't mention to him at any point that you didn't really want to do this.

Admiral DeMars: Oh, no. No, no, no. You know, once again, I was a jaygee. You do what you do in the Navy, but I clearly didn't want to do it. So here I had to go back and tell Margaret, "Okay, we're going to leave our house and rent it. Hopefully we can rent it; we won't go broke." And I had to come off sub pay, because in those days unless you were attached to a submarine you didn't get sub pay. All that changed. There was no nuclear power pay; I never got paid nuclear power pay. I always kind of stayed ahead of the groundswell of people they needed for that.

Paul Stillwell: Well, going back to *Capitaine*, how would you describe her mission during the time you were on board?

Admiral DeMars: Training, largely. Training of the surface forces.

Paul Stillwell: Target ship.

Admiral DeMars: Yes. We did bottom once and have an ASR come over and lower down the bell on us, and I went up in the bell.* That was kind of a nice experience. So

---

* ASR is the designation of a submarine rescue ship, equipped with a chamber designed to be lowered to pick up crew members from a submarine stranded on the bottom. Such a chamber was used successfully to recover men from the USS *Squalus* (SS-192) in May 1939.

we were a training boat, basically.

Paul Stillwell: Did you deploy at all?

Admiral DeMars: No. Never did.

Paul Stillwell: Well, that left a lot of nights at home.

Admiral DeMars: Yes. Well, I was standing one-in-four watch, though; you didn't have a lot of nights off. We only had, I think, eight officers at the most. And they were good. It was a good crew, good officers, good crew, nice people.

Paul Stillwell: What lessons did you carry forward from that diesel boat that you applied the rest of your career?

Admiral DeMars: Audacity. I mean, Leisk was an audacious guy. Audacity. Attention to detail. Of course, that whole qualification thing brought home you'd better that know your boat, better learn your stuff, because of the lessons that the division commander had gone through in the *Cochino*. So that was it. I had good petty officers. While I was on there, I was the supply officer first, then I was the communicator, and then I was the weapons officer. You changed about every six months.

Paul Stillwell: Did you reek of diesel fumes when you went home?

Admiral DeMars: Oh, yes. [Laughter] Margaret would make me undress in the foyer or something and just throw all my clothes in the washing machine. Yes, everything smelled. You didn't realize when you were on the boat but, oh, God, when you got off and you got home you think, "God, I really do stink."

But it was nice. A deployment for us was to go up to Puget Sound, and we did that twice. Once we were tasked, when we were up there, between carrying reserves on the weekend, to do a war shot sinking of this old ammunition ship that the Navy had there. They said it was only inert ammunition, weapons and that on board, and so we were out in the ocean, not in the Puget Sound area. So we had a Mark 14 torpedo. We made it ready, stood off, I don't know, about 2,000 yards or something like that, shot at it, hit it, blew it up. Ah, that's great. So we surfaced there, went over the top to see if there was anything still floating. We just about got over the top of it and there was this tremendous explosion from down below there. Something there was still not inert. Blew up and, boom, the boat went whoom, like that. I thought, God, I'm glad we got on the surface. That was interesting.

Paul Stillwell: I take it you'd been taught about torpedo maintenance and use during Submarine School.

Admiral DeMars: Oh, yes, how to make them ready and all of that. But that was very interesting.

Paul Stillwell: And you learned the torpedo data computer at some point?

Admiral DeMars: Right. Oh, yes, yes. Those things weren't exactly human-engineered very well. The most important thing you had to do on the TDC was then to make the settings down on the bottom that would go into the torpedo.* And you had to squat, with not enough room to really set these things up properly. Who designed that? Hmm.

But, no, I learned a lot, and I continued to have fun in the Navy. Just enjoy what you're doing, play it as it lies, take whatever comes and make the best of it. And fortunately I married a wonderful gal, and she was the same way. She just never complained, threw herself into everything. There was a good wives' group on *Capitaine*. There was no wives' group on the two APAs. Never got together; you never knew anybody. But on *Capitaine* they all got along very well. We had good wardroom parties and ship's picnics and that sort of stuff, so it was a whole different world.

I validated that I'd made the right decision on going into the submarine service.

---

* TDC – The torpedo data computer was a piece of analog equipment that figured approach courses for torpedoes to take on their way to a target and set the torpedo gyros prior to firing.

Paul Stillwell: How would you compare the quality of the enlisted crew in that boat with the nuclear submarines you served in later?

Admiral DeMars: I think they were every bit as good. It was just a less complicated platform, but they were every bit as dedicated and as good. The best crew I was on, on all my ships, was the *George Washington*, and I'll talk about that when I get there. It was the first SSBN, first ballistic missile submarine, and therefore they really loaded it down. The wardroom and the crew were the most talented of any boat I'd ever been on in my life, before that and after. I mean, everybody in the wardroom was wearing dolphins; they were all qualified in submarines. And it was very, very capable. I mean, it was just remarkable how good they were.

But the *Capitaine* was a good boat. It was a great first boat. I learned a lot, and I felt I was making a contribution, even when I was the supply officer. It was interesting, because in those days you ordered things, and then you just gave them to the division that ordered them. You didn't have centralized storage. They wanted a widget or something, they filled out a little chit, they gave it to you, you processed it up through the system. A storekeeper went up, picked it up, you signed it over, and they put it somewhere on the boat [chuckle]. It was up to them. It was theirs. So it was a totally different operation.

Paul Stillwell: How good did you get at ship handling during that tour?

Admiral DeMars: Very good, because it's an easy ship to handle. I mean, two screws, and you could twist it, you could do this and that. And you gained confidence, but it was hard to hurt it. I mean, it had a big superstructure around the bow, and you had these fenders that people hung over the sides, so if you hit it too hard you didn't scrape anything. A lot different from a nuke, which is very tender up forward.

Paul Stillwell: I take it that the deck gun had been taken off by then.

Admiral DeMars: It had been taken off. Because this was an old World War II boat, we still had the battle surfacing hatch, which was right off the control room, and you had a little chamber. The gun crew guys would go up in there, and you'd shut the hatch down below and they'd be in that one up there. Then you blew the tanks very slowly and tried to hold the boat down. And then when you just about couldn't hold it, you changed the angle on the planes and blew the tanks, popped up, they'd open up this hatch, rush out, load the gun, and shoot. So we had that, and we had an ammunition scuttle in the galley where you could pass shells up through this little sort of double-ended torpedo tube. So it was an interesting boat. Reduction gear, slow-speed main engines. Interesting boat.

Paul Stillwell: Well, please proceed to Nuclear Power School.

Admiral DeMars: Yes, Nuclear Power School. This was in the early days, so classes were small. I went to Nuclear Power School up in Mare Island Naval Shipyard.[*] There were two; there was one in Mare Island and one in Bainbridge. I went to the West Coast one. There were only 12 in our class, which was very tiny. The curriculum was impenetrable. You didn't understand any of it. It was unbelievable. I ended up standing right in the middle; I think I stood number six out of 12. The instructors were young guys right out of college that Rickover had interviewed and hired and then sent out.

Paul Stillwell: Civilians?

Admiral DeMars: Well, no, they were all naval officers, but either OCS or NROTC.[†] So they were brilliant in their fields. You know, one guy would be writing with one hand and erasing with the other. Aww.

Stan Severance was my running mate there.[‡] He became a submariner, retired as a two-star, good guy. We'd go to school in the morning. We lived in Wherry Housing, which was right near the building.[§] So we'd go show up at 8:00 o'clock in the morning,

---

[*] Mare Island Navy Yard, Vallejo, California, began operation in September 1854. It was the Navy's first shipyard on the West Coast. Shortly after World War II, the title was change to Mare Island Naval Shipyard. It was decommissioned in April 1996 as the result of the Base Realignment and Closure process.
[†] OCS – Officer Candidate School.
[‡] Lieutenant (junior grade) Laverne Stanard Severance Jr., USN.
[§] Kenneth S. Wherry served as a U.S. Senator from Nebraska from 1943 until his death in 1951. Wherry Housing for military families was named for him.

work all day, we'd get home around 3:30, we'd kind of lounge around for about an hour, and eat. Then one night he'd come down to my house, and the next night I'd go up to his house. We'd study till, like 10:00 o'clock at night, trying to make something out of this stuff. I mean, it was math, physics, and nothing was translatable to what we thought we were going to have to be doing, either at the land-based reactors we were all going to go to after that, or on the nuclear submarine. I think it was just some quirky thing that Rickover had in his mind that nobody talked him out of, or could talk him out of. I don't know what they were trying to make out of us. It was the biggest goddamn waste of time I've ever been at.

So, anyway, we got through that. Our daughter was born there.* One afternoon I came home at 3:30. All the wives were sitting out on the lawn in front of our unit there, and they said, "Bruce, you'd better get Margaret to the hospital." She's about to have her second baby.

I said, "Oh, okay." We had a Volkswagen, so we got in, I pulled up at the emergency entrance and went running in, they came out. As Margaret was getting out of the Volkswagen her bag burst, water all over the place, so they put her on the wheelchair, rode her in. I went and parked the car. By the time I got back in, I had a daughter.

Paul Stillwell: Wow! [Laughter]

Admiral DeMars: I said, "Margaret, you can't be that blasé."
She said, "Well, it just went easily." So yes, that was it.

Paul Stillwell: A whole lot better than a long labor.

Admiral DeMars: We almost had the baby in the Volkswagen. But, anyway, that was a great story.
So we got through that, and, as I said, I ended up in the middle. I think Stan Severance ended up number 11 out of 12, or something.

---

* Margaret A. DeMars was born 17 May 1960.

Paul Stillwell: Did you gradually start penetrating the impenetrable?

Admiral DeMars: It never made sense. A couple of things, a little bit on radiation and that, you learned a little bit about that. But the physics and the math, the math particularly, you know, it was just, "Why are we learning this?" You could memorize enough, and I think the instructors knew what they were doing also, so they graded on a curve. But it was terrible. Anyway, I went back there as an instructor later, and it was a little better.

Paul Stillwell: Was Admiral Rickover getting frequent updates on your progress?

Admiral DeMars: I had no idea. Once again, I'd had enough of Rickover by then, having been thrown out twice. That's all I have on Nuclear Power School.

We went from there to the land-based reactor site, which was in upstate New York. We lived in Saratoga Springs. It's called West Milton, which was just a little township there. And once again it was a small class. There were about three officers per shift. We were running eight-hour shifts so that would have been what—nine, ten officers there. And there were four reactors up there then—three or four—and I was on the S3G, which was the *Triton* prototype, the two-reactor one.*

Paul Stillwell: Ned Beach's boat.

Admiral DeMars: Ned Beach's boat.† And it really was a surface-ship steam plant, with the steam being made by a reactor. Because it was large; it was massive. The thing I remember most—and this was a wonderful experience and great practical training. This was more like Submarine School. I mean, your job was to learn how to stand all the watches, enlisted watches and chief watches, and then stand the top watch, engineering

---

* USS *Triton* (SSRN-586) was a nuclear-powered radar picket submarine, built by the Electric Boat Division of the General Dynamics Corporation, Groton, Connection, and commissioned on 10 November 1959. She was ostensibly a radar-picket submarine but actually a test ship for a two-reactor propulsion plant. The S3G designator meant it was the third type of submarine reactor manufactured by General Electric.
† In the spring of 1960, the *Triton*, commanded by Captain Edward L. Beach, USN, made the first submerged circumnavigation of the world.

officer of the watch. So you really had to set to. You had all these qualification cards. You had to get signatures and trace out systems and answer questions. Most of it was in-hull. Very little of it was outside the hull in classroom.

The thing I remember most, we had a de-aerating feed tank, which was a big tank that heated up the water before it got sent by the feed pumps into the steam generators. And you had to be very careful about how you used the feed pumps, because you could quench the DFT, which means you put out the steam bubble, and then things went to hell in a hand basket. But more importantly, when you shut that plant down, you had to make sure you filled up the steam generators high. So you filled them up high, you shut the plant down, everything cooled down, they contracted a little bit. Because the feed pumps were steam driven, so without steam you couldn't feed the boilers. And where did you get your steam from? From the boilers.

Paul Stillwell: Catch-22.

Admiral DeMars: You got things going, and everything had to be choreographed. I mean, to light off these feed pumps you were opening these big gigundous valves to let steam into them. It was really interesting. It was very, very fascinating.

So we had a good time there. My running mate, the other guy that was in my section, was Phil Bonz, who went from there to go to *Triton*.[*] And interestingly enough, I was in Norfolk later. I had been to *George Washington*, I had been teaching at Nuclear Power School, and I had been on *Snook*, and I was at the Armed Forces Staff College in Norfolk. He was still on *Triton*. In those days Naval Reactors did a dumb thing. They didn't think people were smart enough to learn those one-of-a-kind ships like *Triton* or, you know, *NR-1*, or the *Narwhal*, it was direct drive.[†] So they would fleet up. The

---

[*] Lieutenant Philip E. Bonz, USN.
[†] *NR-1*, a nuclear-powered, deep-submergence research and ocean-engineering vehicle was launched 25 January 1969 by the Electric Boat Division and delivered to the Navy on 27 October 1969. She was 140 feet long, had a beam of 12 feet, and displaced 400 tons submerged. She was taken out of service in 2008. USS *Narwhal* (SSN-671), a fast-attack nuclear attack submarine, was the only ship of her class. She was commissioned 12 July 1969. She was 314 feet long, 38 feet in the beam. She displaced 4,450 tons standard and 5,350 tons submerged. She had a top speed on the surface around 20 knots and a speed in excess of 30 knots submerged. She was equipped with four 21-inch torpedo tubes.

engineer would become the XO, the XO would become the CO. Well, later on they found out you never got any fresh ideas that way.

Paul Stillwell: Good point.

Admiral DeMars: Isn't that interesting? Oh, isn't that a surprise? So poor Phil had been kept on that way. He was getting out. I said, "Well, that's the only way you're going to get off *Triton*."

But it was a wonderful plant, it was a great time. As I said, the curriculum was very practical. I was the first one to qualify, finish all my qual cards and everything. So because of that I stood first in my class. You can tell it was very practical; this was not a theoretical course.

Paul Stillwell: How demanding was the schedule?

Admiral DeMars: You were eight hours on, 16 hours off. And then you kept rotating so one week you'd have days, the next week you'd have swings, the next week you'd have midwatch. So you were kind of coming and going. And every now and then, because they had to shut the plant down to do something, then you'd have some training classes on radiation or something of that sort. It was a very demanding schedule. You didn't have much time off.

Paul Stillwell: Who were the teachers that were guiding you in this?

Admiral DeMars: For the most part it was General Electric employees. They were very good. There was obviously a commanding officer who ran the military aspects of it there, but the whole site was run by GE, West Milton, by the Schenectady nuclear power lab. They were very good, they were very patient, they knew how to do this, and it was very good training. Since I qualified first, got everything done, they put me on the watch bill as the senior instructor for one section. [Laughter] So here, a week before, I didn't know anything; now I was the senior instructor for one section, and I was teaching other people. So that kind of impressed me.

Paul Stillwell: How much emphasis was there on safety?

Admiral DeMars: Very much so. Very much so. Safety and radiation health. You weren't allowed to get too much radiation.

Paul Stillwell: Did you wear dosimeters?

Admiral DeMars: Oh yes, yes, you wore all that stuff. It was very interesting. The most radiation I got—I forget, I got something like 2.8 Rem my entire naval career. Of those Rem, I got 2.5 of them at the prototype and on *George Washington* and on *Snook*. By then the technology of water chemistry was better perfected to where you didn't allow crud to build up and irradiate and move around, and so on and so forth. And so I hardly got any the next 30 years in the nuclear power business, although I had a batch of nuclear power jobs. So that was very instrumental in that.

But I was first to qualify, and eventually all these other guys qualified, and they were all getting orders off somewhere. So I went in to see the personnel officer there, the Navy guy, and said, "They forget about me or something?"

He said, "I'll give them a call, Bruce. Drop in tomorrow." Well, he called me at home that night and said, "You've got to leave immediately." Once again, BuPers—give me a freakin' break. He said, "You've got to leave immediately and join the crew of the USS *George Washington* in Groton, Connecticut, to fly to Holy Loch."* And I had like about four days to do that.

We had to get out of our apartment there. And in the back of my mind I was always worried about my house in San Diego—"Can I keep renters? If that goes empty

---

* The keel for the Polaris ballistic missile submarine *George Washington* (SSBN-598) was laid on 1 November 1957. She was launched on 9 June 1959 and commissioned on 30 December 1959. Her first deterrent patrol began in November 1960. She served until being decommissioned on 24 January 1985. Commander James B. Osborn, USN, was the first commanding officer of the blue crew. The submarine had two crews, blue and gold, that alternated in manning her.

I'm going to have to declare bankruptcy and on and on." So I took my wife and children, put them in the car, drove to Chicago and turned them over to my in-laws, and flew to Groton, New London, and departed the next day with the blue crew to Holy Loch, Scotland.* So once again, BuPers. Or maybe it was just DeMars. They said, "We've got to screw somebody royally, and this is the guy we've picked for this decade." [Laughter]

Paul Stillwell: That's an honor!

Admiral DeMars: But it was amazing.

Paul Stillwell: But this was after you asked for orders. What if you hadn't asked?

Admiral DeMars: Oh, I'd have been flying to Holy Loch by myself. Yes, it was amazing.

But the prototype was a good experience. It was very satisfying. I mean, we all had the old-fashioned lunch baskets that opened up, the black metal ones. We all kind of became working stiffs. You wore civilian clothes to the site, and then you changed there into your uniform, then you went on. Not sure why we did that, but that's what they told us to do. But it was very practical. I mean, you were confident you knew how to operate a steam plant and a reactor plant when you left there.

Paul Stillwell: Did you wear coveralls, or khakis?

Admiral DeMars: Just khakis, wash khakis. We didn't ever wear safety hats or safety glasses or safety shoes. Maybe they do now. Probably they do now. But it was a very practical education, very well designed, very well administered. I felt like I learned an awful lot. I was ready to go, very confident to go off to a nuclear-powered vessel and stand watch.

---

* When the Polaris program was established, the range of the initial A-1 missile was so short that the submarines had to operate close in to the Soviet Union. To facilitate operations, the submarines and their assigned tender were based in Holy Loch, Scotland. The base was used until the early 1990s, when the advent of the long-range Trident ballistic missile made overseas basing unnecessary.

Paul Stillwell: What happened when you got there?

Admiral DeMars: It even got better. As I said, I met the rest of the crew the next morning, and we all got on buses, went to Quonset Point, Rhode Island, got on a Navy airplane that flew to Prestwick, Scotland via Iceland, where we stopped to refuel.* Then we got on buses that took us to Holy Loch, got on a boat, went out to the ship, and we were there at the *George Washington*. Which is really where, on that ship, I got most of my engineering experience, because I was on there for three patrols and three upkeeps. I was the main propulsion assistant and the damage control assistant, so I stood a lot of watches. I never stood forward watches, always in the engineering spaces. And I was involved in fixing things during the upkeep, and on and on. So it was a great experience.

People ask, "Aw gee, wasn't it boring?" The challenge in that ship was to make everything run and work, because this was the first upkeep in the Holy Loch. I joined for the second patrol; the first patrol went out of Charleston. This was the second patrol out of Holy Loch by an SSBN, so everything was new.

We had some squirrelly things on that ship. We had a station-keeping anchor, which was a big mushroom anchor that housed in the bottom of the ship and, I forget exactly how much, but like 3,000 fathoms of 1-inch nylon cord that wrapped around sort of a fishing-rod sort of deal inside the hull. And so the thought was that there was a part of the ocean that had been very rigorously bottom-contour surveyed, and you had special charts that told you where those were. So if you had concerns that you had lost your navigational capability or that, you'd go over to this spot. You'd take some star sights and then go over to this spot, put the anchor down, and go and ride on the anchor. So you knew where you were, you could still fire your missiles if you had to. So we would lower that every now and then and try it out. You had to be very careful, or you'd get the world's biggest bird's nest. You know what that is if you're a fly caster or a bait-casting fisherman.

Paul Stillwell: No.

---

* Lieutenant (junior grade) DeMars reported to the crew of the *George Washington* in April 1961.

Admiral DeMars: If you don't use your thumb right, the thing all winds up and it takes you an hour to undo it.

Paul Stillwell: That's an awfully long anchor cable.

Admiral DeMars: Oh, yes. Well, there were deep spots up there. And the range of the missile was only 1,200 nautical miles, so we were up in the northern Norwegian Sea, pretty close to bad stuff.

Paul Stillwell: What are your recollections of Commander Osborn as a skipper?

Admiral DeMars: Let me finish these other two crazy things.

The other thing we had was a precession gyro, which was a giant gyro. It would barely fit in this kitchen. It spun up at tremendous rpm. And the purpose of that was, if you had to fire from the surface for whatever reason you didn't want the missiles to go off and maybe fall back on the submarine. You spun this thing up, and then you precessed the ship over with that, about 15 degrees worth, so you shot the missiles out that way. It's a crazy thing. Once we were down about 200 feet, 300 feet, in the northern Norwegian Sea steaming along at three, four knots, and the ship started rolling about 15 degrees. The IC electrician down there, who was running the PMs, had screwed up, and he was precessing the entire ship.* (Laughter)

We had an oxygen generator that was called "missile tube number 19" because occasionally it blew up. And so we had a lot of crazy things.

But Jim Osborn was remarkable. I mean, I was very fortunate. This was my second CO. Bill Leisk on *Capitaine* was a great guy. Jim Osborn was great in a different way, obviously. He was brilliant. He was absolutely brilliant. He was tough. He was easy to get along with, but I mean just a wonderful guy. The wives loved him.

Paul Stillwell: Tough in what way?

---

* Shipboard gyrocompasses are maintained by enlisted personnel in the rating of interior communications electrician (IC). PM – preventive maintenance.

Admiral DeMars: Taskmaster. I mean, you had to do your job, and you had to do it well, you had to work hard, you had to work as hard as him. Nobody could ever be as smart as him. He was brilliant.

He and the chief sonarman had determined somehow that the BQR-2B, which was our main sonar, was cut to the wrong frequency for Soviet submarines. So they invented a mod electronically and put it in. Of course, with their judgments it worked wonderful now. So they came back, and he was a little proud of that.

Unfortunately, we turned the ship over to the gold crew, and while they were on patrol they decided that—shows you how different it was in those days—they decided that the steam generator alarms for the steam generator level were set too high. You had plenty of time when those alarms went off; we should set them lower so that you really had to take action when they went off. Well, Rickover about went hermantile when he heard they had changed these setting, so he just beat up on SubLant, SubLant beat up on everybody, and all of a sudden unauthorized alterations were a big no-no.[*]

So—and I know this story is true because Admiral Daspit, who was deputy ComSubLant, which was in Groton at that time—

Paul Stillwell: He got demoted when it went to Norfolk and three stars.

Admiral DeMars: Right.

Paul Stillwell: Joe Grenfell.[†]

Admiral DeMars: Right. But Daspit was in Groton, because we didn't have any submarines in Norfolk. And I knew his aide personally. Osborn went in to make his call before we were going to sail on the next patrol, and they went through the whole thing. Daspit said, "Now, that alteration isn't in there now, is it?"

---

[*] SubLant – Submarine Force Atlantic Fleet, the type commander.
[†] Rear Admiral Lawrence R. Daspit, USN, served as Commander Submarine Force Atlantic Fleet from 13 January 1960 to 2 September 1960. Vice Admiral Elton W. Grenfell, USN, served as Commander Submarine Force Atlantic Fleet from 2 September 1960 to 1 September 1964. The change was made because of operational control of the Polaris submarines going to Commander in Chief Atlantic in Norfolk. After Admiral Daspit was relieved as ComSubLant, he remained in Groton as deputy type commander.

"Oh, no, no, sir. No, Admiral, it isn't."

Okay, fine, good. So Osborn got up to leave, and the aide was sitting over in the corner. Just about halfway to the door, Osborn turned around and said, "Admiral, that mod's not in there now, but you can bet your butt it's going to be in right after we get under way." [Laughter]

Daspit didn't know what to do. He just—ah, ah, ah.

Paul Stillwell: You're talking about the sonar mod.

Admiral DeMars: Yes, the sonar mod. And so he did. We put it back in before we got under way. But that's the kind of guy he was. He was a remarkable man.

You had to be careful when you were reporting. After you'd finished your engineering officer of the watch, you'd come forward and report to the captain everything's fine, etc., etc. You had to be careful. If the light was on in his room and he was doing something, you'd think, "Oh, shit, how do I get in and out of there?"

Because he'd sit you down. "Bruce, let me show you," blah blah. You'd have another hour in there as he was going over something with you.

But he was a very personable guy. He was a good man. But, as I said, the wardroom and the crew were the strongest I ever served with. It was clear they had all been handpicked. Everybody in the wardroom wore dolphins. They were all lieutenants or lieutenant commanders.

Paul Stillwell: And you had a doctor.

Admiral DeMars: And we had a doctor. So, I mean, I didn't have any trouble fitting in because I was qualified in submarines and I'd been on a submarine, I'd been on two surface ships, I'd been around the block a little bit. But it was a very talented crew.

Well, the whole ballistic missile program, from the time Eisenhower said, "I want one," to shooting the first missile, was four years.* And when Eisenhower said, "I want one," we didn't have a missile, we didn't have a warhead, we didn't have a guidance system, we didn't have a submarine. Four years later they shot the first missile. I mean, nowadays it takes you that long to process the environmental impact statement.

Paul Stillwell: It obviously had high priority within the Navy.

Admiral DeMars: Very high priority.

The other thing is that those early COs had a different relationship with Rickover. They called him "Rick," and they didn't take any crap. Our engineer—this was the patrol before I got aboard, the first patrol, during getting ready for it or something—they had accidentally boiled a steam generator dry, because the indication system had failed and they hadn't recognized that. Shep Jenks was the engineer; it wasn't his fault that it happened.† So Rickover told his staff, "Tell Osborn to fire the engineer."

Osborn said, "I'm not going to do that; it wasn't his fault." Well, this became a ba-ba-ba, you know.

Rickover was on the phone yelling at Osborn, "You've got to fire that engineer, goddamn it, or I'll fire you."

"Well, fire me. Fire both of us. That's your prerogative."

Osborn finally said, "I've got to put and end to this tit for tatting. I'm going to go down and see Rickover." So he made an appointment to go down when we were in the off crew. He went down and he came back, he relayed the whole thing to us. But he went in and saw Rickover, they talked for about 45 minutes, and the subject never came up. It was all over. I mean, that's the kind of guy Osborn was. He'd go to bat for you. It was a great illustration of leadership and loyalty.

(Interruption for change of tape)

---

* Dwight D. Eisenhower served as President of the United States from 20 January 1953 to 20 January 1961.

† Lieutenant Commander Shepherd M. Jenks, USN.

Admiral DeMars: Most of the early Polaris skippers had either been in World War II or at least the tail end of World War II, and so they weren't fresh caught. They'd all had commands of diesel boats and done important things in life, and so they weren't going to be kicked around.

I was the main propulsion assistant on the ship, and, as I said, that's where I got most of my real engineering training in the business. I had a great chief machinist's mate. I mean, he really was good. He taught me an awful lot. We were in the dry dock during most of this refit, and so I got to get through all of that stuff. But I did get a majority of my good engineering training on this ship, because it was three patrols, and all I did was stand engineering watches. And the six-week upkeeps were really hectic. I mean, you had to fix everything, get it done, and you had to fix all this stuff at sea that was brand new and didn't operate the way people thought it would.

Paul Stillwell: Were there bugs that had to be ironed out?

Admiral DeMars: Yes, there were bugs, there were unknowns, there were other things that just didn't work right. On the second or third patrol I was shifted, became the damage control assistant, DCA, and the missile stations diving officer. But one caper I had, as A division officer/DCA, I was in charge of the atmosphere control equipment. Freon is used in the air-conditioning and that. There's a certain level of Freon you're supposed to maintain. I forget what it was, it was something like 50, or 30, or something, ppm, parts per million. And we had an atmosphere analyzer that read things out. He kept saying that I had 50, you know, where the limit was 30—and I forget the exact numbers. I thought, "This can't be right."

The captain was always on me, and when my auxiliarymen got off watch, I had them take the halide torch and go around to all the joints. It would burn a different color if Freon was there. So I thought, "I'm going to fix this." So near the end of the patrol I got an empty little gas canister, hooked it up to the control air compressor, which was 120 psi air compressor, and I pumped down the atmosphere and filled this thing up and pressurized it and pulled it all off. When we got into port, I sent that over my signature to the Naval Research Lab here and said, "Would you please analyze this, particularly for Freon?"

They came back and said the Freon was 300 ppm! But unfortunately they sent the letter back to the command, not to me. Well, Osborn got the biggest kick out of that. He said, "Well, Bruce, you were trying to do the right thing." But, see, that's the kind of guy he was. He wouldn't get mad at you for something like that.

We had a little O-club at the Royal Marine Hotel in town, which was really just a corner of the main lounge area.* But the COs would go up in there, and they'd shoot dice and they'd play poker. We didn't get ashore very much, but I was coming back one weekend from just walking around Dunoon, and there were all these protesters lying on the pier that you had to go out on to get to the boat to go back out to the tender. An old Scottish bobby was on the end of the pier. He said, "Awk, lad, don't pay them a heed; they're all up from London." [Laughter] So the relationship with the locals was very, very good.

Paul Stillwell: Did they try to block your path?

Admiral DeMars: No, but you had to walk so you didn't step on them. They were just being a pain in the ass.

I had to qualify as engineering officer of the watch, and so Osborn told the engineer, "Talk to him." So the engineer walked me around and asked me a few questions, and then I sat down with Osborn and we largely talked about sonar and other things. He said, "Okay, you're a qualified engineering officer of the watch. Now, we're going to get other new guys. How about write an instruction on how we're going to qualify engineering officers of the watch from now on, because we don't have an instruction for that. And you're going to make the first startup." So I made the first reactor startup on the ship. But it was not a big deal, because I had done it at the prototype, and the fundamentals are the same, pressurized water reactors, and I had a good crew. So we got through that fine. Then when we got back in I made the first shutdown. But that was very interesting.

---

* The town was Dunoon, Argyll, Scotland.

Paul Stillwell: Would you talk, please, about how a patrol went, what you would do while you were under way.

Admiral DeMars: Well, you were always sort of sleep deprived because you were four hours on and eight hours off, four hours on, eight hours off. Plus there was training and there were drills, although we never did engineering department drills in those days. Osborn said, "I'm not going to drill; we've got to keep the plant on line." And there was no nuclear propulsion examining board in those days. That made a big difference. Nobody trained. So you stood watch, you got off, you ate, you watched movies. Osborn wouldn't allow movies in the wardroom. He said the wardroom was for the officers' relaxation. Nobody said the obvious. [Laughter] So you watched movies out in the crew's mess if you wanted to watch a movie, and the crew understood that, the officers understood it.

Then you had to supervise all your equipment and take care of the bugs, the things that weren't operating right and looked like they needed to be fixed, and all that sort of stuff. So you were busy. There was no real time. My bunk was in the XO's stateroom; he never slept, and so I'd get in there and the lights would be on. But then I found a pallet on the deck way back in the missile compartment. I'd go back there and sleep. [Chuckle]

Paul Stillwell: Who was the exec?

Admiral DeMars: Shep Jenks. Good man, good man. He had fleeted up from engineer to XO and then went off to get his own command.

Paul Stillwell: Did you get any association with the weapons?

Admiral DeMars: No. Just walked past them going to and from the engineering spaces. I'd go in the missile control center and ask questions, see what they were doing, and got to learn a little bit about it. I think we ran that ship with 11 or 12 officers. That's all we had, so there was a lot for everybody to do. I mean, that's a big ship. Nowadays they have, like 16. But it was a busy time for us.

The second patrol was the most interesting. This was Osborn's last one that I was on. I was on two patrols, and then he was relieved by Ed Cooke, who was a good guy.[*] But the last patrol, we got under way and Osborn called all the officers into the wardroom and said, "We're going to be pulled off station after about a month. We're going to come back into Holy Loch, we're going to take off three missiles and put on three missiles without warheads, and we're going to do the first,"—I think they were called ORRT, operations readiness and reliability tests. So, okay, everybody was excited about that.

We came back in, loaded not only the missiles on, but we also loaded three Air Force officers—one brigadier and two colonels from Omaha that were in charge of all this stuff—and Martin Agronsky.[†] You remember him?

Paul Stillwell: NBC newsman.

Admiral DeMars: Yes, NBC newsman, and he had a soundman and a cameraman with him. And a Navy captain, a PAO guy.[‡] I remember him because he would watch movies in the crew's mess wearing a silk bathrobe. The crew really rolled their eyes at that one [chuckle].

So we went out, and we went down to the southern Atlantic missile range. We were getting ready to go. We were spinning up the missiles, getting ready to launch, and one of them had a problem. So the missile techs went in, opened up this hatch right near where the problem was, went in and put a new thing in, boom boom boom, tested it. It took like about 20 minutes. These Air Force colonels from Omaha couldn't believe it. "You did that? You're allowed to do that?" See, their people aren't trained like that.

So we did that, we went down. I was the battle stations diving officer, which meant I had to maintain the ship at 120 feet, essentially half a knot speed, which meant you had to get in beautiful trim, while the missiles were being fired. What I would do, if

---

[*] Commander Edward W. Cooke, USN.
[†] The Strategic Air Command was at Offutt Air Force Base near Omaha, Nebraska. It has since become a joint service command, Strategic Command, rather than Air Force only as it was then.
[‡] PAO – public affairs officer.

I was on watch I was back in the engineering spaces and I'd just head forward. My relief would be there, and we'd turn over quickly, like "You've got it,"

"Yeah, I've got it," in the tunnel, and then I'd go up. I always had standing orders with the chief, who was the normal ballast control panel operator, diving officer under way, "When that alarm sounds, start pumping out," because they're always heavy. Start pumping out. So I'd get up there, and the hovering system, which was supposed to do all this automatically, was horribly undersized, horribly undersized. And we would practice doing this; that's why I knew it was undersized. So I would parallel the trim and drain pump with the hovering pump. So I'd be pumping out everything, or flooding in, etc., etc., etc., and so as the ship continued to slow down you became more and more aware of what your trim conditions were. Usually we could get a very good trim by the time they were ready to shoot the first missile. This was about 20 minutes.

So we were all ready to go, but once they started shooting the missiles it was all over. I was convinced, based on this one test, that after three missiles we'd be firing the rest from the surface, because you just couldn't maintain the depth with these big changes in volume of water. So I wrote my qualification-for-command thesis, which you had to do in those days—the only requirement to get qualified for command was to write a thesis—and so I wrote it on launch depth control on the *George Washington*-class submarine. And I sort of really blasted the Bureau of Ships and SP for allowing this to happen.*

Ed Cooke was the CO when I finally got this done, it was the next patrol, and he sort of said, "Bruce, do you really want to say this about these people? They're not going to like you for it."

I said, "Captain, why would I care?" [Laughter] They're EDs, they're techies, why would I care?"† He was a very nice man, but he was a little worried about that.

So we did, we fired it all off and everybody was happy. They took a lot of movies of it. I think it became a special or something.

I remember I was reading *Conversations with Stalin*, which was a book by

---

* SP – Special Projects Office, which over the years has managed the U.S. Navy's submarine-launched ballistic missile programs.
† EDs – engineering duty officers.

Milovan Djilas, who was the foreign minister for Tito of Yugoslavia.* He had been to Moscow and talked to Stalin.† It was just a small book. I had Agronsky autograph the front of it for me as a memento of the thing.

So that was very exciting to do that. Then we went back on patrol for another couple weeks. Well, we went back to Holy Loch, dropped all these other guys off, and then went back out for a couple more weeks of patrol.

Paul Stillwell: He had a long-running TV show in Washington, "Agronsky and Company."

Admiral DeMars: Yes, he did. He was a very personable guy, a very likable guy. Could sit down and talk, and he liked junior officers, too; he talked to all of us. Very nice man.

Paul Stillwell: Well, this was an era when Admiral Rickover was trying to get public attention. I mean, the *Triton* was part of that program to sell nuclear submarines.‡

Admiral DeMars: The only one other—and I'm kind of monopolizing this with all these stories, but—

Paul Stillwell: That's the purpose of it!

Admiral DeMars: The final one I'll tell you is a humorous one, not that the others weren't. On one patrol, the XO called me in and said, "Bruce, the Navy's got a new program. They're going to put reserves on nuclear submarines."

I said, "Okay."

---

* Milovan Djilas, *Conversations with Stalin* (New York: Harcourt, Brace & World, 1962).
In 1945 Josip Broz Tito established a Communist government in Yugoslavia. He broke ties with the Soviet Union in 1948. He remained the nation's ruler until his death in 1980.
† Joseph Stalin ran the Soviet Union essentially as a dictatorship from the late 1920s to his death on 5 March 1953.
‡ In the spring of 1960, the USS *Triton* (SSN-586), commanded by Captain Edward L. Beach, USN, made the first submerged circumnavigation of the world. Beach wrote about the voyage for the media and later published a book about it.

He said. "We're going to get one of them, and I'm going to put him in your division," because he's not nuclear trained, obviously. That was when I was DCA, it had to be the second patrol. "Because you're A-gang and you can use a fireman. He'll be a fireman. The squadron commander is really interested in this program so you've got to do a good job. You've got to make sure this guy gets qualified, he's squared away, etc., etc."

I said, "Sure, fine." How hard can that be?

Paul Stillwell: Was that Commodore Ward?[*]

Admiral DeMars: Right, exactly. Good job. He was a nice man too.

So this kid showed up, John Melvin. He was from Boston, 18 years old, never been to sub school, never been to boot camp. He had spent about three weekends at the armory drilling. I mean, this guy didn't know how to wear a uniform, how to fold his clothes, anything. But he was hardworking, dedicated, a nice young guy. So we said, "Okay, God, we'll take this aboard and get on it." So we did get on with him, worked him hard, and he responded to everything.

I was coming back from the tender doing something over there. We were in the dry dock, and Melvin was topside watch under instruction, the guy that uses the MC system and that, makes sure everybody that goes down below decks is authorized to go below decks.[†] We were loading pyrotechnics at the time, flares and smokes, and the routine was that every five minutes the topside watch passed the word "The smoking lamp is out topside and below decks while loading pyrotechnics." Okay, fine. So I saw, oh, good; Melvin's getting that qualification out of the way, it's working out. He was a hardworking kid. And so I went down below, and the word got passed every five minutes.

Then all of a sudden the mike got keyed, chhhhhhhhh. That usually meant the

---

[*] Submarine Squadron 14 was established in 1958; the initial members worked in the Pentagon to do planning for the Polaris-armed submarines. Later the squadron received and operated the SSBNs as they went into commission. The first squadron commander was Captain Norvell G. Ward, USN; the oral history of Ward, who retired as a rear admiral, is in the Naval Institute collection.
[†] 1MC is the designation for the shipboard general announcing system.

person didn't think about what he was going to say before he keyed the mike. Now the mike was keyed and they're thinking, so chhhhhhhhh. I thought, "Oh God, Melvin." Melvin came on, very confident, and he said, "The smoking lamp is out topside and below decks while loading prophylactics." [Laughter] Oh, my God, where can I go where the XO won't find me? I mean, this is a story that's down to this day a legend in the submarine force; that was where it happened. He was a character.

Once Melvin came into the wardroom. We were all eating lunch, and Osborn was sitting down at the end. Melvin was the messenger of the watch, learning how to be planesman, driving the submarine, and all that. He came down and he addressed me and said, "Lieutenant DeMars, the oxygen generator has shut down on high differential pressure. It's shut down now, and the chief IC-man and the chief auxiliaryman are looking at it."

I thought, "Jeez, that was great, Melvin." I said, "Thank you very much, Melvin."

Now, the routine in the Navy is they give that report to the officer involved, then to the commanding officer. The commanding officer usually says, if he starts it, "That's fine. I've got it." Melvin turned to Osborn and said, "That goes for you, too, Captain." [Laughter] I mean, he can't have been 18 years old. Osborn just broke out laughing. Meanwhile, the XO was looking at me.

So Melvin served two patrols, and then I left. He was still on. He served three patrols total. I was sitting in the Pentagon almost 30 years later, a three-star now, OP-02, running all the submarine programs, one of the barons.* Somebody on my staff came in and said, "There's a John Melvin on the phone wants to talk to you"

I said, "Melvin? Gollee!" And so I got on the phone with him. We must have been on the phone for 45 minutes. It turned out that he was the second largest heating and air-conditioning vendor in the greater Boston area. He said, "I owe that all to my time on the *George Washington* and the training I got and the discipline I got." And I was thinking, "This guy makes more money than I do." [Laughter] Isn't that a good story?

---

* Vice Admiral DeMars served as Deputy Chief of Naval Operations (Submarine Warfare), OP-02, from November 1985 to October 1988.

Paul Stillwell: It's great.

Admiral DeMars: Yes. That just shows you, people are important. He was so proud of what he had done to learn in the Navy and that. But he was a dedicated young guy, and we helped him. So I felt very good about that.

Paul Stillwell: Well, coming in cold he learned a lot.

Admiral DeMars: Yes, exactly. Well, he was a hard worker. You know, he was a hard worker.

Paul Stillwell: What contacts did you have with the *Proteus* and Captain Laning?[*]

Admiral DeMars: Oh, quite a bit. They were good. And he was brilliant. When I was head of Naval Reactors, we went back to the ceremony that closed down the Holy Loch. I forget when that was. That would have been—

Paul Stillwell: Around '92.

Admiral DeMars: Yes, something like that. And so I big-dealed an airplane from the Navy and then I offered rides to certain people, including Laning and Hal Shear.[†] So we all flew over, and I got to talk to all of them on the way over. Laning was a brilliant guy. I mean, a smart, smart guy, and a very nice man. So I got to know him quite well then. I didn't really have much to do with him when he was CO. But they did good work because they had to. I mean, we had, I think it was a 28-day refit, so we had to get everything done in 28 days and then go out for two months.

---

[*] Captain Richard B. Laning, USN, was commanding officer of the submarine tender *Proteus* (AS-19), which serviced the ballistic missile submarines in Holy Loch from 1961 to 1963. Laning's tour on board ended in 1962.
[†] Admiral Harold E. Shear, USN (Ret.) had been the commanding officer of the USS *Patrick Henry* (SSBN-599), which in March 1961 was the first ballistic missile submarine to enter the Holy Loch.

Paul Stillwell: What did you do during the time in between patrols?

Admiral DeMars: Back when you weren't on the ship? Training, largely. In those days, it wasn't overloaded because everybody recognized you were away from your families for essentially three months and now you were back for a couple of months, then you're going to go away for another three months, and on and on and on. We usually took about a month off and didn't do anything, and then every division had training and you had the attack centers and the damage control training. You had to keep working on the training because the crews kept changing. I mean, you had new guys all the time. So you stayed reasonably busy but not overly so.

Paul Stillwell: Were the replacement people as good as the ones that had been there originally?

Admiral DeMars: Absolutely not. I mean, it was clear. It was clear. Not so much in the enlisted, but in the officers. It was different. In those days we had very competent chief petty officers. It's not the case nowadays, the best I can tell, because they make it too quickly. You'll have a chief who's been to sea for four years, max. In those days the chiefs had been to sea a lot and they knew their stuff, and they were good leaders. And so they were pretty much held up, but the other people were brand new and they were learning a new ship, and on and on and on. But that first *George Washington* crew, it was clear they'd been handpicked. Clear.

Paul Stillwell: I remember interviewing Admiral Ward, and he said it was a great challenge to write fitness reports on the skippers because they were all superstars.

Admiral DeMars: Yes, I bet. Yep. No, they were all good. Chuck Griffiths was one of them.* He was my boss in OP-02 when I was 22B, deputy attack submarine division. But it was a good experience on *George Washington*. I think of it very fondly, and so did

---

* Commander Charles H. Griffiths, USN, was executive officer of the USS *Robert E. Lee* (SSBN-601) and later commanding officer of the USS *Simon Bolivar* (SSBN-641). He was OP-02 from 1977 to 1980.

Margaret. It was a very close wardroom. We had good parties and did good things among our group when we were home.

Paul Stillwell: Is there anything on your outline that we've missed?

Admiral DeMars: I don't think so. I've been sort of tracking on down. God, did we get through all three of these?

Paul Stillwell: Yes. Down to the very last item. Maybe that's the best place to start next time.

Admiral DeMars: Yes, that was interesting. I mean, this was once again a conundrum. They sent me then to teach at Nuclear Power School. Most of my contemporaries, *all* of my contemporaries, either went off to PG School or went off to be engineers. But I didn't think about it. I was so happy to get some shore duty and go back to the West Coast and see if our house was still rented, that I didn't complain. But in retrospect it's strange.

I was a late bloomer, clearly. I wasn't high up on a list of things, although Osborn helped me out. He was the one that got me the job as XO on *Sturgeon*, because Margaret and I had dinner with him and his wife when he was the chief of staff at SubLant when I was at the Armed Forces Staff College.

He said, "What do you want to do when you leave there, Bruce?"

I said, "I'd like to be the second XO on a brand-new attack submarine."

He said, "Oh, okay." That's the job I got. Clearly, he did that. He was a wonderful guy.

But I was selected three years running for postgraduate school at the University of Oklahoma in petroleum engineering [chuckle]. And I was almost going to write a letter to BuPers and say, "Can I get an honorary degree? You keep selecting me but not sending me." [Laughter] But I didn't.

I just traveled in a different group. It's almost as if they were training me to be NR, but they had no idea they were doing that. But, I mean, I went to teach at Nuclear

Power School, I went on the Nuclear Propulsion Examining Board for three years, and I did the Pentagon stuff, so it was good training for what I ended up doing.

Paul Stillwell: It is often only in retrospect that you can appreciate those things.

Admiral DeMars: Exactly. Also, as I said, it didn't bother me, because I always had this lingering thing: I wanted to be the commanding officer of an attack submarine on special ops. And if I did that, I was happy with the Navy. I could go off and do anything else after that, I didn't care. And that's the way it worked out. You know, two Secretaries of the Navy tried to fire me, and I thought, "Well, that's okay; I can always do something else." And that's the way I felt. I mean, the Navy was not the be-all and end-all for me. It was very interesting, important stuff until I finished my command. Then I thought, "Anybody can do the rest of this stuff." [Laughter]

Paul Stillwell: Well, maybe not.

Admiral DeMars: The same thing wasn't driving me. It was just sort of that Chicago thing again: I think I can do other things.

Paul Stillwell: I remember interviewing one of the skippers of *Skipjack* and he said he was addicted to adrenaline. [Laughter] He loved to be under way and doing things.

Admiral DeMars: Yes, it's a very unique business and we're all fortunate to have taken part in it.

Paul Stillwell: We're off to a great start today. Thank you very much.

Admiral DeMars: Jeez, I didn't think we'd plow through all of that. You're a good listener.

Interview Number 2 with Admiral Bruce DeMars, U.S. Navy (Retired)

Place: Admiral DeMars's home in Alexandria, Virginia

Date: Thursday, 10 May 2012

Paul Stillwell: Admiral, please proceed. You mentioned that you wanted to have a few add-ons at the beginning of this interview.

Admiral DeMars: Yes, Paul, just one. It's too good a story to pass up, and it fits back in when I was at the land-based reactor site out in West Milton, New York, undergoing initial training.

My shift mate was Phil Bonz.[*] We were both lieutenants. We were bombing into work one day there in a heavy snowstorm, either in my Volkswagen or his Austin-Healy, both low-slung cars. It was about 7:15, and we were listening to this New York City radio station. We thought we heard the guy say, "If you can answer how much energy you can get from the fissioning of one gram of uranium-235, we'll give you $250.00."

So we said, "Hell, we know the answer to that." [Laughter] And we said, "Well, we're going to be late, but screw it." So we turned around and drove back into Saratoga Springs, where we both lived.

We went to the drugstore, bought two postcards, filled them out with the answer on them, and went to the post office. It had just opened at 8:00 o'clock, and we asked the clerk to postmark ours first. He said, "Oh, we're not allowed to do that, but I'll put them right here on top; they'll get postmarked first."

So we sent those in. We were really happy, until about a week later, listening to the same station, the announcer said, "Oh, we have two winners so we're tied, so we're going to give them both a prize," but it was 250 Belgian Congo francs. [Laughter] And that was the time the Belgian Congo had just gone up.[†] I forgot what it's called, Zaire or something now. But we got the letter with the Belgian Congo francs.

---

[*] Lieutenant Philip E. Bonz, USN.
[†] The Belgian Congo achieved independence on 30 June 1960. At that time it became the Republic of the Congo, and was later renamed the Democratic Republic of the Congo. From 1971 to 1997 it was known as the Republic of Zaire.

Paul Stillwell: And still got the actual bills.

Admiral DeMars: And so they sent them to us, and that was a fun thing. And, as we suspected, nobody at the reactor site even knew we were late. So that's a little postscript to stick in there, just too good a story to pass up.

Paul Stillwell: Well, that's an odd question to be asked of the general public in a radio program.

Admiral DeMars: Yes, it is. It is. I don't know why they got on to that.
So, go ahead.

Paul Stillwell: In your outline for the next phase of duty you have NPS MINSY, which I decrypted as Nuclear Power School, Mare Island Naval Shipyard, so please proceed with that. And you mentioned that the CO, Jack Fagan, was brilliant.[*]

Admiral DeMars: Yep. Yes. I was sent to be an instructor at the school I didn't like [chuckle], Nuclear Power School, because I didn't think I learned anything there when I was a student. So they sent me back to be an instructor, but it turned out it was wonderful. Jack Fagan was the CO of the school, and he was a brilliant man.

The school was just in an old World War II building on the northern end of the shipyard. I say he was brilliant because, when we gave exams you'd have to get the exams cleared by the CO. And, instead of just sending them in and writing things down, he'd say, "Bring them in, bring them in." Then he'd go grab a pencil, and he'd work out all the answers. And many times he wouldn't use the processes we were teaching. And he'd say, "Is that close?"

I'd say, "Jesus, it's right on, Captain." He was a very pleasant man anyway, very nice. He and his wife were very socially oriented.

Paul Stillwell: How would you describe him as a leader?

---
[*] Commander John F. Fagan Jr., USN.

Admiral DeMars: Wonderful. Wonderful, because he led by his personality and the force of his intellect. He was a warm human being to begin with, but he was just brilliant. You knew he would cover for you if anything went wrong, and a few things did, which I'll talk later on.

Paul Stillwell: Where did the curriculum come from?

Admiral DeMars: The curriculum we developed ourselves. I guess it was approved by Naval Reactors, but I'm not sure. Because we also had a Nuclear Power School at Bainbridge, Maryland. They have a training center on the East Coast, and this was the West Coast one. We had to stay together, because we were providing the same kind of students, and we gave a comprehensive exam at the end of the year, the same exam to both schools. So we had some kind of curriculum. I taught the enlisted for a year, then the officers for a year. But when I reported aboard, the fellow I relieved just gave me his notebook and said, "Here's the notes." So I modified that. I wish I'd have kept it, because it was very straightforward exposition of certain things that they didn't teach before there.

Rickover had certain rules for the place. We had a lot of instructor officers, but you were allowed only three officers that didn't teach. And so not only were we running the school, we were responsible for the admin business for the students coming through. And the classes were starting to pick up. They were getting bigger and bigger as the program expanded. So Jack Fagan taught a course. I forget what he taught, but he'd do that. Of the three that didn't teach, one was the admin officer, as you might expect; another was, we had a chief petty officer that ran the barracks and that, because he applied the same rule to the chiefs; and I forgot what the third one was. Those three just kind of did all the other stuff you have to do to keep an eye on 300 or 400 sailors and 30 officers. So it was an interesting rule, but typical of Rickover sort of rules.

Paul Stillwell: Was there an executive officer in that hierarchy?

Admiral DeMars: There was, but I don't remember him at all. He sort of ran the officer department, I think, and taught a course up there. Yes, there was, and his name just escapes me.

Many of the instructors were people who were brought in by Rickover right out of college, NROTC, OCS—no Naval Academy graduates.[*] He interviewed them at his staff, the same as I did when I had his job later. They would get three interviews rather than just two if you were going out to the fleet [chuckle]; you only got two interviews by the staff, they would get three, and then they showed up. So they were all very smart, and they were very good. I couldn't detect any of the sort of oddballs that were there when I went through as a student that wrote on the blackboard with one hand and erased with an eraser in the other hand as they were trying to teach us some esoteric form of math. So it was a little different curriculum.

But it was a great place for the family. We lived in Vallejo, out in town, not in Navy housing. My wife taught Sunday school. There was a beautiful chapel on Mare Island Naval Shipyard, redwood and Tiffany stained glass, just a glorious chapel. I played in shipyard golf tournaments. We had a little team from Nuclear Power School. I forget what name we used, because if Rickover had ever found out, hell would have broken loose. We played golf there, and they had a little golf course at Mare Island, probably still do.

Paul Stillwell: He did not condone golf?

Admiral DeMars: He didn't condone anything except work, and we all understood that. [Laughter] We all sort of knew what Rickover was all about. But, as I told you before, growing up in Chicago you knew there were rules and rules, and some were important and some weren't that important. We didn't think that not playing golf was an important rule, so we didn't follow it. But we never told the CO we were doing it. We swore the people at the base newspaper never to let it get into print. [Chuckle] We even disguised the name of our team; I forget what we called it.

---

[*] NROTC – Naval Reserve Officer Training Corps; OCS – Officer Candidate School.

Paul Stillwell: Were you teaching students going to both submarines and surface ships?

Admiral DeMars: Yes, yes. In some cases they didn't know then. The majority of them were going to submarines, because we didn't have many nuclear-powered surface ships then. They were just getting built.

We won a dog there. My wife and I liked low-impact hobbies. One of the things we did with our two kids was go to dog shows, so we were down at the Golden Gate Kennel Club show at the Cow Palace in San Francisco. We spent a whole day there walking around. I think our kids were two and four in 1962, something like that. So we were leaving and dragging the kids along, and there was a booth from the *San Francisco Examiner*: "Win the dog of your choice from our want-ads."

So Margaret said, "Here, take care of the kids." She went over there and signed up. About five weeks later we got a call. Out of 5,000 entries we won. So we traveled all around the Bay Area looking at all these dogs. It was the first time I ever saw a rottweiler. We went in a house where they were raising rottweilers. They're beautiful, big dogs. And we finally settled on this English springer spaniel raised by a lady in a big compound she had north of Oakland in Hayward, California. She had raised springer spaniels for 30 years. We got a pedigreed dog and had her for, I don't know, 15 years. So that was fun out there.

Paul Stillwell: What was the basis for winning? Was there an essay with it?

Admiral DeMars: No, no need. It just was random. They just picked our name out, so we were quite lucky.

Paul Stillwell: I remember the Cow Palace was where President Eisenhower was nominated for a second term at the '56 Republican National Convention.

Admiral DeMars: Yes, yes. A lot of conventions. I mean, it was a big place.

San Francisco was a lovely place. We used to go down there regularly, visit San Francisco, go to Napa Valley, Bodega Bay, Treasure Island, on and on and on. It was a lovely place to have some shore duty.

Another big fiasco there—wine at the base package store. Napa Valley, Sonoma Valley wine, $1.35 a bottle. And then Congress or the state of California passed a rule that it had to be within 10% of something other, etc., etc. It went up to $1.65. Everybody was complaining. Who would pay $1.65 for a bottle of wine?

I taught the enlisted for one year and the officers for one year. I taught practical courses—radiological controls and systems operation. I was the only fleet-experienced officer in the officer department when I went up there. I enjoyed teaching the enlisted. They were all essentially motivated. They wanted to be there, and they wanted to learn something. Many of them hadn't ever applied themselves in school, and so they tended to drag you off into minutiae, and that was okay—for a while. They asked you a lot of questions, and on and on. So finally we'd start off each class, I'd write "SUAC" on the board and say, "Look, when we get going into a lot of things and we're sort of not moving on, I'm going to write this on the board."

One of them said, "Well, what does that mean, Lieutenant?"

"It means: Shut up and copy." [Laughter]

Paul Stillwell: Had all these officers and enlisted been vetted by Rickover before they got to the school?

Admiral DeMars: The officers were, but not the enlisted. Enlisted, they just grabbed them.

Paul Stillwell: Where did they come from?

Admiral DeMars: The fleet or directly out of boot camp. They had high enough scores and a clean record. So they were mostly very junior. Most of them were out of boot camp.

Paul Stillwell: Was the course sort of generic in that it could apply to a number of different reactors?

Admiral DeMars: Oh, yes, absolutely. It was absolutely generic. I mean, it was basic fundamentals. Generic in that radiation is radiation, and pressurized water reactors are pressurized water reactors, so it doesn't matter that much. I thought it was a great course. I thought I was a great instructor.

Paul Stillwell: You get a satisfaction when you see the light bulb go on in a mind.

Admiral DeMars: Yes, absolutely. And you see young people really wanting to learn. I like to teach. I subsequently taught at sub school. I do enjoy instructing. But you're right, you get a great satisfaction out of seeing people that want to learn, and they all want to learn. It was a six-month course. It was tough and rugged.

    We did have two sort of scandals there. One was an officer situation; I call it a cribbing scandal. They had gotten ahold of, and not a great surprise, previous exams, so they were passing those all around. I think that was more a hit on us officers who wouldn't make up new exams. [Chuckle] But all of a sudden they came to light, so I didn't know what the hell to do. I confronted the guy that had them, and he gave them to me. The senior officer in the course—this was the officer course—was then-Commander Jim Doyle, who later commanded a nuclear-powered ship and went on to get three stars.[*]

Paul Stillwell: He was OP-03.

Admiral DeMars: He was OP-03.[†] A wonderful man.

Paul Stillwell: And a prime mover in the Aegis program.

---

[*] Commander James H. Doyle Jr., USN. As a captain Doyle commanded the nuclear-powered frigate *Bainbridge* (DLGN-25) from 1966 to 1970. His last sea assignment, as vice admiral, was as Commander Third Fleet in 1974-75

[†] Vice Admiral Doyle served as Deputy Chief of Naval Operations (Surface Warfare) from August 1975 to September 1980.

Admiral DeMars: Yes, yes. He was a wonderful man. It was an achievement to go through Nuclear Power School as a commander with a whole bunch of lieutenants. So, instead of telling the CO or telling the head of the officer department that we had this scandal, which I thought would blow it all up and then it would get back to Rickover, I remember I called him up. I went to his townhouse out in Vallejo one Saturday afternoon. Sat down, I told him the whole thing. He said, "Well, Bruce, how about if I just grab ahold of the class and talk to them?" I said that would be wonderful. That's what he did, and nobody else heard about it or knew about it. So, once again, sort of Chicago rules, DeMars's rules: "Don't make a big deal out of something that doesn't have to be a big deal." Because it wasn't really cheating. It was more malfeasance, I thought, on our part for not changing the exams enough, regularly and routinely. So that worked out well. And Jim Doyle still is a very close friend of mine. He's on the board of the Naval Historical Foundation, which I'm the chairman of nowadays.

Paul Stillwell: Did you run the risk at all that one of the Rickover intelligence agents might discover this?

Admiral DeMars: We didn't have any there, at Nuclear Power School.

Paul Stillwell: Oh, okay. [Laughter]

Admiral DeMars: I guess Rickover thought we were *all* his guys, or his gang. But if he did, he'd yell at me, but what was he going to do? I always had the feeling that if I had to, I could get out and do something else in life. I always enjoyed what I was doing in the Navy, but it wasn't my whole life. I thought there were other things to do, and I could do other things. So, anyway, no, that didn't bother me.

Paul Stillwell: What was the pass/fail rate for the two groups, officer and enlisted?

Admiral DeMars: The officers, pretty much everybody passed. The enlisted maybe 10% didn't make it. But it was mostly not smarts; it was just they didn't want to work that hard. And that cropped up after the first couple of months. But most people worked very hard. We had extra study hours in the evening and had instructors there to help people that needed help. And the barracks that they lived in were right across the street. And in those days sailors weren't married, by and large.

Paul Stillwell: Couldn't afford to be.

Admiral DeMars: No, they couldn't afford to be. So the ratio was pretty good getting through.

Paul Stillwell: I presume they had been screened at some point at boot camp that they had the native smarts to do it.

Admiral DeMars: Yes. They looked at the tests they took and that they had the capability to do it if they would apply themselves.

We had one scandal, too, in the enlisted department that was even a little more humorous. About three days before we were going to give this comprehensive exam, which was given to both Bainbridge and Mare Island Nuclear Power Schools, we found that the sailor who ran the mimeographing room was selling exams on the side. [Laughter] So, oh, God. This one, you had to tell Rickover. Well, Rickover went through the roof. "Oh, you're not being..." blah blah blah, blah blah blah, blah blah blah.

The exam had been made up by Bainbridge. You took turns, one made by Bainbridge, the next made by Mare Island, back and forth every six months. And so we set to, and in one long evening we made up a new exam, sent it to Bainbridge, and we gave the exam on time. But what happened was, our students did average on it, as they always did. Bainbridge, almost everybody came close to failing it or failed it. So then Rickover got on a new tirade: Bainbridge is teaching the exam, because they made up the exam that we threw out; now Mare Island makes up an exam and most of their guys fail it. So all the pressure came off us and went on Bainbridge, for teaching the exam.

Paul Stillwell: Well, how did you determine whether an exam was too easy, too hard, or right on?

Admiral DeMars: We tried to keep track of which questions people scored okay on, which they had the most mistakes on, tried to do that. And most of it we had taught, obviously; you shouldn't give exams where you don't test the people on what you had taught them. It wasn't that kind of a school. This wasn't a course in philosophy or something. But you sort of knew after you were there a while. And we did keep sort of rough records of questions and passing rates on questions.

Paul Stillwell: Was it the typical Navy multiple-choice format?

Admiral DeMars: Some were, some weren't. Some were math questions that you had to work out, or physics questions. But some were multiple choice and some were written answers. Then you had to grade all this stuff.

So, anyway, it was a good time there. I thought the curriculum was good. I thought it had improved in the two years I'd been gone, both the officers and the enlisted. That was probably because everybody complained so much.

Then right after I went up to teach in the officer department, the nuclear power program once again figured out they didn't have enough officers, which they seemed to do regularly during my career. And they sent a press gang down to the Naval Postgraduate School in Monterey, California. Everybody who was eligible, which means almost everybody, got ordered to Nuclear Power School. That didn't mean if you were two months within getting your master's degree, or had been there only three months. It didn't matter whether you were a surface officer, a lieutenant, or a lieutenant commander. And so they just sent them all up. Well, there were a few malcontents in that group [chuckle], and I ended up teaching them when I first got there. Most of them were, oh, really whizzed off, but like good naval officers nobody tried to fail out. But most of them said, "I'm not going to be a goddamn submariner." Most of them became submariners once they saw you got paid extra.

Paul Stillwell: But what happened to their coursework at the postgraduate school?

Admiral DeMars: That was it. It was just all over. Period.

Paul Stillwell: They didn't get the degrees?

Admiral DeMars: Didn't get their degree. I mean, it could have been done a little smoother, obviously.

Paul Stillwell: Yes. [Laughter]

Admiral DeMars: But that was the Navy in those days. I mean, it was just, you know, stand by. Boom.

Most of those guys did convert to submariners, and many of them rose up to command. Usually SSBNs, not attack boats. You had to have a little more experience to run those around. And they were all good officers, did a wonderful job. But for some reason it was a big failure of the nuclear power program. We were always lagging in the number of officers.

Paul Stillwell: I interviewed Admiral Train, who was in BuPers around that time.[*] He said there was almost a one-to-one match of nuclear submarine officer billets and trained officers.

Admiral DeMars: Yes.

Paul Stillwell: So there wasn't any slack. And a lot of new submarines were being built then.

---

[*] BuPers – Bureau of Naval Personnel. See the Naval Institute oral history of Admiral Harry D. Train II, USN (Ret.).

Admiral DeMars: Right. We were building the 41 for Freedom, all the Polaris class, and we were building SSNs.* We were building at Mare Island. We launched three or four submarines out there in the two years I was teaching at the Nuclear Power School.

Paul Stillwell: You had a note on here about radcon and system operation. What did that involve.

Admiral DeMars: That was basically what I taught. The enlisted I taught broader courses; they even let me teach some math and that in the enlisted courses. But for the officers—radiological controls is radcon, and it's all about why it's important, what the limits are, and how you protect against it and keep track of it, on and on and on. System operation is fundamentally how a generic pressurized-water reactor works and how it all manages to fit together, and on and on and on. So that when they would leave from there and go out to the land-based reactor site, they'd have some fundamental idea of how it worked, and then they'd learn, practically speaking, how to operate it there.

Paul Stillwell: Did your school typically feed into Arco, and Bainbridge into West Milton?†

Admiral DeMars: No, it fed anywhere. I'm sure the Bureau of Naval Personnel was as careful as they assigned people as they had been with me in my career to date, which had been terrible. So they just went shooting off in all directions, no East Coast, West Coast.

Then from there I was ordered to *Snook*, which was in Mare Island shipyard getting the Water Boy system, WLR-6, installed.‡ It was the latest and the first new

---

* "Forty-one for Freedom" was a motto for the 41 Polaris/Poseidon-armed ballistic missile submarines of the *George Washington* (SSBN-598), *Ethan Allen* (SSBN-608), and *Lafayette* (SSBN-616) classes. All were named for distinguished Americans and allies. The first was commissioned in 1959 and the last in 1967.
† Arco, Idaho, and West Milton, New York, were sites where students qualified on working reactors.
‡ USS *Snook* (SSN-592), a *Skipjack*-class nuclear submarine, was commissioned 24 October 1961. She was 252 feet long, 32 feet in the beam, and displaced 3,075 tons surfaced and 3,500 submerged. She had a top speed on the surface around 15 knots and a speed in excess of 30 knots submerged. She was armed with six 21-inch torpedo tubes.

really integrated electronic surveillance system, and that was a big deal. I joined the ship there about a week before they went back down to San Diego.

We got back into our house, thank God. It was still there, and we hadn't gone bankrupt because tenants had moved out. And *Snook* was a great tour. I learned most if not all of my submarine tactics and submerged ship handling on that ship, simply because of what we did, and we did a lot of it. We did a lot of special operations.

The CO when I first got aboard was Bill Yates, very briefly, just for a couple of months.* He had a great World War II record, and he was a phenomenal leader. After that he became an SSBN CO. Subsequently he was my commanding officer at Submarine School when I taught there.

Paul Stillwell: What examples would you cite of his leadership?

Admiral DeMars: Well, he was very calm, he never got excited, never got upset, was a very good leader. You just felt this guy knew what he was doing and wasn't going to get you in trouble. I was very fortunate except for the one I'll talk about at the end of my *Snook* tour. I had great COs in everything I did, whether it was at Submarine School, Nuclear Power School, or any of the ships I was on. I just had remarkable leaders, and I learned an awful lot from them. So that as you advanced up and you became XO you knew how to be an XO before you got the job. You knew how to be a CO before you got the job, because you'd seen great leaders and you'd spent so much time on submarines at sea.

Paul Stillwell: Well, and the good ones make sure their juniors have a chance to operate the ship, handle it and learn.

Admiral DeMars: Yes, exactly. Exactly. They cut you loose, and they're very confident of what *they* can do, and that came through very clear.

---

* Commander William K. Yates, USN, commanded the *Snook*, 23 February 1963 to 14 November 1964.

Paul Stillwell: The S5W was the plant du jour at that time, and *Snook* was in *Skipjack* class, so she was smaller than the earlier ones in the *Skate* class.*

Admiral DeMars: Right.

Paul Stillwell: So did that make her more maneuverable?

Admiral DeMars: Oh, yes. Fundamentally very, very maneuverable. You could be steaming along at 350 feet, you know, 15 knots, going somewhere, and you could go up and copy a broadcast at periscope depth.† You could get to periscope depth, clearing the baffles on the way, in a minute. Have the periscope up—say you do it safely—periscope up, antennas up, looking around, in a minute. It just was a very maneuverable ship. And we could make 30 knots. But it was very tight, very cramped. All the equipment, including the steam turbines and the reactor pumps and everything, was hard mounted right to the hull, so we were very noisy.

The sonar was terrible. I mean, you saw contacts through the periscope before you heard them. But fortunately the Soviets were noisier and had even worse sonars than we did, so we had undersea superiority, but it was clear that the move had to be toward more quieting and better, more sensitive sonars. But every time you relieved the watch as officer of the deck submerged at periscope depth, you'd almost broach the submarine up. You'd put the periscope up as high as it would go, and you'd look all around before you got relieved. Then you'd go back down. Because you didn't want your relief to come in and say, "Hey, I just saw a target." And then you did that right after you took over, because the sonars worked, but not very well.

Paul Stillwell: What was the doctrine on active versus passive sonar?

---

* S5W was the designation of the fifth model of submarine nuclear plant produced by Westinghouse. It was used in both ballistic missile submarines and attack submarines built in the late 1950s and into the 1960s.
† The broadcast refers to a series of messages sent to ships of the fleet, either individually or collectively.

Admiral DeMars: Oh, you never used active. In fact, I think we pulled the circuit breakers out of that when we deployed. Never used it. You kept your Fathometer in operation and used that, single ping, very judiciously, if you had to. But I'm not sure the Soviets had any intercept receivers subsequently that they could pick up sonar very well. We did, but I'm not sure they did.

Paul Stillwell: Were these Fathometer pings for navigation?

Admiral DeMars: Yes—well, just to keep you off the bottom in unfamiliar waters. The navigation gear was very tenuous, and I was navigator near the end of my three years on *Snook*. We had basically Loran Alfa.[*] There aren't many stations in the Pacific, and it's not very accurate. We had RDF, radio direction finding, where you could pick up a beacon—whether it was Japanese, Soviet, American [chuckle]—and get a one-line bearing on that. And we had a sextant in the periscope, which I used a couple of times. It was a lot of work, and you really *had* to know where you were to use that because it was painful. But it was very fundamental stuff.

Now, the second CO there was Jim Watkins, who was really brilliant in all respects.[†] Very smart, great sense of humor, great at handling people and enlisted. I mean, he was very well liked. He was also very tough. *Very* tough. I mean, demanding.

Paul Stillwell: To the point of being feared?

Admiral DeMars: Only by the XO, Ron Thunman.[‡] [Laughter] Ron's a good friend of mine, still is; he was my boss in OP-02 and I was his deputy. But Watkins would take most things that went wrong out on Thunman, which is the way it should work.

And there were a lot of things to take out, because it was a very weak wardroom. I was beginning to see how diluted the talent was getting as the submarine force

---

[*] Loran (long-range aid to navigation) is a system of electronic navigation that involves the reception of pulse signals transmitted simultaneously by paired stations ashore.
[†] Commander James D. Watkins, USN, commanded the *Snook*, 14 November 1964 to 13 December 1966. As a four-star admiral he later served as Chief of Naval Operations from 1982 to 1986.
[‡] Lieutenant Commander Nils Ronald Thunman, USN. Vice Admiral Thunman served as Deputy Chief of Naval Operations (Submarine Warfare), OP-02, from July 1981 to November 1985.

expanded. It was a very weak wardroom except for Lieutenant Mike Barr, who was the officer that they put in charge of the Water Boy system.* He was the electronics material officer in addition to other things. Brilliant, smart. I don't think he'd ever been to PG school or anything; he was just smart. He ended up being a two-star; he was Commander Submarine Force Pacific Fleet before he retired.† Very, very thoughtful, smart, fun guy. And Thunman was good, obviously; he had to be to withstand all of that.

We only had nine officers. You ran submarines very modestly in those days. Nine officers, because you only had nine bunks on board [chuckle]. And when we went off on a special operation, carried another lieutenant, who was the intel officer; he handled all the special sonar riders and the CTs, communication technicians. He would sleep in a bunk in the wardroom. Usually we'd watch a movie at night, and that would interrupt his sleeping. So he'd pull the curtain back and watch the movie with us, and then when the movie was over he'd go back to sleep.

Paul Stillwell: What examples do you recall, various incidents of Commander Watkins's brilliance?

Admiral DeMars: Well, the way he handled and managed the very delicate operations you had to do. We did things such as underwater hull surveillances, going underneath ships or submarines that were on the surface, going underneath them and looking at the bottoms of the vessels with our periscopes. Which meant our periscope was three to four feet below the bottom of the enemy ship. So we had to do that very carefully. One, it takes great maneuvering to stay underneath. And then it takes great judgment to film everything and to take pictures of everything. It takes great trust in your diving officer.

We also did missile tracking stations, where we would sit off a target barge that the Soviets were firing their missiles into. We recorded the electronic signatures as they came in so that the Navy could develop countermeasures against them. He would position the ship beautifully and hold it there.

---

* Lieutenant Jon Michael Barr, USN.
† Rear Admiral Barr Commanded Submarine Force Pacific Fleet from July 1993 to February 1996.

Then we would close on Soviet submarines submerged and record their signatures, getting within about 1,000 yards of them. Go from beam to beam and do all of that. Just handled the ship beautifully and calmly, not excited, and just very measured. So you watched all of that.

He just had a great sense of humor too. On the way back from a special operation, he'd always have a briefing for the entire crew in the crew's mess of what we did. Everybody had a clearance, and obviously you didn't go into things they shouldn't know. But once he said, "I'm going to prove to you how calm and talented we are up there when these things are going on, and the remarkable control I have over everything." So he played, I think it was a missile-tracking tape that we had made, but he played it at, like, three times the speed. "Raisethescopeputthedownscopeupmarkbababababa." It went on for about three minutes, and the crew was almost wetting their pants they were laughing so hard at it. Well, you could do things like that.

He was a great leader. You know, I was very fortunate with the leaders I had, as I said. Jim Osborn on *George Washington*, Bill Leisk on *Capitaine*, and him. They were all just wonderful leaders. But the thing was, they knew their business, they didn't get excited, and they were great teachers. They were great teachers. But they were firm. They were firm, tough guys.

Paul Stillwell: Was the WLR-6 the vehicle for picking up these transmissions?

Admiral DeMars: Yes, yes. We did several ops off of Hainan Island to get all the radars there so they could try and map it so that our planes going in there would know the best routes and the best countermeasures, and our jammers had the right kind of jamming.[*]

We also did one circumnavigation of the Sea of Okhotsk. Went in through the Sakhalin island chain, and at periscope depth went around the entire Sea of Okhotsk, like at four knots. And there's nothing up there except beautiful scenery [chuckle], and a bunch of puffins floating in the water. So we played a lot of cards, watched a lot of movies. But it was absolutely gorgeous. We got way up the northern end, which is

---

[*] Hainan Island, part of the People's Republic of China, is in the South China Sea. It is near what was then North Vietnam, the target of U.S. aerial bombing in the Vietnam War.

where the town of Magadan is, and that's where the Soviet ships would go in and take in the prisoners to go up and work in the mines up in Siberia. I was then, still am, a student of Soviet history and all of that, so that was quite a thing for me to see that place. So that was fascinating. But we did that because we had the WLR-6, the Water Boy.

The other interesting thing is that we did the OpEval for the WLR-6 on the first two spec ops we did on the first deployment.* And we carried the civilian program manager from Sylvania aboard, and a commander—I can't remember his name right now, Polish name—from NSA, who was a PhD in physics or electronics or something.† Both of them were on board to make sure this was all done properly and kept all the right records and everything. The Navy was so interested in getting this thing into operation we did the OpEval on two spec ops.

Paul Stillwell: Were the tapes made of these?

Admiral DeMars: Oh, yes, yes. We made large reel-to-reel one-inch tapes.

Paul Stillwell: And then sent somewhere, presumably.

Admiral DeMars: Oh, yes. We'd usually go to Naha, Okinawa, as we came off station, and then they'd be given there to some NSA person who would send them back or take them back or something, all the sonar tapes and all the electronic tapes.

Paul Stillwell: This was before they could be recorded digitally, I presume.

Admiral DeMars: Right. Yes, it was the reel-to-reel tapes.

Paul Stillwell: You haven't said what your job was. You mentioned navigator during part of the time.

---

* OpEval – operational evaluation.
† NSA – National Security Agency, which does electronic eavesdropping on communications.

Admiral DeMars: Yes, that was at the end when it was really fun. I got put as MPA *again*.* Maybe that's why they never made me an engineer, because I didn't have to do it. I stood all my watches forward as officer of the deck.

I had to qualify as engineering officer of the watch. I had to *re*-qualify. And the only thing I did for that, the engineer said, "Well, why don't we just run one drill for you? If everything goes fine, I'll tell the captain you're qualified." So what drill did they run? A fast scram recovery. Well, from the time I'd been on my previous nuclear submarine, the *George Washington*, till now we had lost the *Thresher*, Naval Reactors had come out with a fast scram recovery.† Previously, when the reactor scrammed you shut the main steam stops and took the main turbine off the line, and you went up to periscope depth and snorkeled and went on the battery. Well, the new procedure was to not shut the steam stops but to continue to bring steam back, run at least one turbo-generator, and you could run the main turbines very, very slowly while the reactor was cooling down because you're not critical, and while you're using the water in the steam generators, because it was hard to start a feed pump under those circumstances. I had never done one of these. I had read about it in the reactor plant manual. And that was the first drill I got. Bam—fast scram recovery [chuckle]. Well, fortunately I had a good crew in the maneuvering room. I followed the procedure, and we got through it all okay. So I became an engineering officer of the watch again. But, as I said, I fortunately stood all my watches forward.

Paul Stillwell: Were there any SubSafe modifications made after the loss of the *Thresher*?

Admiral DeMars: Not to us, no. That came later. Because we were due, at the end of this tour, for an overhaul. Right after I got off, they went in the shipyard, and that's when they had that done.‡ But there were main things done, like obviously the SubSafe

---

* MPA – main propulsion assistant.
† "Scram" is a term used for the emergency shutdown of a nuclear reactor. The nuclear-powered attack submarine *Thresher* (SSN-593) was lost with all hands on 10 April 1963 while operating east of Cape Cod. The presumed cause was a reactor shutdown during a dive.
‡ On 19 March 1967 the *Snook* left her homeport of San Diego to go to the Puget Sound Naval Shipyard at Bremerton, Washington, for a 14-month overhaul that also included her first nuclear refueling.

program, the new procedures for repairs, maintenance, special handling of your spare parts that were in the SubSafe boundary. All that got imposed, but nothing involving welding or anything of that nature.

Paul Stillwell: But it certainly got your attention when it happened.

Admiral DeMars: Oh, yes. Yes, absolutely. And everybody was much more careful, and we realized we were susceptible to that sort of terrible thing.

Paul Stillwell: I wonder if there were any noticeable effects you remember from the *Albacore* hull, because this class had it, whereas the *Skate* class had not.

Admiral DeMars: Oh, yes. I mean, it was fast. We had the S5W reactor but, as I said, we'd go 30 knots. And just very maneuverable. I mean, you could turn on a dime, you'd go up and down, you could slow the ship down. The reason we could arrive at periscope depth and ready to go at three knots or less was, as you were going up at all stop you were fishtailing the rudder back and forth to slow yourself down, and making a big, wide turn to listen what was behind you with the terrible sonar that wouldn't have heard anything anyway, but we cleared the baffles and went through all the motions. But it was a fun ship to operate, just an absolutely fun ship to operate.

Paul Stillwell: Did the noise from the propeller at times overwhelm the sonar?

Admiral DeMars: Ah, well, you couldn't tell. *Something* overwhelmed the sonar. [Laughter] I think it was mostly design. But no, we were always very careful not to cavitate, because cavitation, the making of the little bubbles and the collapsing of those bubbles, can travel a long distance, and I think even the Soviets could have heard that. So we were always very careful not to cavitate. But, as I said, the Soviets were worse in both the noise they radiated and the sensitivity of their sonars. We know that because we got up and close and personal to them, and we were sure they never knew we were there or they would have done something. So we were sure. And so we were always careful to try and stay back in their baffles, back beyond their beam, but we never got in any position to feel that we'd been counter-detected.

Paul Stillwell: Well, one thing, in getting so close to the enemy shore and the enemy ships, the captain has to suppress the normal caution factor that lives in everybody's mind, but do it judiciously.

Admiral DeMars: Yes, you have to do it in a thinking way. But as long as you know you do have that undersea superiority of your sonars and your radiated noise, it works. So you have to do it very judiciously and carefully, but it's a doable do.

Paul Stillwell: You mentioned you had CTs and sonar techs on board.

Admiral DeMars: Yes, we must have carried probably 8, 12, 14 extra people on every spec op, which means you hot-bunked.[*] But they were great guys. They did this for a living, they enjoyed it, it was just in them, and they wanted the ship to do well because that added to their professional luster. But on the way to station they had to study and do their homework and get everything ready to go. But while we were on station they'd engage in field day. Where do you want them to clean? You want them to clean in the engine room? They'd clean in the engine room. Torpedo room, they'd do that. And they were just part of the gang, very, very good shipmates. So it was a pleasure to have them. They didn't get a lot of sleep; they worked hard. You had linguists, you had the special communications guys. Usually a senior chief ran the sonar techs, and a lieutenant ran the CTs. So they were great shipmates.

Paul Stillwell: Was there any sense of getting immediate operational intelligence, or was this mostly building a library?

Admiral DeMars: It was immediate operational intelligence if you were looking for an event. You sometimes got tip-offs there was going to be a missile firing, and many times

---

[*] Hot-bunking refers to different individuals sleeping in a specific bunk at different times.

we might receive that before other national systems received it. It went down through the intelligence community and broadcast out to us. So we'd get that. We could sometimes get tip-offs that submarines or important surface ships were getting under way, and so we could intercept them, take pictures and do all that sort of stuff. So you received operational intelligence also, not just stuff to tape and take back.

Paul Stillwell: Who laid out the schedule for the ship? Who said where to go and when?

Admiral DeMars: The captain, wherever he wanted to go, and based on all this intel and the regular broadcasts that told you what was going on where. It was his job. Obviously he spent a lot of time with the lieutenant who was in charge of this sort of stuff and listened to him, what he thought, because there's a lot you can learn from broadcast analysis even if you can't break the code. Who's calling whom on something. There's a sort of a very stylized way of analyzing that, and our lieutenant rider would do that. Then he'd caucus with the commanding officer and the XO, and they'd decide where we'd go with it.

But there were certain places that a lot of ships went through. And so if you went and you lingered there, you'd run into—well, "run into" is the wrong word; you would encounter something. It was exciting, but the captain had freedom to position his ship wherever he thought he'd get the most gain.

Paul Stillwell: Did you do periscope photography?

Admiral DeMars: Oh, yes, all the time. And that was wonderful to watch. You know, Watkins is about, I don't know, 6-foot-4. Thunman's about 6-foot-5, or -4½. And to watch the two of those on the periscope stand, trying to stay out of each other's way, was a real show. Watkins would take all the pictures, and Thunman would put the camera on and take it off. But watch the two of them, they really filled up that periscope stand, but got it all done.

Paul Stillwell: Kind of a do-si-do?

Admiral DeMars: Yes. We had two cameras. One was a Nikon, which was a nice little one that went right on, but you had to take the periscope eyepiece off, hook this thing on. The other was a Hasselblad, which was a giant one. It was about the size of two shoeboxes together, and you cranked it to take the picture. It depended on which one you wanted to use, and sometimes you did both of them. So it was something to watch. But, once again, that's why the crew liked the captain; he knew how to do that stuff, and he just did it well.

Paul Stillwell: It sounds like he made them part of the routine, so it was a vicarious experience right directly.

Admiral DeMars: Oh, yes, absolutely. Sailors could come up, as long as there weren't too many of them, and stand around in the corners of the control room and watch what was going on anytime. And when you were officer of the deck looking out through the periscope, if there was nothing going on you'd say, "You want to take a look through the periscope?"

The sailor would say, "Is that Russia over there?"

"No, that's the Soviet Union, it's not Russia." [Laughter] No, he had a great way with that, and it rubbed off on the rest of us, obviously.

We visited some foreign ports over there but not many, because they had to be specially cleared. We went to Naha, Okinawa; Sasebo, Japan, which was a very nice place; and we were the first nuc into Yokosuka, Japan. There were about three days of rioting, and then we left. The rioters were really farmers who were paid the equivalent of about a buck a day to march outside and chant. But no violence. It was just a very orderly thing.

We did get some flights to Hong Kong from Naha, and I went to Hong Kong once with the CO and the XO. That was when I was ops officer, I think, and we gave a briefing to the commander of the Seventh Fleet on his flagship in Hong Kong. So we stayed there about three days at this beautiful hotel up on the top of the mountain in Hong Kong.

All that went well, because the things we were doing were really the first of a kind because of the suite we had, and because of Watkins, obviously.

Paul Stillwell: I was in a ship that was home-ported in Yokosuka at that time and I remember the demonstrations, which were ritualistic. They had been choreographed and practiced and all that. I also remember being in the barber shop and seeing an officer in tropical whites. He had gold dolphins on and a dosimeter, and I thought, "Well, they don't get many of those in here." [Laughter]

Admiral DeMars: After seven or eight weeks on station, we'd go into Naha, Okinawa, and we'd all get a bus up to Kadena Air Force Base. Go to the barbershop, and you got a shave, a facial, a haircut, a shoulder massage, all of that. You just became new people.

Paul Stillwell: For about a buck or two.

Admiral DeMars: Yes, yes. And we all smelled terribly because submarines have that sort of diesel smell that just permeates everything. But you came out just glowing. It was easy to please people in those days.

Paul Stillwell: On your outline you've got some abbreviations: UHS, MTS, and SPL. What are those?

Admiral DeMars: Oh, that's what I said before, the underwater hull surveillances, missile tracking, and the SPL is sound pressure level readings on submarines.

Oh, a very interesting thing here. Watkins called me in one day. I'd been aboard maybe almost two years and done a lot of spec ops. We went to WestPac every year for about seven months and did at least two spec ops every time we went to WestPac.[*] He said, "Bruce, I have a decision to make on you, but I want to see what you want to do. They have this new thing now called the engineer's exam that NR [Naval Reactors] has instituted to make sure people are qualified to become engineers of these vessels. I can

---

[*] WestPac – Western Pacific.

send you back for the engineer's exam; then you'd probably go off and do something else. Or I can make you ops officer and navigator."

I said, "You're really giving me that choice?"

He said, "Yeah."

I said, "Well, I want to stay. I want to be ops/navigator and keep doing what we do."

He said, "Okay, fine." So I became the ops officer and the navigator, which are the greatest jobs on ships doing spec ops like that.

I had a great assistant navigator, Chief Dickieson, whose brother was a Naval Academy graduate and the CO of one of the SSBNs, Bob Dickieson.* The chief had entered the Navy as an enlisted man and eventually came to the *Snook*. This guy was fun, and he was smarter than the devil. I remember we got under way heading to WestPac once out of San Diego, and I'd just been made navigator. I said, "Okay, Chief, we'll start getting everything ready to go, and tonight we'll get a fix." I was a lieutenant commander then; he always called me "Commander," which made me feel good.

He said, "Commander, it's going to take us like two and a half weeks to get to where we're going," which was to go up and through one of the straits in Japan and up off Vladivostok. He said, "The first two weeks there's nothing you can hit. Nothing. So we just steam northwest. Then the last week we start sweating. Where are we and how do we get to where we get through these things? But the first two weeks we don't have anything to do." [Chuckle]

I said, "Okay, Chief, what do you do?"

He said, "We usually correct all the charts and do a little training and this and that." And he was absolutely right.

The other funny thing with him. We had another senior chief who was the head nuc back aft, Senior Chief Machinist's Mate Ruble. Barney Ruble, they called him.† He was short and stocky. They had just issued Polaris coveralls to SSNs; we'd never had them before that. Most people on board didn't wear them. The officers liked to wear

---

* Commander Robert W. Dickieson, USN, was the first commanding officer of the gold crew of the USS *Kamehameha* (SSBN-642) when she was commissioned on 10 December 1965. He had previously commanded the blue crew of the USS *Ulysses S. Grant* (SSBN-631)
† Barney Rubble was the name of a cartoon character in a television program, "The Flintstones."

their wash khakis, and the sailors liked to wear their dungarees. But Barney Ruble came walking up in the control room—we'd gotten under way from San Diego—and he was wearing a set of these khakis. Well, he was so short the bottoms had to be turned up and the sleeves turned up, and he was kind of lumpy looking because of his physiognomy. He said to Dickieson, "Chief, how do I look?"

Dickieson said, "Like a condom full of doorknobs." [Laughter]

Paul Stillwell: That's a colorful description.

Admiral DeMars: I remember that to this day. And everybody in the control room was laughing so hard they were almost crying.

So it was a good ship, we had good people, we had a lot of fun. And now that I was ops/nav, that was great.

Several interesting things happened. On deployment, on a special operation, just at the beginning of it, we had a malfunction of the trash disposal unit, the TDU. The TDU on that class of ship was in the galley and was operated by the cooks. You're supposed to use a torque wrench when you shut it to lock the outer door shut. It was essentially a small torpedo tube with a watertight door at the bottom, a watertight door at the top. And they had over-torqued it or something; they hadn't used the torque wrench properly, and we couldn't get the bottom door to seal. So what the captain and the XO decided to do was that we would pressurize the ops compartment. We shut the bulkhead flappers, we shut the watertight doors, put red tags on them. Then vented high-pressure air into the ops compartment. We were on station, and we withdrew to about 30 miles off of Vladivostok, went to periscope depth, pressurized the ops compartment to just above sea pressure, and then we defeated the interlocks and opened the inner and outer door of this 12-inch tube.

Ron Thunman was the XO, and I was the A Division officer then, and we were down there supervising this. The ship was rolling, and the water would slosh up and go down and I thought, "Oh God, somebody's going to open a bulkhead flapper by mistake, vent off the air in the compartment. We're all going to die." We probed down there with flashlights and did this and that. We could never fix it.

But here you had a fellow that then became OP-02, another one that became Chief of Naval Operations and Secretary of Energy, and one who became head of Naval Reactors, doing something that stupid. [Laughter]

It made a great joke because we had to freeze all the garbage then in the freezer, and the crew would always accuse the cooks of making the wrong breakout: "That's not real soup."

We surfaced before we went into Naha that time, at night, and formed a line and passed all this frozen garbage up and threw it out the hatch. God, what a mess.

Paul Stillwell: Well, when the system was working normally, was there any concern that the Soviets would see your garbage?

Admiral DeMars: No, because we weighted it. It was in mesh bags. We carried garbage bag weights that looked like big hockey pucks. They were just iron, and you put those in there. There's a lot of those on the bottom off Vladivostok and Petropavlovsk and all those places.

Paul Stillwell: What did you do in between deployments, off the West Coast?

Admiral DeMars: Tried to do as little as possible. I mean, we usually took at least a month off and let people catch up and all that sort of stuff. Then you'd do some training, maybe go out a little bit and give some services to the aviators and the surface guys.

Once my wife and I went down to Ensenada on a trip, oh, for about ten days. You could go across the border then; you didn't need a passport or anything. We went down there, got a motel. We had our two kids then still, obviously. We all got huaraches, these sandals made out of car tires, with leather on top. We had a Volkswagen, and I had it reupholstered in Naugahyde down there for next to nothing. We had a great time. So you did stuff like that.

It was a close wardroom also. We had a lot of wardroom parties. I don't think they have those anymore, at least at the fervor we had then. And they were all fun because everybody really was close and had a good time.

While we were gone, the wives would all pile into two cars, and they'd go to Tijuana for a day. Cross the border, park the car, go shopping, have lunch at Caesar's, which claimed the place that invented Caesar salad. Buy, for some reason, bakery down there because it was very cheap. Bring it home and freeze most of it. So the wives did wonderful things that we never fully appreciated till much, much after. But it was a very close sort of thing.

Paul Stillwell: How much were you able to communicate with your family when you were on deployment?

Admiral DeMars: Not at all. Not at all. Even when you got back in port, I mean you couldn't afford phone calls in those days. So you wrote letters. You just wrote letters. Letter was the way to communicate. It was just a different world.

Paul Stillwell: Was there any kind of debriefing when you got back off a deployment? Did you talk to intelligence people?

Admiral DeMars: Yes. We had to make up a full patrol report. That was the XO's job. It was a daily summary of everything we did, what we thought was important, what worked, what didn't work. It had several sections to it, the ops and the material section and personnel section. Very detailed. I mean, it was usually about an inch think. That was submitted. And then many times the CO/XO and the ops officer would come down to Washington to give a full debrief on something and talk to a bunch of the intel people down here. So it was a big deal. It was totally apart from the rest of the Navy. I mean, we were just different.

Paul Stillwell: The World War II submarine patrol reports then got endorsements up the chain of command, not always favorable. Did you get specific feedback from these reports?

Admiral DeMars: No. No, they never did. Never did. You always were sort of told, "Here's your package of awards you might think about making: you know, two of these and three of those." But in those days they didn't give out many awards, which I think was much better than it is today. Today you look at some young sailor that's been in three years, and he's got more medals than I retired with. [Chuckle]

Paul Stillwell: Including a sea duty medal—of all things.

Admiral DeMars: Yes, exactly. [Laughter] But that's a different story.

I got washed overboard once, off of Vladivostok. We had a rattle forward. I think that was when I was A division officer or something and first lieutenant as a side thing. So my chief and I said, okay, we'd go down on deck and see if we could find out what it was. We pulled about 30 miles off, the ship surfaced, dark at night obviously.

Paul Stillwell: Rounded hull.

Admiral DeMars: Yes. We went down, and fortunately they had this track that ran along the deck, and you had on a safety belt that you hooked into the track. We went forward with some wedges and a maul and we pounded them into all these hatches, and we thought we found the noise. So we were coming back, and the ship was slowly going up and down. It went down once, and this big wave washed over the deck, washed us both over the side. Colder than the devil. So here we were, each of us dangling at the end of his own 8-foot line.

Fortunately, there used to be a quarterly information bulletin that came out from SubPac. One of the things it had in it once was a suggestion to tie a knot in the safety line about every two feet, because it's too slippery otherwise. Trying to climb up on that wet, rounded hull with a wet line, if those knots hadn't been in there we'd still be hanging off that thing.

So we both got up on board. The chief went up onto the hull, and then I went up, and we went down inside. We were sitting in the wardroom, and the doc was in there. We were okay, just a little cold. And Thunman still tells this story. One of the first things I said was, "Does this qualify us for brandy?" [Laughter] And it did. We each got two medicinal brandies.

So, anyway, we had a lieutenant attempt suicide, which was a very tragic thing. He was a young guy, direct input into submarines. He was my junior officer of the deck. We were on station. He didn't show up for watch, so they sent down. He was in the head. He had stabbed himself with this knife he had bought in Okinawa. He had also taken a bunch of pills beforehand that made him sleepy, and probably saved his life. So obviously there was something wrong with him. He was doing well; he wasn't delinquent in qualification or anything. Doing well. So the doc kept him alive on the wardroom bench while we steamed as fast as we could go to Okinawa. We went in there about 2:00 in the morning, got him off, and there were several intel agents waiting on the pier to escort him up to the hospital, because he had all this knowledge. That was the last we saw of him. So it was a very tragic thing. And what did we do? We went back on station.

Paul Stillwell: But now one officer short.

Admiral DeMars: Yes, now one officer short. But you could manage that.

Paul Stillwell: Did you ever hear afterward what became of him?

Admiral DeMars: He got out of the Navy. I sort of kept in touch as best I could. Can't remember his name now. He called me a couple times and said everything was fine now, but you never know. It was a very tragic thing. Because ostensibly you couldn't figure it out. I mean, there was a bunch of other guys you could say, "Jesus, it wouldn't surprise me if they did it." But he just had some problem. I'm not sure what it was.

Paul Stillwell: Well, living in a submarine is an unnatural environment.

Admiral DeMars: Yes.

Paul Stillwell: Maybe that would exacerbate whatever was there.

Admiral DeMars: It could be. It could be. You get very insular, and you work very hard. You don't have a lot of free time.

One other little story here I had. When I was navigator there was a device called the DRAI, dead reckoning analyzer indicator, and it takes an input from the log, the pit sword, and from the compass, and it dead reckons you along.* It projects a beam of light up, and you put a chart on there, and you set it all up, and it projects where you are on this chart by dead reckoning.

Paul Stillwell: It's like a DRT.†

Admiral DeMars: Yes, yes. But no input from current or wind or anything like that. So on one WestPac deployment this thing stopped working. It's kind of a pain in the butt because you use it quite a bit. So we took it apart and looked hard at it. Best we could tell, the ball bearings may have been screwed up in this thing, had gotten flattened or old or something. So we sent a message in for the next time we went in to Okinawa. And waiting on the pier was this Air Force captain in a fancy little red sports car with no top on. He said, "Who's the navigator?"

I said, "I am."

He said, "I'm here to help you find some new ball bearings."

We'd sent it in a message about them. I said to him, "Well, God, that's good service." So we jumped in this car, and he went bombing down the road. We went in this local market. It was all open-air sheds. There was this one shed that must have had hundreds of pie trays full of ball bearings just sitting there. I'd brought a micrometer with me, and the lady that ran it was a little Okinawan lady and *she* had a micrometer. I had several of what I thought were the bad ball bearings. We miked those up and we must have got a dozen ball bearings, and I think they cost me like five cents each. So I

---

* A pitometer log provides the speed and distance of a ship's travel through the water by measuring pressure on a pitot tube that extends from the hull.
† DRT—dead reckoning tracer, a mechanical device used in the combat information center to maintain a plot of the ship's movements.

paid for those, I gave her a nice tip, we got back in, we put them back in. The DRAI worked for about a week and it crapped out again. [Chuckle] It makes a good story, anyway.

Paul Stillwell: Was Okinawa your main source of logistic support?

Admiral DeMars: Yes. That was the place you could go.

Paul Stillwell: Because it was still under American control.

Admiral DeMars: Yes. We did a number of things there and that's where we transferred all our intel packages, and we got to know Naha, Okinawa, quite well. Not a garden spot of the world.

Paul Stillwell: There was an LST ramp there, and my ship used to go in there regularly.* We couldn't go directly from Japan to Vietnam for political reasons, so that was a way station.

Admiral DeMars: So you know that idea.

Watkins got relieved in Sasebo, Japan, which was a very interesting change of command. He was relieved by Ken Loposer, who went on after this to, I think, command an SSBN, but I'm not sure.† A totally different personality, but I'll get to that later.

The change of command was in Sasebo aboard the repair ship *Ajax*, and so we mustered up on the deck there. Watkins's mother had been a big figure in the Japan-American Society in the '30s, and so we had a number of Japanese at the ceremony all dressed up, and they came up. We didn't have a band, obviously; neither did the *Ajax*, so we got a recording of the Japanese national anthem and a recording of our own national anthem. We had a bugler there for honors, etc., etc. I was one of the ushers, and I was

---
* LST–tank landing ship, an amphibious warfare ship capable of putting her bow directly onto a beach, opening bow doors, and lowering a bow ramp to permit vehicles to exit. The interviewer served in the USS *Washoe County* (LST-1165) from 1966 to 1969.
† Commander Avery Kenneth Loposer Jr., USN, commanded the *Snook* from 3 September 1966 to 5 August 1969.

busy getting people seated. Jim Watkins's older brother—I guess he's dead now—was a naval aviator, and he was so different from Jim. I mean, he was a *naval aviator* in every sense of the word, and our CO wasn't that type.

Paul Stillwell: Gung-ho, derring-do.

Admiral DeMars: Oh, yes, absolutely. He had the most arrested carrier landings of anybody ever when he finally retired. He retired as a captain. He was a CO of another ship over there.[*] He was doing a deep-draft command before getting a carrier. I don't know if he ever got a carrier. Anyway, he came over in his gig and came up with a young WAVE lieutenant on his arm.[†] He said, "Hi, Bruce, how you doing?"

"Oh, nice, Captain, nice to see you."

I was showing them to their seats, and he looked over at the bugler and said, "What's that?"

I said, "Well, we don't have any music. We got a record for the Japanese national anthem."

He said, "Seat her; I'll be right back." He ran over, [whistle], called his boat back, went down and got in his boat and took off. Well, the ceremony was in about half an hour, and I wondered, "What's this all about?"

He came bombing back about ten minutes later with about eight musicians. He was carrying around one of the bands in WestPac on his ship. He'd big-dealed it that way, because he got a lot of mileage out of them in social events and that. This chief musician came up, and he looked at the Marine and said, "You can leave. We'll take care of this."

Then I said, "Well, we do have a record for the Japanese national anthem."

He said, "We know the Japanese national anthem. Don't worry about that. Just tell us what the program is." I told him. He said, "Okay, you can relax, Lieutenant Commander." So they did it. The thing came off wonderfully, the Japanese national

---

[*] Captain George C. Watkins, USN, commanded the stores ship *Mars* (AFS-1) from December 1965 to December 1966. He had been a fighter pilot and test pilot. He did not command an aircraft carrier. Watkins retired as a captain and died 18 September 2005. His nickname was "Gorgeous George."
[†] WAVE was a term used at the time for a woman in the U.S. Navy.

anthem, all of that. The next day Jim got off, and we took off for station again with Ken Loposer on board.

Well, there was a big change in the ship. Loposer had been on the *Tullibee*—the very little submarine that went 12 knots, I think. Never really did any spec ops. And he had been on SSBNs. So we were up on station the first day, and I was the officer of the deck. We saw a Soviet submarine coming over the horizon on the surface. Buster Bilyeu was the XO by then; he had relieved Ron Thunman.* Buster went down to tell the captain about the contact, and I was positioning the ship so we could take pictures as it went by, and sound pressure level readings and everything. Buster came up and said, "The captain says just go ahead and do it."

I said, "What?"

He said, "Yeah, as usual he's laying on his bunk reading a cowboy novel, and he said. 'Just go ahead and do it. You guys know how to do it; I don't.'" [Laughter]

I said, "Well, shit, he's not even going to come up and watch?" No. So he didn't. He went up and we did it, we went in, we took pictures, we did the recording, we did everything you were supposed to do, Buster and I working our butts off. Well, we knew how to do it. We'd done it.

I went down and reported to him after the watch. I said, "Captain, here's what happened on the watch."

He said, "You probably wondered why I didn't come up."

I said, "Yes, sir, I did."

He said, "Well, I figured you guys knew how to do it and I didn't, so I just let you do it."

I said, "Is that the way it's going to be?"

He said, "Yeah."

I said, "Okay." I had a big smile on my face.

So Buster and I got together, and he said, "Okay, Bruce, you've got to come off the watch bill, and you and I will be the senior watch officers." We had another guy we could make an OOD, and just have the poor engineering officers of the watch go port and

---

* Lieutenant Commander Roland C. Bilyeu. USN.

starboard.* "And you and I will do all of this." And we did. For the next six weeks we did everything we had to do: underwater hull surveillances, missile tracking, anything that was required done. And we loved doing it. And we didn't hazard the vessel. We knew how to do it. We were very confident, because we both had great experience. Buster had been on another SSN out of San Diego, and was a great guy. He lives down in Charlottesville now. Great guy. And so the CO sat it out.

We got back into port. I had orders to the Armed Forces Staff College, and I left the ship in Okinawa, I guess. I flew back. The ship came back to the West Coast and went in the shipyard, so it was a good time to get off anyway.

Paul Stillwell: The captain's reaction there says two things. One, he had a lot of confidence in you, and the other thing is, surprisingly, he didn't have the curiosity to see what was going on.

Admiral DeMars: He was a different kind of guy. I always thought we ought to check him for a pulse. [Laughter] I mean, wouldn't you even want to come up and learn?

Paul Stillwell: Right.

Admiral DeMars: Or say, "I don't want to do that. That's too dangerous." But we loved it. Buster and I loved it. Here were two lieutenant commanders running a spec op.

Paul Stillwell: And it would have been on the skipper's head if anything went wrong.

Admiral DeMars: Absolutely. Absolutely.

The Armed Forces Staff College was funny. These orders came in, and they just said, "Ordered to ASFC."

So I said, "Christ, where the hell am I going now? Air Force Supply School or something?" So we looked it up in the book: Armed Forces Staff College, Norfolk,

---

* OOD – officer of the deck.

Virginia. I said, well, once again, they can't send me to PG school [chuckle] but they're sending me to Armed Forces Staff College, which is good.

Paul Stillwell: Had you applied for PG school?

Admiral DeMars: No, no. As I mentioned last time, I had been selected for PG three years running but not made available.

So that was the end of *Snook*, which was a fun ship, a fun tour, obviously. Learned an awful lot there, awful lot.

Paul Stillwell: That experience made you into a professional submariner.

Admiral DeMars: Yes, it really did. You know, the *George Washington* made me an engineer, and the *Snook* made me a tactician. I got filled up on both of those, and they served me the rest of my career. The rest of my career. And I had great COs. Up until Loposer—that was really, I couldn't believe it—I thought all COs were great because that's all I'd had. Couldn't believe it. I subsequently got disabused of that when I went to the Nuclear Propulsion Examining Board; I saw you had all different kinds of COs.

Well, I don't know if you're tired.

Paul Stillwell: Ready to keep going?

Admiral DeMars: Okay, let's do at least one more.

Paul Stillwell: Please tell me about your experiences at the Armed Forces Staff College.

Admiral DeMars: Well, as I said, I got off the ship in Okinawa, and back to San Diego. As I remember, that's when we sold the house finally, got rid of it, and piled into our Volkswagen and once again drove cross country with two kids, a dog, and a cat. Drove cross country from San Diego to Norfolk, where the Armed Force Staff College was. I think that was the third and last time we drove cross country, but we loved it because it was a free vacation in those days.

When I got to the Armed Forced Staff College, it was a great six months. The reason I was there, Lieutenant Commander Noel T. Wood had been the diesel detailer in the Bureau of Naval Personnel. He had been one of my first classmen at the Naval Academy, and he was getting ready to leave as detailer and go off and command, I think, a diesel submarine. He wanted to enjoy himself a little bit, so he ordered himself to the Armed Force Staff College. And he wanted to have some friends there, so he ordered a bunch of his submarine friends there, and I was one of his submarine friends. We had the biggest submarine class that the place has ever seen; there must have been 30 of us [chuckle]. So we had a great time, and it was all because of N. T. Wood.

Paul Stillwell: What was the atmosphere at that transition time between nuc and diesel submariners?

Admiral DeMars: Very good. Very good, because the nucs realized, either then or later, that we couldn't run the submarine force without the diesel submariners. They had all the hard staff jobs, they commanded all the tenders, they commanded all the bases, they had all the jobs on SubLant, SubPac, the squadron command jobs, until you got enough nucs. So they were very, very vital to the operation of the Submarine Force. And the majority of them took it well. They understood that. I never saw any problems. There was some nascent here and there "diesel boats forever" bullshit and that. I mean, that's fine, but you've got to grow up after a while. But none of it ever got very serious. I never gave it another thought, quite frankly.

It was a great six months. We lived in base housing, which was very nice. They were little modern townhouses. And we would visit the entire area on weekends and establish locations that we still use today: Cape Hatteras, Chincoteague, Assateague. Visited all those places and then later on went back fishing, and on and on and on.

I learned much about the other services while I was there, and I was very glad I was in the Navy [chuckle]. I validated that the Navy was the best service, for me, certainly, and I don't say that to denigrate any of the other services, because we had good people there.

Paul Stillwell: What gave you that impression?

Admiral DeMars: Oh, the people were just easier to get along with. Army was very difficult to get along with, very difficult. The Air Force seemed very diverse, and they didn't seem like they were in the military. [Chuckle] It was just that they had a different approach to life. We didn't have many Marines there. So I just felt the Navy was easygoing; everybody got along. I mean, the Army was always worried about what corps you went in and that. And although the Navy gets accused of having the three big unions—aviation, surface, and submariners—it's not the way, really. They all get along well, at least they did in those days. And so I just felt I was in the best service. Of course, I was a little parochial looking at the Navy.

Paul Stillwell: Well, there's a stereotype that the Army people are better at staff work because they have to do something in between their operational tours.

Admiral DeMars: Yes, absolutely. The other difference, I think, that drives it is that Navy people rarely live on a base. They usually live out in the community. Air Force and Army people always live on a base—always. And so that kind of makes you narrower, I think, and less broad-based toward the community, and that sort of thing. I mean, all their stuff is done on the base. Their kids play their sports on the base, you go to the O-club, on and on and on. Whereas when we lived in Mystic, Connecticut, for 12 years that was wonderful. We lived in San Diego. We weren't on a base. Lived in Mare Island, we weren't on a base. I think that drives it a lot. Plus, in the Army in those days a deployment meant you went and lived on a base in Germany.

Paul Stillwell: Did you encounter any of your classmates from other services later in your career?

Admiral DeMars: No. No, because I got dumped right back into the narrow world of submarines and nuclear power. But it was a good time then. Later on they toughened it up. They actually had exams and that sort of stuff. Then we just had seminars, had a weekly speaker, you had to make book reports and that sort of stuff. One of the things I found was my love of reading served me well there, because I felt I was a little broader than most. I had read things that were very broad—history and biographies and all that sort of stuff—and I just sensed that I was a little more broader educated than most.

Great social life. Everybody got along well. I remember this Air Force officer—I think he was a captain or lieutenant colonel—had a Kentucky Derby party where he would make mint juleps. I mean the real mint juleps, with the sugary syrup in them and just on ice and bourbon. And then he had a country ham there, which is very salty, which makes you want to drink more, and everybody went staggering home. Fortunately everybody lived on base there.

So it was a great place, and very broadening for me because we had a speaker from Washington every week. It was a good time.

Paul Stillwell: What were the subject matters you got into?

Admiral DeMars: Political-military sort of things, relations with other nations and allies, and that sort. It was all strictly a military-oriented approach.

Paul Stillwell: Was there anything in the curriculum about making up op orders?

Admiral DeMars: No. No, not that I remember. If there was, I can't remember it. No, it wasn't that; it was more broadening, because all the Army and the Air Force guys knew how to do that stuff; the Navy guys didn't care [chuckle].

Paul Stillwell: So you were just sitting there absorbing knowledge.

Admiral DeMars: Absorbing things. It was run on a seminar sort of thing. We had this Air Force colonel was our seminar lead, wonderful man, and we would have topics and we'd have to do some reading. Then we'd have to discuss it in the seminar.

Paul Stillwell: Did you write papers?

Admiral DeMars: Yes, we had to write papers. One of the big things we had, you had to take a book and go into it in a great amount of detail. And it had to be on Vietnam. So I picked *Hell in a Very Small Place*, which was on the Battle of Dien Bien Phu.[*] I can't remember the author. He subsequently got killed in Vietnam.

Paul Stillwell: Bernard Fall?

Admiral DeMars: Bernard Fall, that's the one.[†] I went into it in great detail, and I read a couple of other books on the battle so that I could write up a great report, and I got the highest mark in my seminar for my report. *Hell in a Very Small Place.* Terrible thing.

Paul Stillwell: This was a time when the President and McNamara and so forth thought that the war was still winnable.[‡] Did you get into that kind of thing?

Admiral DeMars: Well, nobody in the audience felt that way, even those that were flying there and endangering themselves, the Air Force and the Navy pilots. None of them felt that this thing was winnable. In fact, we were just burning up people. The Army I don't remember, because they didn't talk much about it.

But it was kind of funny. The Air Force guys were always on the phone to their detailer saying, "I need a tour in Vietnam. It's for my career, it's for my career." And

---

[*] The Battle of Dien Bien Phu took place between 13 March and 7 May 1954 in what was then known as French Indochina. Communist Viet Minh troops defeated the French Army garrison at the time peace negotiations were getting under way in Geneva Switzerland. The French surrender on 7 May paved the way for French disengagement in the region and the later establishment of North and South Vietnam.
[†] Bernard B. Fall, *Hell in a Very Small Place: the Siege of Dien Bien Phu* (Philadelphia: Lippincott, 1966).
[‡] Lyndon B. Johnson served as President of the United States from 22 November 1963 to 20 January 1969. Robert S. McNamara served as Secretary of Defense from 21 January 1961 to 29 February 1968.

the Navy guys were on the phone saying, "I don't need my third tour off Vietnam on another carrier." [Chuckle] "I've done my bit." So it was a different approach.

But it was an absolutely fun place. Margaret and I had dinner there one night with Jim Osborn and his wife. He was the chief of staff for SubLant then, still a captain. And I remember him saying, "Well, Bruce, what do you want to do next?"

I said, "I'd like to be the second XO on a new construction SSN." That's what I got.

Paul Stillwell: Why second instead of first?

Admiral DeMars: Because the first one has to go through the shipyard.

Paul Stillwell: Ah! [Laughter]

Admiral DeMars: And do the shipyard. I didn't want to do that. I didn't want to do that. I'd never been in a shipyard in my life except a small battery replacement on the diesel submarine *Capitaine*. I got just what I wanted, and so it worked out. Although it was a great job because it went right back into the operations stuff once again, on a thing that was operating the whole time that I was there.

So I got ordered to *Sturgeon* as XO.[*] It was a great, great tour. We bought a house, an 1880 Victorian colonial sitting way up on top of the hill in Mystic proper, right near the library. Looked out over Long Island Sound. It was an octagonal base, the main room and then the living room off that. Above that was an octagonal bedroom. Above that an octagonal glassed-in widow's walk that you could see the Sound from. Jeez, I think we paid $44,000 for it, which we had to scrimp and save.

Paul Stillwell: Big bucks in those days.

---

[*] USS *Sturgeon* (SSN-637), the name ship of her class, was commissioned 3 March 1967. She was 292 feet long, 32 feet in the beam, had a maximum draft of 29 feet. She displaced 3,856 tons surfaced and 4,630 tons submerged. She had a top speed on the surface around 20 knots and a speed in excess of 30 knots submerged. She was armed with four 21-inch torpedo tubes. Lieutenant Commander DeMars reported to the submarine in June 1967.

Admiral DeMars: Very big bucks in those days. But it was great. It was a good move, because I ended up having three tours there, essentially. That was a period of time when the government ran out of money to move people, so what they did was not move people. So if you were stuck in Missouri or something, then you were in tough times. If you were in Mystic, you thought it was a good deal.

Our kids went to the same schools for that period of time and had a great time. They had jobs there. My son shucked oysters and peeled lobsters and worked as a lifeguard. They enjoyed it immensely. So it was a good time.

The first CO was Commander Curt Shellman, who was the commissioning CO.[*] The ship had been commissioned and was on shakedown now, I guess. He ended up a two-star in Washington, and got out and went to work for EB.[†] Had he not had a heart attack down in the yard, I'm convinced he would have been the president of EB. He was that smart, he was that good. He was a tremendous engineer, and very hard working—he was a nuc's nuc, a very hard-working man. He was a fine engineer but a very cautious tactician. But a fine engineer, and a wonderful man too. He was big and burly, but he had been a dash runner at New London High School, which was where he went and where his wife went. He was a very nice man.

His dad was a retired chief quartermaster, and he used to work second shift at EB. I remember I'd go through the ship and I'd look at the logbooks from the security watch and that and it was so neat, and it was Curt B. Shellman. So one day I either got in early or stayed late and talked to him, and, sure enough, it was his dad.

I turned out to be the only one on board with spec-op experience. None of the others had ever made a spec op in their life. Now, fortunately, I had illegally brought all my spec-op paperwork with me from *Snook*—the parties, what you manned, the procedures to do the particular evolutions you have to do. So I started off on an intensive training program for the wardroom. I also put a new twist in. I picked three young enlisted men and made them junior officers of the deck, gave them the same training, so that we had extra people to work in the control room while we were on spec ops. And it worked out quite well, quite well.

---

[*] Commander Curtis B. Shellman Jr., USN.
[†] EB – the Electric Boat Division of the General Dynamics Corporation is a long-time submarine building yard in Groton, Connecticut.

Paul Stillwell: It had to be very satisfying for them to get that opportunity.

Admiral DeMars: Yes, they did. They did. In those days you couldn't get medals, but I always got them a citation from ComSubLant or something that was presented to them.

We did a special operation in the Barents before our post-shakedown availability, which was very unusual. I think it was because we had the first reelable towed array.[*] You had a big tube down the side of the ship that went off just far enough outside the propeller so you wouldn't cut it off, and then it came through a wiper and an O-ring and that. Then it had a reel in the forward bow compartment that you could reel this towed array in and out. They wanted to get us to sea quickly to evaluate that, so we did it. It was a good spec op but not great. Shellman didn't like to hazard himself, hazard the ship, so it was cautious. It was too cautious for me, but that was the way it was.

Paul Stillwell: And obviously the advantage of the reel is that the sonar could go through different thermoclines to detect something.

Admiral DeMars: Yes. Absolutely. And also the aperture width is long, because it's like 100 feet at the end of it are the sections with the towed array in it. So you can pick up much lower frequencies.

The new CO was Bo Bohannan.[†] He lives up in the Groton area to this day. He came aboard, and all he had was a diesel submarine and a ballistic missile submarine background. He had been one of the latecomers into the nuclear power program. He was a charismatic leader. I mean just a charismatic leader. And a risk taker, quite a risk taker. But he and I got along well.

While we were getting ready to go off and do that special op, we went down to do something in the Caribbean, testing out something or that, and off of Fort Lauderdale he got pneumonia. So we went into port, and we took him up to the Air Force hospital there. The next day I went to see him, and the doctor said he couldn't leave for two

---

[*] A towed array consists of passive sonar sensors, as opposed to those mounted directly on the ship's hull. By being on a towline, the passive array has the advantage that it can be lowered through thermal layers that would otherwise inhibit sound propagation and reception.
[†] Commander William L. Bohannan, USN.

weeks. I said, "Oh, God." So I went in and saw him and I said, "Well, Captain, I guess I should sent a message or call SubLant and say we're going to have to cancel this test we were going and doing out there."

He said, "Hell, no. You go off and do it."

So I said, "Can I?"

He said, "Yes, absolutely. You know, I've been with you long enough. You can run the ship." So he called SubLant and, I was amazed, NR approved it, SubLant approved it. I took the ship under way for, I think it was ten days. The first thing I did when I got under way I sent a message: "Under way with XO in charge." [Chuckle] I still have it on my wall down in my basement. But that's the kind of guy he was. It wouldn't occur to him at all not to do that. And he was that way with everything. That's why everybody loved him. The crew just couldn't get enough of him, and particularly compared with Shellman, who was very cautious. This guy was: "Roll the dice and let's go see what happens."

Paul Stillwell: Did you ever have to restrain him if things got too wild?

Admiral DeMars: Yes, all the time. [Laughter] All the time. That had to be a careful act, because I wanted to keep his confidence, and he did good things. But, you know, I had to say, "Captain, should we just be a little deeper?" Or, "How about positioning over here, do you think that would work better?"

And he'd say, "Ah, yeah, Bruce. You're always right." But, you know, all the time.

Paul Stillwell: I take it there was no resentment when you said things.

Admiral DeMars: Not at all. Not at all. He was that kind of a guy. I mean, he was just a wonderful, wonderful man.

We did three more spec ops in the Barents against the newest of the Soviet Navy. And, as I said, Bohannan was great, but he was a risk taker, and so I had to make sure I restrained him when he should be restrained. But he was good.

I instituted division cooking night as XO, where every division could cook for a special night. And it really got that way by the second spec op, when people knew I was really serious. One division had an Italian night, and they'd bring in Italian flags and put them up and they'd make pasta and all special things. And they'd buy special things to bring aboard, on their own money, and do it. And we even had one where the officers did it. But you had to clean up also, afterward. And this really gave the crew an appreciation for how hard the cooks and the mess cooks worked.

Paul Stillwell: Good point.

Admiral DeMars: Yes, that really gave them an appreciation for that. Because by the time you get done feeding all these guys, you're bushed, you're done. So that was good.

We carried wine in the CO/XO shower. And then at the halfway point we'd have a wine night and everybody—the chief of the boat and I were in charge—everybody got a glass of wine. It was interesting, because several other boats were doing this too. Then the flotilla commander, Admiral Wilkinson, came out with a very beautifully worded message to the COs and said, "I understand why you're doing this, and I can't argue with the thought, but you've got a nuclear reactor aboard, you've got nuclear weapons on board; knock that shit off right now."[*] So we threw it all overboard, we didn't do it, and it just went away. But that's the way the submarine force was in those days. I mean, whatever your boss said, you did it—boom. So that went by the way.

Paul Stillwell: Did drugs rear their heads as a problem at that point?

Admiral DeMars: No, not then. Not then. It hadn't gotten there yet, fortunately. It was probably there; we just didn't know it. I don't know.

---

[*] Rear Admiral Eugene P. Wilkinson, USN, served as Commander Submarine Flotilla Two in 1969-70. The oral history of Wilkinson, who retired as a vice admiral, is in the Naval Institute collection.

Bill McHale, my yeoman, wrote a book on that.* He was one of the junior officers of the deck that I made. He went to the University of Rhode Island and left after a year or so, joined the Navy, came aboard as a seaman, a very smart young man, obviously. He fit in well, did everything well. I picked him as the second yeoman. You usually had a yeoman and then a striker, somebody who wanted to be the yeoman. Picked him, and he did everything well. He was very good, very talented. Made him a JOOD. And he subsequently wrote a book on his three years on *Sturgeon*, and it's very well done. I helped him with it a little bit. He characterized the two COs. And at first it was a little harsh against Shellman, I think, because McHale was a young guy, and all he could remember was the hero parts of it, so I got him to tone that down, look at it more carefully, what did they do afterward in their careers, and on and on and on. It's a very good book. I had to talk the Naval Institute Press into doing it, and they did. It's been quite a bestseller. It's been very well received.

Paul Stillwell: Well, it really captured the day-to-day life of the sailors on board.

Admiral DeMars: I think it did. Yes, and how they worked. *I* learned a hell of a lot. You know, *I* learned that sailors swore like sailors when they were by themselves. They didn't swear on board around the officers. It was just respect.

Paul Stillwell: Well, and he said in the book that he had toned down the actual language.

Admiral DeMars: Right, exactly. When he wrote it the first time, the Naval Institute said. "We can't publish this." [Laughter] But we're still very close friends. He lives in New York City. He's made his living in the musical comedy and stage play business. He's an actor and a singer. A very nice man.

Paul Stillwell: Well, speaking of yeomen, what do you recall about the administrative side of your job?

---

* Gannon McHale, *Stealth Boat: Fighting the Cold War in a Fast Attack Submarine* (Annapolis: Naval Institute Press, 2008). His given first name was William, but he chose the name Gannon in his work as a professional actor and used Gannon also as his pen name.

Admiral DeMars: It was very easy, except writing that goddamn patrol report when we were on spec ops, because I had to do all the stuff I had to do as senior watch officer. When the captain went to bed, I stayed up all night long, and I was the senior watch officer. We just did that port and starboard. So I had to get some sleep in around that, I had to write the patrol report, and I had to do all the other stuff. But the basic bureaucracy, the paperwork, was sort of minimal, really, in those days.

Now, when I came aboard I relieved a guy, an XO, who spent all his time in his stateroom. He had one of these pull-out files—I forget what they're called—with the little cards on it. He had a card on every sailor on board. And everything was in there. That guy's service record and that. When I relieved him, I saw that. God. I told all the wardroom officers, "Stop by the wardroom one at a time; you're getting these goddamn cards. I'm not keeping them." [Chuckle] "And you don't have to keep them either. You keep whatever records you want on your people." He used to drive the yeoman nuts. He had a bell in his office, and he'd ring the bell. The yeoman would have to leave his office and come one door over. That XO was a different kind—never left his room. So it was easy to relieve him.

But I was tough. I didn't put up with any crap. And I always had a penchant for cleanliness on board. I had field days and would inspect things and get down and look with flashlights with the chief there and the officer who ran it. I thought McHale put it right when he said the crew thought that I was tough but fair. And I think that's what the XO should be. You know, let the CO be the hero and all of that.

Paul Stillwell: Well, there's a lot to be said for management by walking around too.

Admiral DeMars: Absolutely.

Paul Stillwell: You pick things up.

Admiral DeMars: Every day when I was XO or CO, twice a day I'd just walk all the way to the engine room, both levels, machinery space both levels, all the way forward, torpedo room, crew's mess, everything, and just talk very briefly to the sailors. What's going on, this and that. Twice. Do that twice a day. And when I was CO I did the same thing. Even on spec-op station, go off and do it. Find out what's going on, etc., etc., etc. You learned a hell of a lot.

Paul Stillwell: People will tell you things in that atmosphere that they wouldn't come see you about.

Admiral DeMars: Yes, exactly. Yes, exactly. But I enjoy that. I like sailors, and I've always enjoyed dealing with them.

Paul Stillwell: Well, and it shows them you care too. You're interested.

Admiral DeMars: Yes, absolutely. Which you ought to be, because they're the lifeblood of the ship.

When I was relieved, I took my wife to Europe for two weeks. [Chuckle] We sent the kids back to Indiana to live with her parents, and we flew to Prestwick, Scotland, took a train down to London. Couple days in London, took the ferryboat across to Le Havre and then the train to Paris. A couple days in Paris, then the train up to Amsterdam. A few days there and the ferry back across to Scotland. Rented another car and drove back to Prestwick and came home. My last patrol on *Sturgeon* my relief rode. I had him do the patrol report. And then when I stepped off I was relieved as XO, so I didn't have to do any of that. And so we went off and did that, had a great time.

Paul Stillwell: Well, you have a note here about "against the newest of the Soviet navy." What did that involve?

Admiral DeMars: Well, their newest submarines were out then, and they were getting quieter. But our sonars were very good. I mean, the sonar on *Sturgeon* compared to *Snook* was unbelievable. I mean, it was a great sonar. And, of course, we were quieter. Everything was sound mounted on *Sturgeon*; nothing was hard mounted to the hull. So we had kept that undersea superiority advantage against them, but clearly they were starting to get into the business, and that's why we'd get in close and make these recordings. Then we sent them back, and the intel community would say, "Yeah, they're getting quieter. They're marching down the same path we did." But they had the newest missile submarines, the Deltas and the Victor class—it's started to come back now.[*] And so we went up against all of them. I'm not sure we weren't potentially counter-detected a couple of times because of Bo Bohannan's tactics, but we never got held down or anything, and they never reported it, and on and on.

Paul Stillwell: I take it there were some trail operations involved in this?

Admiral DeMars: Oh, yes. Well, you had certain requirements. If you saw this kind of submarine or surface ship, the intel people were very interested in this sort of data. If a new ballistic missile submarine left port, you should try and trail that as far as you could and try and find out its operating areas. So in case the war got hotter, we could send attack submarines in there to get ready to take them out. So there were certain intel requirements on just about everything, and you tried to fulfill all those.

Before you went on patrol they had all the patrol reports from the last two years up in this vault in Groton in the intel spaces, and all the officers were supposed to go up there and read them. And we read them all before we went on patrol, so you had all the latest dope, and on and on. So it was a very serious business. That was what we did for a living.

Paul Stillwell: Did you again have special riders?

Admiral DeMars: Oh, yes. We had the same kind of riders we had on *Snook*—CTs and sonar techs. And once again, they loved Bohannan because, Christ, he'd do just about anything they proposed [chuckle].

---

[*] Soviet Victor I-class nuclear-powered attack submarines entered active service at a rate of two a year from 1968 to 1975. They displaced 4,300 tons on the surface and 5,100 tons submerged; length, 312 feet; beam, 33 feet; draft, 23 feet; speed 30 knots. They were armed with torpedoes and SS-N-15 surface-to-surface missiles.
Soviet Delta I-class nuclear-powered submarines entered active service from 1972 to 1977. They displaced 9,000 tons on the surface and 11,750 tons submerged; length, 459 feet; beam, 39 feet; draft, 28 feet; speed 25 knots. They were armed with torpedoes and ballistic missiles.

Paul Stillwell: And maybe wanted to do more. [Laughter]

Admiral DeMars: So they enjoyed riding *Sturgeon* because we were an exciting boat then. So it was *Snook* redux, but just on a much better platform, much quieter platform, much more reliable platform. Slower platform.

Paul Stillwell: Because you had a bigger ship.

Admiral DeMars: Yes. And it had, essentially, the Water Boy system built into it now, the WLR-6 or whatever. So it had all that, and it was a good ship. It turned out it was the first of the 637 class. I subsequently commanded the last of the 637 class.

Paul Stillwell: *Cavalla*.

Admiral DeMars: *Cavalla*. So I got bookends on that baby.
    After I left, the *Sturgeon* made an op into the Med and had a collision with a Soviet submarine. Now, I'm not saying it's because I wasn't there, but it just happened.

Paul Stillwell: Was Bohannan still the skipper?

Admiral DeMars: Yes, he was still the CO.

Paul Stillwell: Did you have any deployments or parts of deployments that weren't special ops?

Admiral DeMars: No. That's all we did. That's all we did [chuckle]. Go off for essentially three months, come back, work up. Well, we did go down and fire a SubRoc missile at AUTEC, the Tongue of the Ocean range down there.* We went down there

---

* SubRoc was a submarine-launched antisubmarine ballistic rocket, fired from underwater and guided to its target by an inertial system. Development began in June 1958, and it was approved for service in 1966. It had a range of about 35-40 nautical miles. AUTEC – Atlantic Underwater Test and Evaluation Center, based on Andros Island in the Bahamas.

and did a couple of other things like that. We all fired in those days five or six Mark 48 torpedoes for proficiency. Which is the strength of the submarine force; they actually fire their weapons. We try and do them down there where you can recover them and get all the tracking data and everything. So we did stuff like that, but most of it, it was basically two spec ops every year. So six there, and six in the Pacific.

Paul Stillwell: Did you get any overseas liberty ports?

Admiral DeMars: No. The guys that got the overseas liberty ports were the ones that went to the Med. But they would go to the Med for six months. So we just went north, because of our special equipment and the quality of what we could do there. And the other lesser capable boats would go to the Med.

Paul Stillwell: What kind of demands did the patrols make on your stamina?

Admiral DeMars: Well, you were younger. I did find out when I was CO that I could stay up doing something demanding for 36 hours. Then I was out of it. And this was either trailing somebody or waiting for a missile to come in or go out, and on and on and on. And then I'd just tell the XO, "You've got it," and I'd go crash for four hours, and then I'd reenter the fray. But you were younger then. You could do a hell of a lot more of that kind of stuff. I mean, now I have to take a nap every afternoon. No, stamina never came in as a problem.

Paul Stillwell: Adrenaline was probably helping also.

Admiral DeMars: Yes, oh yes, all the time, all the time. Well, you wanted to have a good run, because there was a lot of competition between the boats, a lot of competition. You wanted to do it well and you wanted to come back and be proud of what you did.

Paul Stillwell: How were the judgments made among the competitors? Was this from the patrol reports?

Admiral DeMars: Oh, you could tell. How many sound pressure level recordings did they get? Because, you know, when I was CO and when I was XO with Bohannan and when I was on *Snook*, every submarine that you saw, you went in for a recording. You didn't say, "Well, I don't know, I'm a little tired." You just went in and did it. So the gross number that you brought back. And then the quality of those recordings and the type of submarine. And then watching ballistic missile launches by a submerged Soviet submarine, we did that. The quality of the recordings you got and the data you brought back, all that was evaluated. And some boats did very well because they were very aggressive, and they were very well managed. They gathered the data the way that analysts like to get it, and so the analysts would say, "Hey, this is a good run." So it was subjective but not totally.

Paul Stillwell: You could draw a comparison in a way to the fleet boats in World War II because you had some skippers who were more highly cautious, and some who were more aggressive.

Admiral DeMars: Yes, exactly. Yes, exactly, that sort of thing. But it was fun. One of the reasons I stayed in the Navy—in fact I told Bob Long that once, and he kind of looked at me.* I said, "The reason I'm staying in the Navy is I want to be CO of a spec-op boat." He looked at me. "That's all?"

I said, "That's all." [Laughter]

Paul Stillwell: At some point you become too senior for that.

Admiral DeMars: Yes, but until you get the job, that still ought to be your goal. And that was my goal. And then after that I sort of thought, "Well, I can do other things in the world; this is not the be-all and end-all for me." But it was, up until then, because I'd gotten so inoculated on *Snook* with the good COs.

---

* When the ballistic missile submarine *Patrick Henry* (SSBN-599) was commissioned on 9 April 1960, Commander Robert L. J. Long, USN, was commanding officer of the gold crew. Long later became Deputy CNO (Submarine Warfare), Vice Chief of Naval Operations, and Commander in Chief Pacific. His oral history is in the Naval Institute collection.

(Interruption for change of tape)

Admiral DeMars: So Margaret and I were back from Europe, and the kids were back from Indiana. We were still in our house in Mystic, and I was now at Submarine School.* Once again, they couldn't make me available for postgraduate work or to be an aide or anything, but I was teaching again.

It was a pleasant tour, once again. We continued to love Mystic, so I wasn't complaining to anybody. I was the director of the executive division in the officer department—diving trainers, attack trainers, damage control trainers, tactics—that sort of stuff. We had a supply course, although we were beginning to put Supply Corps officers on nuclear submarines then, so this course was getting a little unnecessary.

Paul Stillwell: What was the classification level in the course?

Admiral DeMars: Confidential, I would say.

Paul Stillwell: So you didn't get much into spec ops.

Admiral DeMars: No, no. Not any.

I initiated and led a total redo of the curriculum, because I thought we either did that or put mothballs in it. It had never been re-upped at all. And so my staff and I looked at everything and changed some things, and primarily updating to make it more relevant. It was still kind of a diesel-electric submarine course, and now we sort of updated it to be a more nuclear-preparing course.

Collisions with Soviet submarines had continued. I mentioned the one the *Sturgeon* had had. We were having them with more regularity, which indicated a number of things. One, that the Soviets *were* getting quieter, and it was more difficult business.

Paul Stillwell: And the Soviets were deploying more.

---

* Lieutenant Commander DeMars reported to the staff of the Submarine School at Groton, Connecticut, in July 1969.

Admiral DeMars: Yes, and just the opportunity was greater. But I always characterized these collisions as parking-lot fender-benders, because they were at low speed and nobody ever got killed in either one. Nobody ever let water into either submarine on these things [chuckle]. *But* they were big political problems, obviously, and the Soviets always tried to exploit them, because they saw it as a wedge to drive us out of our patrol areas, and say this is bad, etc. And the White House never liked them when it happened.

Paul Stillwell: In surface ships at that time Soviets were harassing U.S. ships. Was there any of that in submarines? I mean, deliberately trying to embarrass, coming too close, or something?

Admiral DeMars: Well, they couldn't do it when we were up on station because they didn't know where we were. But they did try it with our ballistic missile submarines going in and out of Charleston. We know that. They would try and come too close, and so you escorted them out farther with tugboats and that sort of thing. You have a long run on the surface on the East Coast before you can dive. But I think it reminded the Soviets of their inferiority. That was one of the problems, that the admirals couldn't continue to say that they were the best submarines in the world.

But a new manual was written to try and codify all the lessons learned, and a lot of people without a lot of experience had to read up on what they should do. And some new rules were put in, how close you could get, etc., etc. I and a young lieutenant who had come off *Ray*, I think, nuclear-trained lieutenant, very smart young guy, initiated pre-deployment training for local submarines. We said, "Why can't we put together a course and teach them what they need to know before they go up on station to do it, using mostly the attack teachers, where you can simulate a target, etc.? Well, we'll simulate a target and then we'll ask the submarine to—you have the control room there—drive in on that target, do certain things, etc., etc., etc. We can turn that target around. All you're feeding is bearings back to the people to plot." And so this is very difficult business to do because it's not active. This is all passive tracking. Very difficult.

So what we did, we set it up two days. The first day was in classrooms on plots and tactics for officers and enlisted, and the second day was 24 hours in the attack center, run 24 hours around the clock, with the lieutenant and I—we got plenty of sleep before this—and the attack center crew that ran that, they would go on shift work. And it worked out quite well. People felt much more confident when they finished. It only took two days. And it was on kind of a voluntary basis. The local submarines would come up and say, "We'd like that before we deploy."

So the CO, sub school, sent me down to SubLant to brief down there when we were doing.

Paul Stillwell: Who was the CO?

Admiral DeMars: Don Hall, a very tough-minded nuc.[*] So I got down there, and I was in front of the entire senior SubLant staff—there must have been 12 captains in there and SubLant himself—and made the pitch of what we did and that. SubLant right there said, "I want every submarine to go through that before they deploy." Whether they're in Charleston, Norfolk, or Groton. So that kicked off pre-deployment training, and the lieutenant and I thought it was a great success. I think most crews that came through also felt that. You turned over people often enough, even if guys had been on spec ops and that, it was good for them to brush up.

So it was a great tour there. I was there two years. Kept myself busy, kept out of trouble.

Then I got ordered to prospective commanding officers' school down in Washington here, before going off to command. Six months in Rickover's headquarters down on Constitution Avenue there. Lectures, self-studies, and exams. My roommate down there was Dwaine Griffith, University of Idaho, electrical engineer.[†] We lived with this lady over in Arlington—Mickey Garverick's mother.[‡] And he was younger, he was an XO of some SSBN at the time, and he said, "Hey, my mom's got a place down there." And so we lived in her house. She was a widow, happy to have us. We paid 25 bucks a week, and we each had a bedroom and kitchen privileges [chuckle]. So it was very nice. We were getting 25 bucks a day, which was munificent money in those days.

---

[*] Captain Donald P. Hall, USN.
[†] Commander Dwaine O. Griffith, USN.
[‡] Lieutenant Commander Charles Michael Garverick, USN, a nuclear submariner.

We went home every weekend. You were supposed to stay at Naval Reactors till 3:00 o'clock Saturday afternoon, but in order to catch the plane for Groton you had to be at the airport by noon. So we would just leave. [Laughter] "Sneak out" might be a more appropriate term. Every Saturday, Duane and I, and all the other guys would look at us. And we'd walk over to National Airport.

Paul Stillwell: Was this course in Crystal City?

Admiral DeMars: Yes, this was in Crystal City now.* We'd walk over to National Airport, catch the plane up, and get home about 3:00 o'clock. We had to get back on the plane about 5:00 o'clock the next day, on Sunday, to go. But it was worth it. I was redoing the house then, this old 1880s Victorian mansion, sanding floors and painting walls and putting up wallpaper, so I spent most of the time doing that.

You had a six-hour final exam to get out of this school. And after that I had to have an oral with the head of radiological controls, so I must have failed that part of the exam. But he asked me a few questions and passed me. One officer failed out—and mostly on the interviews. He was a kind of squirrelly guy. So he didn't graduate. There were about 12 of us there, I think.

Rickover spoke to us only once. He got us all together in this little conference room and spent about 45 minutes essentially berating us. [Laughter] We all just sat there and took it and thought, "God, I'm glad I don't have to work for this guy real close." So it was a rite of passage, and away we went.

Paul Stillwell: What would happen to that one officer who didn't pass the course?

Admiral DeMars: He'd go off and get some staff job in the submarine force. There were plenty of staff jobs.

While I was at school there I got ordered to be the prospective commanding officer of *Cavalla* at EB, which I was happy to do. Maybe now BuPers was finally

---

* Crystal City is the name for a large modern office complex in Arlington, Virginia, not far south of the Pentagon.

putting two and two together, sending me back to where I had a house. [Laughter] But I had no shipyard experience. This was the first time I'd ever been in the shipyard, really, in my life. But it was great. *Cavalla*, PCO.*

Paul Stillwell: Do you remember any of your cohorts from that class?

Admiral DeMars: Yes. Dwaine Griffith. Frank Kelso became CNO.† And a couple of others. Most of them went on, were reasonably successful. It was mostly self-study, an occasional lecture, and exams, and oral exams. And try and stay away from Rickover. But he never got out and about very much, thank God. Steve White was, they call it head of the line locker there, that's the senior naval officer on Rickover's staff that sort of worried about PCO school and everything.‡

So I was back in my house in Mystic again, happy. The pre-commissioning crew was sent to the ship in advance, and we had essentially me, CO, an XO, an engineer, and three other officers, and a small crew. The rationale for them is that the shipyard didn't have a license to operate the reactor. That reactor belonged to Naval Reactors and to the Atomic Energy Commission and the Department of the Navy, and Rickover held those keys. So the only way they could do some of the testing, the power range testing, and operate the reactor, take it critical and that, was have the Navy crew do it. So unlike surface ships, they build the ship with shipbuilders and take it to sea on initial sea trials with shipbuilders. You can't do that with a nuclear vessel. So that's why you have a small crew there, and then it slowly builds up as the ship moves along toward launch.

The wardroom and the crew were very good. New construction always gets the best people, because they want a good ship; it's got to last 30 years. They want serious people there that are going to work hard and do a good job, so I benefitted from that.

We were the last of the 637 class.§ Thirty-seven of the *Sturgeon* class were built

---

* PCO – prospective commanding officer.
† Admiral Frank B. Kelso III, USN, served as Chief of Naval Operations from 29 June 1990 to 23 April 1994. His oral history is in the Naval Institute collection.
‡ Captain Steven A. White, USN, later a four-star admiral.
§ USS *Cavalla* (SSN-684), a *Sturgeon*-class nuclear attack submarine, was commissioned 9 February 1973. She was 292 feet long, 32 feet in the beam, and had a maximum draft of 29 feet. She displaced 4,193 tons standard and 4,498 tons full load. She had a top speed on the surface around 20 knots and a speed in excess of 30 knots submerged. She was equipped with four 21-inch torpedo tubes.

and, of course, I'd been XO on the first one and CO of the last one. That was both good and bad. The good part was you were at the end of the learning curve for Electric Boat. They knew how to do it. They knew how to do it. Problem, boom-boom-boom-boom-boom-boom. So it wasn't a lot of stress on the crew or the captain. The bad part was the spare parts had kind of leaned down, so sometimes you didn't have what you needed to fix something. They'd have to borrow it off another ship that was in overhaul in Mare Island, California, or something. But that was minor compared with the learning-curve aspect of it.

Paul Stillwell: Did it have more sophisticated equipment than *Sturgeon* had had?

Admiral DeMars: Yes, it had a better sonar, and the WLR-6 had been upgraded to a degree. But it hadn't changed very much and so, and once again it was an S5W reactor, so I knew that like the back of my hand. [Chuckle] It was my third S5W ship.

I had a good crew, I had a great engineer who had been the main propulsion assistant on three ships before me, and they just told him to turn your hat around and now he was going to be engineer. He got out at the end of our tour, but he was a wonderful guy.

Paul Stillwell: Who was he?

Admiral DeMars: Jim Burke.* He really was a wonderful guy. I still stay in touch with him. Lives in California. Got out and made a lot of money in the software business.

We beat all the construction records for the ship. There's one evolution where they do a flush. They put a filter in, and they do a flush of the core and all the systems and that when they're all welded together and that. Then they take this thing like a colander out and inspect everything and make sure there's nothing bad that showed up. And so the chief nuclear test engineer, Haggerty, said, "Captain, you've got to come with me. I have to be able to tell the Naval Reactors rep that the captain looked in the core

---

* Lieutenant James G. Burke, USN.

vessel with me."* So I said okay. The top was off this big vessel that the reactor core goes in. We were looking down there; it was all brightly lit with a flashlight. I said, "What's that over there?" There was a little piece of lock wire about that long....

Paul Stillwell: Two inches.

Admiral DeMars: Yes. It was like a paper clip unrolled. I said, "What?"

They said, "Christ, I've never seen that before." So they got it out. It was a piece of lock wire.

Rickover said, "Okay, put the goddamn strainer back in and flush for another three days." So this set them back on their schedule. And they got paid extra if they delivered early. So we helped them do all that, and we never made any mistakes, we never got shut down. We helped them recover the schedule, and they really appreciated that.

When it was all over, Haggerty came up to me and said, "Captain, you think it would be okay if EB put on a keg for you at Appy's [that was one of the bars right next door to the entrance to the shipyard] to thank you for all that you and your crew have done in building this ship?"

I said, "Yes, that's okay as long as Siskin [who was the Rickover rep] doesn't hear about it, and Rickover doesn't hear about it."†

He said, "This will be a black program. We'll keep it undercover." [Laughter] And so we did, and they put on a keg for us, which I thought was very nice. The crew got a big kick out of it.

Paul Stillwell: Did you have to submit regular reports to Admiral Rickover?

Admiral DeMars: Yes, every month we had to send in the Rickover letter. The engineer would write it, and then I'd sort of look it over and say, "That's fine, I'll sign it."

---

* Thomas Haggerty.
† Edward Siskin, a civilian, had a long career in the nuclear power field.

Twice Steve White, who was the captain in Rickover's office, called me and said, "Bruce, Rickover is upset because you never say anything in your letters."

I said, "You know how hard it is to write a letter like that. Well, we never have any problems."

He said, "No, come on. Put some meat in there." Okay, fine, fine.

But we did shift work during power range testing and engine room steaming, where you went on shift work for, like, five, six weeks straight. And you had a senior supervisory watch, which was either the CO, XO, or engineer. We each took an eight-hour tour. I'd always get days, XO would get swings, and my poor engineer would have the midwatch.

There was a local Naval Reactors rep there and a small group that works with him, four or five guys. It was Ed Siskin. He was easy to get along with, great guy. I really like him. We still are friends to this day. Because he was a reasonable guy. And he was the buffer between you and Naval Reactors.

They had a PCO fund that was in the ship's contract. I, as the PCO, got $10,000 worth of work that I could have done. So I had to figure out what to do with that. Well, I noticed we had a bunch of tall guys in my crew. They were taller than the submarine bunks were long. So I had EB draw up some plans and make a little extender at the foot of four enlisted bunks, one wardroom bunk, and one chiefs' quarters bunk. Make a nice little thing, cut it out, put CRES around it, a little door to open it, a little mattress in there, so that the guy could stretch out.* It was only about that big. So that was a big seller.

One of my pet peeves during my time in submarines was that when you took a down angle or an up angle, any toilet seat that was left up would bang down. So I had non-banging toilet seats put in. You have this thing you have to push it down to keep it down. So I became known for that, you know—the captain only worries about the crapper—in the submarine force. [Laughter] But it was a good thing.

Then I had them build blackout curtains to go around the periscope stand so that when you rigged for red to go to periscope depth, and you rig for red in the entire control room—still there's a little light and that—you could pull these blackout curtains around and go to periscope depth and it was really dark. And so it was safe. They did a

---

* CRES – corrosion-resistant steel.

beautiful job. They came in, and the guy that did that work was always impressed that, "The captain was right there talking to me how he wanted it," this and that and so on and so forth. So that was fun.

And then I had some special things done. Over the plotting station we had a small camera that was used for something else on board. I had them mount that above, then put the little screen up above the periscope stand so that I could look at the plots that were being done; I didn't have to walk over there and do it.

A bunch of stuff like that. So it was money well spent.

The first big deal was the launch.* The weather was fierce. It was raining, the wind was blowing sideways. I got permission to have my son be up on the bridge with me for the launch. We went sliding down into the river.

Paul Stillwell: I was at EB for the launching of two submarines, the *Groton* and the *Annapolis*, and it is such a thrill. I mean, you get this emotional feeling.

Admiral DeMars: Yes, really. For the last one when I was at Naval Reactors, the last "slider"—they do them all in the land-level facility now—I went up and I put on my khakis because I was going to go to a party afterward. It was the one that Hillary Clinton christened, *Columbia*.† But I went down below. All the yard workers were down there with their families. You looked up at the ship, and then when it started sliding it was really something to see from down there. That was a big treat for me.

After the launch of the *Cavalla*, we got off on boats and went off to the party at the Mystic Inn. Congressman Price later was the chairman of the House Armed Services Committee.‡

Paul Stillwell: Mel Price.

---

* The *Cavalla* was launched at Groton, Connecticut, on 19 February 1972.
† The nuclear-powered submarine *Columbia* (SSN-771), sponsored by First Lady Hillary Clinton, was launched at Groton, Connecticut, on 24 September 1994.
‡ Charles Melvin Price, a Democrat from Illinois, served in the House of Representatives from 3 January 1945 until his death on 22 April 1988. He was chairman of the House Armed Services Committee from 1975 to 1984.

Admiral DeMars: Mel Price. Wonderful little old guy. His wife, Geraldine, christened the boat. Party was at the Mystic Inn. [Chuckle] My mother was born down in Gillespie, Illinois, which is just east of East St. Louis, which was Price's district. And so she was over there talking up a storm with him. They were shooting the breeze, and I went over. Who are they talking about? Who's the sheriff now, you know. [Laughter]

So I was there having a good time. I was going out of my way to try and stay away from Rickover, which is my usual penchant. That didn't bother him. But then one of the wives—we only had five officers on board—came over and said, "Captain, could we get a picture with Admiral Rickover?"

You can't say no to that. I said, "Of course."

So I went over to Rickover, and I said, "Admiral, some of the wives would like to have a picture with you."

He said, "Oh, of course. Send them over." He was yelling for the cameraman, "Come over here, come over here." We all went over, the husbands and the wives, and we were all lining up around Rickover. Rickover said, "Only the wives." [Laughter] He shooed us all away, and he posed with them. I'll show you the picture on the way out. My wife cut out just her part of it and it's in our hall of heroes there. You know, "Only the wives." What a character.

Then we had initial sea trials, which was always a monumental thing, because Rickover rode on them, as I later rode. I rode 42 of them when I had Rickover's job. And there's all rationale to that, because you require the top guy from the shipyard and who owns them, chairman of Tenneco or chairman of General Dynamics, to ride also. If anything goes wrong, you can really light into them. That's what Rickover did, and that's what I did later when I was NR. So that if you really do that well for the smallest things, then nothing bad happens. They build the ships better, and they inspect them better, and on and on and on.

Because it was kind of a harrowing thing, thinking back. It was the first time at sea for many of the sailors. They'd only been in the shipyard. And so everything's got to work right, and you've got to keep your head screwed on.

The ship before me was the *Batfish*, and the prospective commanding officer of the next ship always rides the ship ahead of him to see how initial sea trials work.* So we were out doing the full-power run south of just where the ledge drops off in the Atlantic, south of Groton/Mystic. You do a racetrack there at 400 feet. I was standing in the control room just watching things. The captain was in the control room, and Rickover's rep was in the control room, and the ComSubLant rep was in the control room. The Fathometer operator kept taking a sounding every minute and reporting it, and the soundings were like 600 feet, 600 feet, 600 feet. 450 feet. 400 feet. 350 feet. All of a sudden everybody was alerted. What had happened, the ship kept turning toward land, which you never want to do. I mean, that's what a long time in submarines had taught me: always turn away from land. And so it was slowly making its way toward the continental shelf there. Well, we ended up emergency blowing when the depth under the keel got to about 80 feet. They were stopped, they were back emergency, emergency blow. Well, Rickover just went hermantile, obviously. Oh, shit, I mean it was something to watch. He could really chew ass.

So we got up on the surface. Now we had to replenish the air banks because they'd used all that air [chuckle]. So they had to run the air compressors and go back down and redo the whole thing. We were about ten minutes to go on the four-hour full-power run.

So the subject of navigation became a big topic for the next sea trials. I didn't mind that too much, because I was pretty experienced in that area. But what I did was put a chart of where we were going to do the sea trials up in my stateroom, and then an area where the deep dive was going to be. I put red tape around that chart, on and on and on. When Rickover's guys came aboard the day before, I took them in my stateroom and they said, "Oh, what's that, Captain?"

I said, "That's just what I use to keep track of where we are," etc.

"Oh, explain that to me." We went through it. "You're going to have this up when Admiral Rickover is here?"

"Yes, if you want me to."

---

* USS *Batfish* (SSN-681) was commissioned 1 September 1972. The first commanding officer was Commander Richard E. Enkeboll, USN.

"Oh, yeah. Have that up. Bring him in here; explain that all to him." They loved it because they didn't know anything about this. And that all of a sudden gave a whole new luster to me. I loved it.

As I told you, being from Chicago, it's the town of the possible. You think of things in a different way. And I thought, "How do I ease their minds? I make them think I'm an expert in navigation." Which I almost was, but they didn't know that. So I put this up, and it went well.

There was another humorous thing. You had to get books for Rickover to read on the initial sea trials. And so Ed Siskin came down and he gave me, I don't know, 30 or 40 bucks. He came down, and he said, "Bruce, do you read?"

I said, "Goddamn it, Ed; yes, I read."

He said, "Would you buy some books for Admiral Rickover on the sea trials?"

I said, "Sure."

So I went out and I bought one book. I think it was *Is Paris Burning?*[*] I brought it back. He came down about a week later and said, "Did you get the books?"

I said, "I got this one."

He said, "No, no, no, no, no. Three. Three books."

I said, "Ed, we're only going to be gone 30 hours."

He said, "No, we need three books." So I went back out and I got *Freedom at Midnight*, which was when India got set free by the Brits.[†] I knew what Rickover liked to read, same stuff I like to read. And I got one other one that I can't remember right now. So Siskin was happy then.[‡]

Paul Stillwell: *Freedom at Midnight* was about the time when Mountbatten was in charge of partition of India.[§]

---

[*] Larry Collins and Dominique Lapierre, *Is Paris Burning?: How Paris Miraculously Escaped Adolf Hitler's Sentence of Death in August 1944* (New York: Simon and Schuster, 1965).
[†] Larry Collins and Dominique Lapierre, *Freedom at Midnight* (New York: Simon and Schuster, 1975).
[‡] The initial sea trials were in mid-October 1972.
[§] Louis Francis Albert Victor Nicholas Mountbatten, 1st Earl Mountbatten of Burma was the last Viceroy of India as a British possession and the first Governor-General of India as an independent nation. Independence was granted at midnight between 14-15 August 1947. Pakistan became a separate independent nation at the same time.

Admiral DeMars: Right. Yes, exactly, the partition. It was horrible, the Sikhs versus the Hindus, and on and on and on. So he was happy with that.

The next thing Ed brought down was this beautiful silver Parker ballpoint pen, in a case. I said, "What's that for?"

He said, "You've got to put this on the desk in Rickover's stateroom." Rickover was always in the XO's stateroom, which was right opposite the CO's stateroom; the head was in between. And that's what Rickover would sign all these letters out. He would sign something like 600 letters out that had been prepared, announcing the successful sea trials, and they put a little plug in there for nuclear power, and on and on.

But the funny thing was, we were out on the sea trials—and he always signed them on the sea trials, because he said "I'm signing this on the sea trials"—the yeoman brought in the letters and knocked on the door. "Yeah?"

"Your letters."

"Oh, good. Thank you. Just put them down on that [there were two desks] on that desk there." He put them down. And then Rickover looked up and said, "You got a pen?" The guy pulled out one of these black ballpoint pens.

Paul Stillwell: Government issue.

Admiral DeMars: Government-issue pens, handed it to Rickover, and he signed them all with that. [Laughter]

I still have a copy in my archives of *the* Rickover check-off list that my engineer used and, God, it's got everything on there. Some technical, some culinary, some on and on and on. Because it grew over the years. All Rickover had to say was, "I like that," and then they had it for the next trial. It was not because he asked for it, necessarily.

Then I got the closest I've ever been to Rickover in my life. They did three fast scram recovery drills, one for each watch section. You were down 400 feet, steaming along. So Rickover and I were standing in the corner of the maneuvering room, which was about half the size of this kitchen, with three big panels in it, the throttles, and the engineering officer of the watch, and we were scrunched back in the corner. He was literally right up against me, like that. And he said to me, "Where did you stand at the Naval Academy?"

I said, "Well, the first year I was 500 and I was thinking maybe I was going to fail out. But I graduated about 150."

He said, "Eh, that's probably why we took you." [Laughter] That's the only civil interchange I think I ever had with him.

Then we had the electrical operator, who was a first-class, a little older and a little gray in his hair. Rickover pointed to him, and we were about as far away from here to that window, less. He said, "How come he's not a chief?"

I said, "Well, he has a little trouble with exams but he's a great operator, he's a great maintenance guy, and we're trying to help him."

Rickover said, "There used to be a lot of people like that in the Navy." You know, he'd been in a long time.

The procedure on these trials was that what he'd usually do was kill the engineering officer of the watch, tell him "Get out of here; you're dead." And then he would appoint either the reactor operator or the throttleman to make the recovery. We did all this research and looked at what he would do. He never killed the electrical operator, because that was a very complicated panel, and if you didn't do that right you could screw things up. So he said to the engineering officer of the watch, "You're dead; get out of here." Then he pointed to the first-class electrician's mate and said, "You make the recovery."

I thought, "Oh shit." That was the only one we hadn't practiced. We had practiced the permutations with the other ones.

Now, Rickover hadn't scrammed the reactor yet. But the petty officer got up on the 2MC to conn and said, "Conn, maneuvering, the engineering officer of the watch is dead. This is Petty Officer First Class McGarvey. I'm in charge."

Now, my XO, Lieutenant Commander Jim Patton, was forward, and he thought that the electrician had forgotten to say the reactor was scrammed.[*] But we hadn't scrammed the reactor yet. So my XO said, "Reactor scram, reactor scram, rig ship for reduced electrical." He started going through the drill.

---

[*] Lieutenant Commander James H. Patton Jr., USN.

Rickover immediately wheeled on me and asked, "You always have a memorial scram when somebody dies on board?" [Laughter] And he was chipping at me, bababa bababa bababa. Then he said, "I'm going forward. When you get this squared away I'll come back and we'll do the drills."

So he went forward, and I thought, "Oh, shit." My XO came back all sheepish.

I said, "What the hell?"

He said, "Well, I thought that he forgot."

I said, "Well, don't you know when the reactor scrammed you hear things?"

"No, okay."

I said, "Okay, well, forget it. We'll do it right next time."

So now I was only worried about the fact that this electrician, whom we hadn't trained, was going to make the scram recovery, but it was too late to do anything about that.

Rickover came back, and he never mentioned a word of it, which is pretty typical of him, and we had the real scram. Killed the engineering officer of the watch, again told the electrician "Make the scram recovery."

He got up and he said, "Scram the reactor." The reactor operator scrammed the reactor. Electrical operator got on the announcing system: "Reactor scrammed, the engineering officer is dead, this is Petty Officer So-and-so, I'm making the recovery." So he started. The rest of the maneuvering room, the reactor operator and steam plant operator—they knew what to do. They shut the throttles, they did this, they did that, boom boom-boom-boom-boom.

Well, unfortunately the electrical operator wasn't paying attention to his panel [chuckle]. Now, I was one of the few who noticed that, but Rickover didn't know what was going on in that panel; he never knew. That wasn't in his ken. I was looking and realized, oh, my God, that we were drawing so much juice out of the battery, and he hadn't loaded up the MGs and unloaded the TGs and on and on and on.[*] But we got through it okay in any event, and we got the reactor started up again. Then Rickover turned to me and said, "Hah, shows what you know, Captain. You said he wasn't very smart. He just made a wonderful recovery." [Laughter] And then he left.

---

[*] MG – motor generator. TG – turbo generator.

What you did was, change the watch and you had a scram for each section. The other two times he had the steam plant operator and the reactor operator make the recovery. But, God, unbelievable. Those things stick in your mind.

Paul Stillwell: Understandably.

Admiral DeMars: Yes.

So we got done with everything and we were heading back in, and we were going to be on the 30-hour point, which is good, for initial sea trials to be all done in 30 hours. I was sitting in my stateroom totally exhausted, just sort of there, limp, and a little tap came on the door between the XO's stateroom and mine. The door opened, and in came Rickover. Of course, I jumped up, and he said, "Ah, everything went okay." Which is high praise. That is high praise, "Everything went okay."

Then he said, "I've got these three books here, and I've marked some excerpts. Would you please have the yeoman write them down and put the attribution at the bottom?"

Now, I made a mistake of not saying, "Yes, sir." I said, "Well, Admiral, we bought those books for you; you can take them."

"Goddamn it, DeMars, do what I tell you to do, and don't," you know, blah blah blah blah.

"Yes, sir. Yes, sir. Yes, sir."

So I got the yeoman, and he made out the cards and delivered the cards to Rickover. I found out later, and I'll talk to you in a subsequent time about where all those things go.

Then Rickover said, "I'd like to speak to the crew."

I said, "Yes, sir." So we went up in the control room, up on the diving stand. He picked up the 1MC and started to talk into it, but he was not holding down the button.* So I grabbed his hand and pushed down the button. So here I was, holding hands with Admiral Rickover while he was telling the crew they did a good job, sort of in spite of the officers. That was what I got out of it. [Laughter] But it was a good talk. I mean, all the

---

* 1MC – the ship's general announcing system.

crew knew what he was like, and they ate it up. He really was a good leader from a different viewpoint.

But I sort of got back at him. I took the three books, and I told the XO and the chief of the boat, "Pick out three guys, only one of them can be a nuc, that contributed heavily to initial sea trials." They gave me the names of these three guys, and in each one of the books I wrote: "To Petty Officer So-and-so, you did great work on the initial sea trials." Signed "H. G. Rickover," and I forged his name. [Laughter] So at quarters the next morning, the morning after, before we had to get under way again, I went out and presented those. And they still to this day, I'm sure, think that's Rickover's signature on there. [Laughter]

Paul Stillwell: As long as you didn't have to have it notarized.

Admiral DeMars: Exactly. Exactly. So they've probably sold them on eBay.

Paul Stillwell: What were the satisfactions of getting your first command?

Admiral DeMars: Oh, well, it was the thing I always wanted to do. The satisfaction didn't come yet, because we hadn't made any spec ops yet. That was shortly to come. But you could set the pace, you could set the tone, you could really mold a ship that was going to be around for three decades. And so it was extremely satisfying. Just personally very satisfying, to be doing something that important and that demanding. So I thoroughly enjoyed it.

But I also enjoyed being XO. I also enjoyed being navigator. CO is a special thing, but I'd had good tours, so I was very lucky.

Paul Stillwell: Many flag officers look back on an individual ship command as among the most enjoyable tours.

Admiral DeMars: Yes. I would almost say that when I was XO it was tied with that. Because XO, you can rant, you can rave, because you were expected to do that, and you let the CO take all the credit. But if you'd say, "Paint the goddamn ship orange," they had to do it. [Laughter] And so I really enjoyed XO, because you can kind of be a dictator. As CO you can't be a dictator; you've got to be more a presiding magistrate or something. So I enjoyed XO immensely. I enjoyed being navigator and ops officer. I just had a lot of good tours. I enjoyed being MPA on *George Washington*. Had a lot of good tours, and I can't say which is the best. I looked at things a little differently, I don't know.

For our commissioning, Congressman Price came up, and he was the speaker. That was very nice. Then we went out on shakedown in the Caribbean. We had the first towed array, as I said, reelable towed array from inside, so we had a lot of different things go on there.

We sort of became the tour boat, and I'm not sure why. Maybe it was because of initial sea trials. I took Deputy Secretary of Defense Clements to sea with several members of his staff for about four days.* I took the Atomic Energy Commission commissioners to sea for two days. All of a sudden I sort of had the feeling that they had discovered DeMars—that I was a late bloomer, and they suddenly had discovered me, because now I was the tour boat for NR.

We did all our pre-deployment training, deployed for two months to the Barents. Again, I was the only one on board with experience. And when we trained heavily, and we did, it was a good run. I still had all my *Snook* papers and *Sturgeon* papers that we had used, and it was a good run.

Then I got ordered to the staff of Submarine Squadron Ten from there. Curt Shellman was the commodore; he had been my CO on the *Sturgeon*, of course, so that was a nice place to go.

So far DeMars was happy, he had done what he wanted to do, be a CO, and so I just kind of looked at everything a little differently now. Still having fun, but I was not hot to do anything else in the Navy. [Chuckle]

Paul Stillwell: Any specifics on the special ops or how they might have differed from previous years?

---

* William P. Clements Jr., served as Deputy Secretary of Defense from 1973 to 1977.

Admiral DeMars: No, they were not that much different, other than we were a brand-new submarine. We had new stuff. We came back probably with more sound pressure levels on Soviet submarines than most guys, because I had been trained by Watkins and Bohannan: "If you sniff anything, go do it." So it was a good run. We had good riders, and it was very credible for the first one by a brand-new submarine. Because everybody else is new on board. Nobody's done that.

Paul Stillwell: Would you characterize yourself in the aggressive class as a skipper?

Admiral DeMars: Thoughtfully aggressive, yes. I didn't shirk from doing it, but at the same time I wasn't going to have a collision and I wasn't going to get counter-detected. Those were big no-nos, particularly having a collision. But counter-detection was also a no-no; you didn't want that to happen, because that kind of sullied your reputation. That means you weren't smart enough at doing what you were doing. Or maybe you were a little too aggressive. But we brought home the bacon.

Paul Stillwell: Did you counsel your OODs on the possibility of a Crazy Ivan?*

Admiral DeMars: Oh, yes, yes. Well, they got most of that from the reading before we went. You read all this stuff, and then you could tell when it was happening. You always tried to stay at a different depth than the Soviet submarine you were playing around with, so that if anything happened and you got in the exact same water space you wouldn't have a collision. But you sometimes didn't know exactly what depth he was at. You knew from reading intel and all that what depths they preferred, and so you did that as a starting point. But you never really knew that.

We experimented with a lot of new tactics. They were just coming in with Doppler shift in the sonar business where you could tell with the shift in Doppler sort of

---

* "Crazy Ivan" was the American nickname for the maneuver in which a Soviet submarine would reverse course suddenly so the crew could use the sonar to determine if another submarine was behind.

some idea of speed of the other guy, and on and on and on.* And experimented with new plotting techniques and that. So it was a lot of fun.

Paul Stillwell: Any opportunities for innovation?

Admiral DeMars: Yes. I guess the innovation was that I did put the JOODs on the watch again and that worked out well, enlisted men as junior officers of the deck on the watch.

I did institute a program—when you're in these special parties for doing these special things on spec ops or to fire a torpedo and that, the way they train you in Submarine School is, everybody's talking. You know: "What's the angle on the bow, how have you got for this, what's your solution for that?" I said, "I don't want any of that chatter. I want to do a chit system. You write down on a chit what your solution is and you pass all these chits to the fire control coordinator guy, and he'll put all that data down on the big plot. And if we want to know what's going on, we go over to the big plot." Then I had this little television set mounted above the big plot and had the screen up in the attack center so I could look up at that. So it was always very quiet in my control room. There was not all this yahyahyahyahyah. That worked out quite well, and that got quite nice comments when I would have rides by the division commander and the squadron commander. First of all, they didn't believe it would work, but it did. It worked wonderfully. So that was an innovation, I guess.

Paul Stillwell: Did you have any link with the sailors from the *Cavalla* of World War II and subsequently. Did they tie into the new boat at all?

Admiral DeMars: Yes, Herman Kossler was a guest at the commissioning. He had been the CO of the first *Cavalla* when it sank the aircraft carrier.† So that was quite a treat, to

---

* Doppler is an apparent change in the pitch—that is, frequency—of sound or a radio wave caused by relative motion between the source and the listener.
† Lieutenant Commander Herman J. Kossler, USN, was the first commanding officer when the submarine *Cavalla* (SS-244) was commissioned on 29 February 1944. On 19 June 1944, during the "Marianas Turkey Shoot," the *Cavalla* torpedoed and sank the *Shokaku*, one of the Japanese aircraft carriers that had taken part in the air raid on Pearl Harbor in December 1941.

have him there. I had read up on him beforehand, of course, that war patrol of his, which was quite a one.

Paul Stillwell: And he would retire as a flag officer.

Admiral DeMars: Yes, he retired as a two-star.[*]

The original *Cavalla* is down in Galveston, Texas. It's up in sand, but they have a galvanic protection system on it. And they also have one of two remaining DEs down there, the *Stewart*, and it's up on pilings.[†] And there's a little museum down there and it's very, very nice. They had a reunion down there and I went down to it. The sailors asked me to come down and speak, and *Cavalla* sailors were down there, and maybe only one or two of the World War II ones.

Paul Stillwell: This is a convenient breaking place for the interview.

Admiral DeMars: Yes.

Paul Stillwell: Thank you very much.

Admiral DeMars: My pleasure.

---

[*] Kossler's last tour of active duty was as Commandant Sixth Naval District, with headquarters in Charleston. He retired in June 1973, a few months after SSN-684 was commissioned.
[†] The destroyer escort *Stewart* (DE-238).

Interview Number 3 with Admiral Bruce DeMars, U.S. Navy (Retired)

Place: Admiral DeMars's home in Alexandria, Virginia

Date: Thursday, 17 May 2012

Paul Stillwell: Admiral, we have a beautiful spring morning here for our interview. I know you wanted to start with one follow-up from our last interview, and I have a few additional questions also. Please tell me about the *Seawolf* incident when you were in *Sturgeon*.

Admiral DeMars: Yes. When I was XO of *Sturgeon*, Development Squadron 12 was our squadron, and we were running a submarine ASW exercise, SubASWEx, in the Gulf of Maine. *Seawolf* was the target.* It was really to try out the *Sturgeon*'s combat system, because we were the first of the class. We had a *Seawolf* in World War II. This was the second *Seawolf*, and it was the second nuclear-powered submarine. Originally it was built as a liquid metal, sodium, reactor, and then converted very quickly to pressurized water after that because sodium didn't work well. They were running back and forth in the Gulf of Maine, which is very deep, but it shoals up quickly on both sides of kind of a trench. I was the fire control coordinator. We were making an approach on them. Actually we stumbled on them late, so we had to get up and run hard, get ahead of them, came around, and everything was tracking well. We had a good solution.

All of a sudden the solution started to fall apart. I looked at the chart and I looked at the plots. I told the captain, "Well, they must have turned toward us. They couldn't have turned away, because they'd run into shallow water very quickly." The sonar said they had turned away. I said, "That can't be right." The next thing we heard was a tremendous crash over the sonars. They *had* turned away and run aground making,

---

* USS *Seawolf* (SSN-575), commissioned 30 March 1957, was the Navy's second nuclear-powered submarine. The first, USS *Nautilus* (SSN-571) had a pressurized water reactor. The *Seawolf* served as a test bed for a reactor cooled by liquid sodium. The latter was not deemed a success, so the *Seawolf* was later equipped with the pressurized water type. For the first skipper's view, see Richard B. Laning, "The *Seawolf*'s Sodium-Cooled Power Plant," *Naval History*, Spring 1992, pages 45-48.

probably, 25 knots.* Then we couldn't talk to them, of course, because their underwater telephone had been destroyed in the accident.

We went to periscope depth, and fortunately we saw them on the surface. They were in very bad shape. They had leaks in the hull and were taking on water, but they could keep up with that. So we got on the radio and called for assistance, and tugboats were dispatched and on and on. I ended up being the expert navigation witness for the court of inquiry that took place after that. That was a very valuable lesson.

I had done that once before when I was on *Snook* and some diesel boat had run aground in the Pacific. There was a court of inquiry, and I was asked to be the expert navigator for that, so I sort of knew how to do it. In both cases it always astounded me how poor the navigation was on the ships that ran aground. So, anyway, that was quite a lesson and added to my lore and my store of experience on what to do and what not to do on a nuclear—or nonnuclear submarine, for that matter. So I just thought it was important enough to stick it in here.

Paul Stillwell: You said it was valuable. In what way? As a learning experience?

Admiral DeMars: Well, it was valuable in a learning experience, and to make me realize that just because I'd been fortunate enough to serve on good submarines that were well run, well commanded, that I shouldn't be complacent. Bad things can happen. When I was later in command myself, I relieved *my* navigator because he had made three mistakes in a row. I said, "You're no longer a navigator," and made the XO the navigator for the rest of the tour. So it's very touchy, dangerous stuff. It was valuable because it reminded me not to be complacent.

Paul Stillwell: In Gannon McHale's book he also talked about some very rough seas right after that incident. Do you remember that transit, and the boat being tossed around?

---

* The *Seawolf* grounded on the coast of Maine on 30 January 1968. She was towed to New London for repairs. She next went to sea on 20 March 1969.

Admiral DeMars: Oh yes, yes. We always were, whenever we got stuck on the surface on a submarine, because of the rounded hull, no keel. I mean, you take 30-degree rolls on the surface. And usually you had at least one cook who was tough enough he could cook, and he always took a sardonic delight in making stuff like greasy pork chops and things like that to serve to the crew. Nobody ate very much. I was always fortunate. I never got seasick. But there weren't many of us who were still up and about during that transit.

Paul Stillwell: You have, in the enlisted crews in submarines, presumably a higher cut of individual than the Navy norm because the men are volunteers and go through a screening-type process to get in. How were the disciplinary cases when you were CO and XO?

Admiral DeMars: Almost nonexistent. When I was XO I can't remember a captain's mast.* One reason is that we had a good chain of command. We had very fine chief petty officers. They handled a lot of the stuff, didn't let it get up to that point. When I was commanding officer, we had one mast. We had two young seamen, one in the deck gang and one a mess cook. That's not a very pleasant way to live your life, but it's a rite of passage. If a man makes his way through that, then he can strike for a rating and move on.

Paul Stillwell: And somebody has to do those chores.

Admiral DeMars: Yes, somebody has to. The two of them went over the hill. They were gone almost three weeks and then came back. So obviously I had to have a captain's mast on them. Their division officers would obviously be there, and I insisted that their chief petty officers be there also. I used that as an occasion to lecture mostly the chiefs but also the division officers that it was their job to not have these sorts of things happen, and that I was embarrassed that it happened on my submarine, etc., etc. I

---

* Captain's mast is a sort of court in which the commanding officer of a unit listens to requests, awards non-judicial punishment, or issues commendations. Most often captain's mast is used for punishment of lesser offenses than those that merit courts-martial

restricted the two young men to the ship for 30 days. They couldn't leave the ship, which is pretty severe punishment because it was an in-port restriction. I mean, there's no place to go, and on and on and on. They survived that and maybe squared away a little bit.

But in general submarines in those days had very few problems, simply because it was a close-knit crew. People looked out for each other in general, and you had good chief petty officer and leading petty officer leadership.

Paul Stillwell: Please talk more about the role of the chiefs of the boat in both *Sturgeon* and *Cavalla*.

Admiral DeMars: Yes, it's a very unique position. It's grown now to where they even have a senior chief back aft who is an engineering senior chief. And it's grown to the surface ships also to a large degree, where you just don't have the master at arms who goes around writing people up, but you have a senior petty officer—a chief, master chief, or senior chief—who runs the business.

We had good ones in the ships that I was on. They were always selected by the commanding officer, and they didn't necessarily have to be the most senior chief. They were ones that had good judgment, good leadership.

When I was the deputy Squadron Ten at State Pier, I worked for the squadron commander, Curt Shellman, who had been my commanding officer on *Sturgeon*.* So we got along well. We had a squadron boat that was not doing well, *Greenling*, working up to go to the Med. Finally we had done about everything we could, and it was time to deploy. So Curt said, "Bruce, you're going to ride it to the Med and continue to work them up. When you get to Rota, Spain, either you get off or the CO gets off." And I knew Curt Shellman well enough not to mention how hard it was to relieve a skipper.

I just said, "Yes, sir."

Paul Stillwell: But you knew he meant it.

---

* Captain Curtis B. Shellman Jr., USN. Commander DeMars reported to his staff in January 1975.

Admiral DeMars: Yes, I knew he meant it. And he would have done it. He was a good man, the kind of naval officer you liked working for.

So we got under way the next day, about a week later. I toured the entire ship, looking at everything. The ship was a shambles. It was dirty. Well, I had worked them up at sea; I already knew they weren't great! The exception was the torpedo room, which was the cleanest compartment in the boat. They should have served meals in the torpedo room instead of the crew's mess. They had a chief torpedoman who was the head of the torpedo gang. The chief of the boat was a master chief electronics technician. He was a good technician, but he was a terrible leader.

So I went in the CO's stateroom, shut the door, and said, "Okay, the first thing is that you've got to fire the current chief of the boat and make the chief torpedoman the chief of the boat."

He said, "Well, but he's not the senior guy."

Then I told him what Shellman had told me. I said, "We've got a lot of work to do. We've only got four and a half days, and we're going to be there. We've got to get cracking." So he knew I was serious.

So he called both of them in. I didn't sit in for that; I let him do that. But, surprisingly enough, the chief electronics technician felt relieved that he had been relieved of the job. He knew that he wasn't very good at it, and he was happy to go back to doing what an ET does. The chief torpedoman sort of took it in his stride.

About half an hour later the word went over the 1MC, "Now, will all the chiefs report to the chiefs' quarters." It was the new chief of the boat having a meeting. Then shortly thereafter field day was announced, and everybody was cleaning the boat, and on and on. So we knew we had a good first step. We had got a senior leader who knew how to appeal to the other people. Everybody wants to do well on the crew and that; they just need leadership. Nobody wants to be a bozo.

So that's the importance of that senior position, and usually it's filled by a very, very good leader who can inspire the other people to do the right thing.

Paul Stillwell: Well, another benefit is that he can be the two-way communication link to bring things to you.

Admiral DeMars: Oh, yes, absolutely. Very important, that he can say, "You know, XO, this isn't working, what you're trying to do here. The crew doesn't like it, but they don't want to say anything about it, so I thought I'd mention it to you and talk about it." Yes, you're right, it's a two-way street, and it's a very important position.

Paul Stillwell: In reading McHale's book, it seemed as if whenever *Sturgeon* was in port that the crew just took liberty through an alcoholic haze. And I recall reading recently in *Navy Times* that the Navy is even considering breathalyzer tests for guys coming back from liberty. Can you comment on the difference in Navy policy on alcohol in those two eras?

Admiral DeMars: Well, I was never aware of a lot of drunkenness. Now, I say that carefully because I read a lot in McHale's book that I didn't know was going on on the ship when I was XO. [Laughter] He also talks about a lot of swearing and foul language. They never did that around the officers. They were very respectful. They didn't swear. The F-word wasn't used for an adverb, adjective, noun, on and on and on. And so, yes, they went ashore and had a good time, and drank too much for young guys. But they always got back to the ship. I don't think we ever left anybody in port because he didn't show up. Well, the whole country was different then. Everybody drank more in those days.

The breathalyzer thing now, I think is the dumbest goddamn thing going, to have to do that. Can you imagine a breathalyzer on an aircraft carrier? How long is that line? And, okay, if somebody fails it what do you do with him or her?

Paul Stillwell: Well, there's been pushback from senior enlisted.

Admiral DeMars: Do you say, "You can't come aboard; you can't stand watch"? I mean, to me it's stupid.

To speak a little out of school here, I went to the Chief of Naval Operations retired four-star meeting, and he took a lot of gas on that matter.[*] So I don't think it was

---
[*] Admiral Jonathan W. Greenert, USN, has served as Chief of Naval Operations since 23 September 2011.

very well thought out, and it was a knee-jerk reaction. Then once you do it, you look like you're bozos. So that's my answer.

Paul Stillwell: Well, my memory from that 1960s era was that if a man could get back on board and do his job the next day, then it wasn't an issue.

Admiral DeMars: Yes, it wasn't an issue. And nobody went ashore by themselves. If you were running a good ship, your shipmates got you back if you couldn't get yourself back.

I can remember once on *Snook* when we did that Sea of Okhotsk circumnavigation, the captain, Jim Watkins, would play acey-deucy with the intel rider, and they would bet mai tais. We were going to get back to Pearl Harbor after that. The intel officer was a pretty good card player, and he beat the captain just hands down. I think he won 12 mai tais. So we got back into Hawaii and the captain said, "I've been invited up to CinCPacFlt's house for dinner tonight. I know all you guys are going to go over to the O-club, so I'm going to give the intel officer the money to buy the mai tais for you guys."[*] So I think there were a number of us who went. We each had three mai tais. The first one tastes great. The second one not so great. The third one you just can hardly get it down.

But we were coming back to the boat and one of the officers [chuckle], Joe Adams, was just out of his brain.[†] He broke loose from us, went running into the main admin building in CinCPacFlt there and started messing around. We grabbed him and got him back. The only way we got him down below decks was to get a blanket, put him in the blanket, and lower him down. He lived in my stateroom, and we had to drag him into the stateroom and get him in his bunk. So those things happened, but you took care of your shipmates. And he didn't get in trouble for it. He had a giant head the next day, and he felt terrible, but those things happen.

---

[*] CinCPacFlt – Commander in Chief Pacific Fleet.
[†] Lieutenant Joseph H. Adams, USN.

Paul Stillwell: In a previous interview you mentioned having nuclear weapons on board *Sturgeon*. Presumably that was SubRoc. Was there anything else?

Admiral DeMars: Yes, there was a Mark 45 torpedo, which was a wire-guided torpedo; that was nuclear also.

Paul Stillwell: What do you remember about the personnel reliability program and screening?

Admiral DeMars: It wasn't that intrusive. I mean, you had to get signed off by a doctor, and it was in your health record so that anytime you went to see the doctor he knew that he had to take special care and that. But it was a fairly well run program.

Paul Stillwell: Was there screening to keep people out who would, say, have an aversion to nuclear weapons?

Admiral DeMars: No, that screening took place before you ever got on submarines, I think. And times were different in those days. Nobody in the military had an aversion to nuclear weapons that I know of.

Paul Stillwell: What was the role of divers in those submarines?

Admiral DeMars: Largely in-port repairs and inspections, that sort of thing. If you were doing anything really serious, you got professional divers from the submarine tender or the submarine base. But if you were in Naha, Okinawa, and you wanted to inspect your screw to see whether it should be cleaned because there were too many barnacles on it, or it had nicks on it and you were worried about cavitation, then you had your own scuba diver go down and make an inspection, or other things of that nature. It was a special training program and code, and I think they got a few extra bucks for that, but not very much.

Paul Stillwell: I take it that it was a collateral duty.

Admiral DeMars: Oh, yes, yes, absolutely. Absolutely. Usually it was a machinist's mate, somebody in the A gang, or a torpedoman, somebody like that.

Paul Stillwell: What do you remember about your wife's role, both when you were CO and XO, in relating to the wives of the officers and crew?

Admiral DeMars: It was very close in those days. I don't think it's that close now. So much has changed. I mean, they don't have officers' clubs anymore; they don't have chiefs' clubs anymore.

Paul Stillwell: And more working wives, too.

Admiral DeMars: Yes, and more working wives. But Margaret generally had a very maternal protective attitude toward the people. She had a good relationship with the chiefs' wives and the rest of the officers' wives. We all had parties at our houses. We would also have calls made and returned, as you did in the old days. When a new officer came aboard, he was expected to visit. He and his wife would come and pay a call on you and then have a drink and talk for half an hour or 45 minutes. Then, a week or a couple weeks later, you'd reciprocate and call on them in their house. I thought that was a wonderful tradition. That's gone by the board now in the Navy. You got to meet people and know people.

Paul Stillwell: And drop off calling cards.

Admiral DeMars: Yes, you'd drop off cards. There was a certain number of cards, based on how many women there were in the house or something. And if they weren't there, you were supposed to turn up the corner of the card. I think all these rules were from the 1800s. But Margaret liked the process and enjoyed it. She's a very private person, but she knew what her duty was, and she did it quite well. Very gracious. She was always very talented in decorating and dressing and putting on a party and all that sort of stuff. She enjoyed it, I think, and got along well.

The wardrooms were tinier in those days. As I said, I think we had nine officers in an SSN wardroom, and an SSBN maybe 12—not a lot. There are too many now [chuckle]. So she got along well, and if there was anything special with the crew, Margaret and generally the chief of the boat's wife would figure out what they had to do about it. They would help if there was a sick child, for example, or something of that nature.

Of course, when we would deploy to the Western Pacific for seven months, there was no communication with the families except letters. There was no Internet and there were no e-mails. Nobody could afford to make phone calls, so you wrote letters, and that was just the way it was. And your wife just did everything at home.

Paul Stillwell: Was there any system to help a wife who, say, had a broken washing machine, to call in some help from the community?

Admiral DeMars: Not really. Not really. They were really pretty much on their own. But they did a good job, did a wonderful job. I think I've told you in a previous interview, particularly on *Snook*, because Jim Watkins's wife was very outgoing, and they'd go down to Tijuana in a couple of cars and have lunch and buy things down there and come back across. In those days it was very safe. You didn't need a passport to get across the border. It was just a different world.

Paul Stillwell: What do you remember about upkeep of the ship between going to sea, in New London, and maintenance availabilities and what have you?

Admiral DeMars: It was pretty good support, whether you were at the sub base or at Squadron Ten, which was at State Pier and you were serviced there by the submarine tender *Fulton*. It was good service and very well run. In fact, once the *Greenling*, the boat I had to ride to the Med on—and we'll talk more about that later—ruined their diesel generator. They took water down and tried to pump water through the cylinders and just totally ruined the diesel generator. That was when Curt Shellman was the squadron commander. So we had one of our squadron weekly management meetings, and the squadron engineer said to Shellman, "Huh, we're going to have to have that diesel generator replaced. It is just beyond repair; you've got to get a new diesel generator."

But Shellman said, "We can probably do that." I mean, here we were, right across the river from Electric Boat. And the squadron engineer just about turned white. And Shellman said, "Of course, we can get the hull welders from EB to come over and cut the hole in the hull, but we have cranes here and we have all this stuff."

And, I'll be damned, he did it. They found another diesel generator down at Cheatham Annex, down east of Williamsburg, and carted it on up. They cut the hole in the hull and undid the old diesel generator, pulled it out, put it on a truck and took it somewhere, scrapped it, put the new one in, hooked it all up, and it worked. And everybody was so proud once they had done it. But that was another sort of thing why I really admired Curt Shellman. I mean, he would take on stuff like that and *do* it. Do it. And he inspired people to be able to do that. So they did that, basically, with just the tender crew. So the logistic support was very good.

After I retired, they decommissioned about four submarine tenders, which I thought was a big mistake. A big mistake. We only have two of them now, and we wish we had six.

So that the support was good. The sub base was good also.

Paul Stillwell: What do you recall about ship handling around State Pier with the currents that are there?

Admiral DeMars: Oh, it was very dicey. [Chuckle] A funny story as I remember—I think I was deputy squadron commander. We were all standing up in the 02 level or 03 level of the *Fulton*, and some boat was coming in. I think it was *Pargo*. The conning officer kind of misjudged the turn and couldn't turn fast enough, and it was either going to hit the tender or run aground. So he straightened out, went upstream under the bridge all the way to the sub base, turned around and came back and made the landing. So it was very dicey, and you had to learn how to use a tug and do it right. Because the hull on the tender was not that thick, and the last thing you wanted to do was get some tonnage there by sinking the tender. So it was very dicey.

It was the same way down at the sub base also, because the current ripped past there. It wasn't a problem getting under way, but coming back in it could be quite a problem. Generally you hooked up a tug on the bow and used that to control your head. You had plenty of power, you just couldn't steer very well, particularly as you got going slow to make the final approach. So you had to cleverly use that tug.

What I always did was give the tug master the directions myself and not have a pilot do it. I just felt it was my responsibility, and I could tell him what to do as well as anybody. So I used the pilot to relay my communications to the tug, and it worked out fine.

Paul Stillwell: It fit in with union rules, I gather?

Admiral DeMars: Oh, yes, yes. It seemed to. Nobody ever complained about it.

Paul Stillwell: What recollection do you have of polar operations?

Admiral DeMars: Well, we didn't do a lot of them when I was CO or XO. We went under the marginal ice a couple of times, once unexpectedly [chuckle]. Put the periscope up at 100 feet getting ready to go to periscope depth and all we could see was ice, so we figured we'd better not surface there, we'd better not go to periscope depth there.

I did do an awful lot of it when I was OP-02, and we'll talk about that later.

Paul Stillwell: What can you recall about the role of providing services for ASW, for both airplanes and surface ships?

Admiral DeMars: We didn't do a lot of that. There was a certain amount put in the annual schedule because somebody had to do it, obviously, but we didn't do an awful lot of it. We spent most of our time either going to station for a spec op, coming back, or working up getting ready to go, or standing down when you got back. But we did have some time at sea, and we usually enjoyed those periods at sea giving services because they gave you a chance to do things on board the ship you wanted to do, training for your officers and your crew.

We had to carry noisemakers on board to make us noisy enough so the airplanes or destroyers could hear us. But then, as the Soviets got quieter and quieter, the word came down: no more noisemakers. Which I thought was the right thing to do. They have to learn to use their sonars properly against a legitimate foe. But we didn't do an awful lot of services.

Paul Stillwell: Well, and there was usually some kind of artificial restriction that there was a box you had to stay in to make it easier for the ASW people.

Admiral DeMars: Yes. Oh, yes. Yes. But the best services we gave to each other were down at AUTEC, Tongue of the Ocean, because it's a three-dimensional instrumented range. You could run torpedo exercises there, and you could do other things. Then they'd send the track charts out to you, and you could have a good critique after you did things. That was very valuable training.

Paul Stillwell: One of the things that struck me about McHale's book was that he called you the smartest guy in the room. [Laughter] You would obviously win the competition in this room today, but I've seen you in other situations—limited sample, to be sure—but you don't flaunt it. Any observations on your personality, and how you approach things?

Admiral DeMars: Well, I never realized that I might be considered the smartest guy in the room. Maybe that's what kept me so humble. [Laughter] As I've mentioned several times, I've been a different kind of naval officer, a different kind of admiral. I didn't think that becoming an admiral was the be-all and end-all of my life. It was nice. What I really wanted to do was command an SSN on a spec op. Once I got that done, I was happy. I could have got out and done something else but I didn't have 20 years in yet, so I stayed around a little longer. So that's just my personality. And as I mentioned before, growing up in Chicago and the way I got my appointment to the Naval Academy sort of melded my view of life. Chicago's the city of the possible. If you don't follow all the rules—just the right ones—and don't tell a lie, you can get along okay.

Paul Stillwell: When you commanded the *Cavalla*, this was after Admiral Zumwalt had come in and issued his Z-grams.[*] What impact did you see from that at your level?

Admiral DeMars: Virtually none, because most of the things that he put in—and I think they were good for the surface Navy, but I think that the aviators and submariners already did most of those things. We didn't have liberty cards. We didn't know what the hell they were. Why would you have a liberty card? If you had liberty, you went ashore; if you didn't, you didn't go ashore. And we had civilian clothes we could keep on board, and you could put your civilian clothes on and go ashore. The surface Navy didn't have all those things. And so he did good things. The problem was, he didn't do it via the chain of command. Now, maybe he felt that he couldn't, because it was just too hard, and he had to leap over it. But I think what he was trying to do was correct.

One of the things in that nature that went on I remember, the two Bagley brothers came to town.[†] They wanted to talk to 20 officers: lieutenants, lieutenant commanders. I think I was CO at the time. So they got us all in this room. And clearly what they wanted to know was, what didn't we like about what Rickover was doing? [Laughter] And so we were smart enough to fathom that right away. We said, "Oh, we like what he does." And we really played them like a fiddle. I'm not sure they really realized they were being played. But nobody fell into their trap. So that was kind of part of the Zumwalt thing also.

Paul Stillwell: Well, they were both close disciples of his.

---

[*] Admiral Elmo R. Zumwalt, Jr., USN, served as Chief of Naval Operations from 1 July 1970 to 29 June 1974. His oral history is in the Naval Institute collection. Z-grams were consecutively numbered policy directives from Chief of Naval Operations Zumwalt that attempted to deal with such issues as enlisted rights and privileges, equal opportunity, and Navy families. Junior personnel viewed them much more favorably than did their seniors. See *U.S. Naval Institute Proceedings*, May 1971, pages 293-298.
[†] Rear Admiral David H. Bagley, USN; Rear Admiral Worth H. Bagley, USN.

Admiral DeMars: Yes, exactly. And submariners have always felt themselves different, and rightly so, and they've always felt a reasonably close kinship with aviators because we both depend upon our platforms tremendously. And so you pay more attention to maintenance, you pay more attention to your sailors that are doing the maintenance, and on and on and on. But somehow it's different in the surface Navy. They've gotten away from it. They earn their marks nowadays in the political-military field. That was true even when I was on active duty. Or they're cannon-cockers; they like guns and missiles and that. But as far as maintenance, oh, God. Terrible.

Paul Stillwell: There were some ugly racial incidents in ships in the early '70s.* Was there any of that in the submarine force?

Admiral DeMars: Not that I was aware of. And, as you saw in McHale's book, there was one incident in the *Sturgeon*. We had, I think, three or four black guys and maybe the same number of Filipinos on board the ships that I was on. But the incident in the *Sturgeon* where the one black sonarman went ashore with a bunch of guys in Norfolk and this bartender wouldn't serve him a beer. There was one man who was a seaman at that time, having made torpedoman second class several times and got busted. Deeter was his name, big hairy red arms, and he was a biker.† Tattoos and everything. He just essentially told the bartender, "Either give him a beer, or all these guys are going to beat the crap out of you." [Chuckle] And he got a beer. So it was more of that. And Deeter would be the last guy to support civil rights and all of that. It was just, you were dicking around with one of his shipmates, and you weren't going to get away with it.

So no, I never experienced any of that on any of the ships I was on, even way back on the two APAs in the late '50s. I'm sure some of it was around, but I don't think so on the submarines. It's too close proximity to have anything like that happen. And you depended upon everybody having a very important job, and everybody had to know

---

* Racial disturbances broke out in the carrier *Kitty Hawk* (CVA-63) on 12 October 1972; in the oiler *Hassayampa* (AO-145) on 16 October 1972; and in the carrier *Constellation* (CVA-64) on 3 November 1972. See Captain Paul B. Ryan, USN (Ret.), "USS Constellation Flare-up: Was it Mutiny?" *U.S. Naval Institute Proceedings*, January 1976, pages 46-53. See also Gregory A. Freeman, *Troubled Water: Race, Mutiny, and Bravery on the USS Kitty Hawk* (New York: Palgrave Macmillan, 2009).
† Donald Deeter. See *Stealth Boat*, page 11.

the damage control aspects of everything they did, and on and on and on. So you depended upon people like that for your life.

Paul Stillwell: And the qualification process forces that.

Admiral DeMars: Right. Exactly. Exactly. And forces people to get to know each other quite well.

Paul Stillwell: Well, that is my list of questions. We're ready now to return to your list of topics and your time as deputy squadron commander.

Admiral DeMars: Right. I was deputy squadron commander at Submarine Squadron Ten, which was on board the USS *Fulton* at the State Pier in New London. It's no longer there; it should have never been there [chuckle]. I don't know why they did it. I guess we just had so many submarines in so many places we had to put them there. There wasn't enough room at the sub base. Actually they subsequently built more piers at the sub base and did away with State Pier.

Curt Shellman was the commodore, and that was a good relationship because he had been my CO, and he and I got along very well. I already told you that I had to go and ride the ship to Rota, the *Greenling*. And we did. We got the ship clean, we continued the training of what they had to do in the Med. And I was happy to get off at that point. I felt comfortable that we had done everything we could and they were adequately trained up to go to the Med.

Paul Stillwell: Who was the skipper? Do you recall?

Admiral DeMars: Chris Nichols. And we're still friends to this day. I see him every now and then at Naval Submarine League affairs.[*]

---

[*] Lieutenant Commander Christopher Nichols, USN, became CO of the *Greenling* on 14 January 1975.

Every now and then I'll get a letter from the fellow we made the chief of the boat, the torpedoman. He lives up in Wisconsin, and about once every eight years I get a letter from him.

Paul Stillwell: You empowered him.

Admiral DeMars: Well, he was very important.

So, anyway, I was supposed to get off in Rota. Kinny McKee had set it up so I could fly to Naples and see his command setup he put there to run the submarines in the Med.* And so I said sure, I'd do that. They sent a tug out to get me off, and the weather off Rota was so bad I couldn't get off the ship. So they sent a helicopter out.† I was up on the sailplanes with my little bag, with essentially my shaving gear in it and some skivvies. They lowered the cranial helmet you put on, I put that on, and the helicopter was like 15 feet above me. It was deafeningly loud, and you just couldn't see anything. And the helicopter has a hard time seeing. He couldn't see the submarine because we were inside his blind spot. So he was trying to look off to the side and see how high he was above the water, and everything was pitching and rolling.

Then down came the horse collar. And I just got it on when he had drifted forward and dragged me off the sailplanes. I went swinging down like a pendulum. I looked and I saw the pit sword, which is the underwater log, sticking up down there. I sort of tried to put my body to the side, which was good because it would have hit me right between the legs otherwise. It hit me on the left hip, basically broke all my ribs. They got me up. I remembered passing out just as the guy grabbed me to pull me in and laid me down on the helicopter deck. And when I came to, I remember, I was uncomfortable because the ridges in the deck of the helicopter were hitting me in the back.

We went to the naval hospital at Rota, and I spent like three days there. Then I got medevaced to Wiesbaden Air Force hospital in Germany, spent about a week there,

---

* Rear Admiral Kinnaird R. McKee, USN, served from 1973 to 1975 as Commander Submarine Group Eight, commanding both U.S. and NATO submarines in the Mediterranean. As a four-star admiral, he was Director, Naval Nuclear Propulsion from 1982 to 1988. He was Admiral DeMars's immediate predecessor in that billet.
† This incident occurred in April 1975.

and got medevaced back to Bethesda and spent three months there in recovery. So it was a very interesting process.

During part of the time at Bethesda my hospital roommate was a helicopter pilot who was in for a double hernia operation, and he wasn't supposed to laugh or move around very much. I told him every joke I knew. [Laughter] Every joke I knew.

The helicopter pilot came to visit me. His wife came to visit me in the hospital. McKee came to visit me. Everybody was so sorry it happened. I was just happy I was still alive. My wife wanted to come over and make sure I was okay, but they rightly told her, "No, we'll bring him back there; it's easier."

So, anyway, all that worked. And while I was recovering in Bethesda the submarine detailer came and said he'd like to order me to go down to be on the Nuclear Propulsion Examining Board in Norfolk. And so, what did I know? I usually just went wherever they told me [chuckle], and it always worked out.

So we reluctantly had to leave our big house in Mystic, Connecticut. My daughter was overjoyed. She thought it was the boondocks up there. My son was sad, but he didn't raise any objections. He was just entering senior year. He was on the tennis team and the soccer team. Well, we ended up going down to Norfolk, to Virginia Beach. They didn't play soccer down there, and if you weren't in the top two in tennis in transferring out from wherever you come from, they weren't interested in you, so he didn't play either one of those. But consequently his grades got better, and he got into Virginia Tech. So it all worked out.

The only thing that I did wrong was that I sold our Mystic house. We had bought it for, I don't know, $42,000. We sold it for about $46,000, because we needed the down payment for the house down south in Virginia Beach. The house in Mystic must be three or four million bucks by now. But that happens to everybody. And so it was a great time. We lived up there for 12 years in one spot.

Paul Stillwell: What do you remember about family life in Mystic?

Admiral DeMars: It was wonderful. I mean, our basic rule was, and the times were such that, "If you can get there on your bike, you can do it." We never took them anywhere.

My son would bike all the way to the sub base to do something there. He'd go to the swimming pool or do something. My son was a lifeguard at Esker Point. He used to get on the ferryboat, go out to Fishers Island and caddy at the very tony golf course there. It was a very rich area. He used to work at Abbott's Lobster Pound making cole slaw and that. And my daughter, who's less of an activist like that—her closest friend was the daughter of the only black family in Mystic, because it was in her grade. So they used to hang out all the time together.

So it was a wonderful family place. As I said, I had three different tours of duty there, so we got to meet a lot of people. My wife cultivated Harve Stein, an eminent painter who ran a little art gallery in Noank. He was a professor emeritus—he's dead now—from the Rhode Island School of Design. He would have a lot of stuff in his art gallery from families from the old China trade. The families either weren't interested in it or had died out, so on and so forth. And this was in the time when Oriental art was not popular. So our whole house is full of Oriental art from there. People think we bought it in the Orient; we didn't. We bought it from there, for a song.

I remember one particular piece. It's that ivory boat we have. And Margaret never calls me at work. Never. The house could be on fire, she wouldn't call me at work. We were doing power range testing on *Cavalla*, and I was the senior supervisory watch in the engine room. A sailor came up and said, "Captain, your wife's on the phone."

I said, "What?" We had one phone that Rickover had decreed had to be 25 feet from the maneuvering room so it wouldn't interfere with testing. So I went back, and it was Margaret. She said, "You've got to come home early." This was about 4:00 o'clock.

I said, "No, no. Why?"

She said, "There's this wonderful thing Harve Stein has."

I said, "Well, I will be home as usual about 7:00."

She said, "Okay, I'll call him. He'll open up for us." So I went home, we went over there, and they had that ivory boat. It was $1,200. But we didn't have $1,200. So I said, "Okay, we'll take it." The next day I went to the submarine base credit union, borrowed $1,200, and we bought that. I think it's worth ten times that amount right now. But she did that. All our great art we have we got through that connection. So it was a wonderful tour. It was really a wonderful tour. Made up for all the separations we had in life.

Paul Stillwell: To what extent were you able to get involved in your children's school activities?

Admiral DeMars: Not very much, because you didn't do that in those days. [Chuckle] I mean, it just wasn't done. I might go watch my son play tennis a little bit, or play soccer. That was about it. They didn't have a lot of activities for kids. Kids made their own activities in those days. It was a totally different kind of life. Kids were more on their own, the world was a safer place, and it was idyllic. It was just so much nicer than it is nowadays, for families. Nowadays you've got to have two cars in order to keep up with your kids.

Paul Stillwell: Any further recollections on Commodore Shellman?

Admiral DeMars: No, I always liked him very much. I ran into him again, twice more. Once when he was stationed here in Washington, they had us over for dinner. Then he went to work for Electric Boat, and so when I was at Naval Reactors I dealt with him quite frequently there over things. I just thought he was a wonderful man. He was very principled, very hard working, and we got along well. I enjoyed being his XO.

Paul Stillwell: How large a staff was it for the squadron?

Admiral DeMars: Well, we had two deputies, one other fellow and I. We had a squadron engineer, squadron Supply Corps officer, squadron medical officer. That was about it. And then everybody had a couple of lieutenants around. The big staff, of course, was the tender staff, and those were mostly limited duty officers or warrant officers and mustangs, for all the trades that you had. In the machine shop they could make almost anything. It was a wonderful, wonderful facility. So it wasn't a large staff.

Paul Stillwell: A tender is an LDO heaven.*

Admiral DeMars: Yes, yes. And they do good work. As I said, I was very disappointed that they decommissioned four submarine tenders.

Paul Stillwell: Did you have any misgivings going to the Propulsion Examining Board? Those individuals are viewed as the bad guys by the people they visit.

Admiral DeMars: No, I didn't, because I was pretty successful the only couple of times I had them visit *Cavalla*. See, they were invented when I was at Submarine School and when I became the CO of *Cavalla*, so we had two exams from them. And I had a wonderful engineer, I mentioned him before, Jim Burke, who had been the main propulsion assistant on another submarine that was being built at EB. That got built, and they told him to turn his hat around and become my engineer. So he really knew how to do things, set things up, and we got above average in our exams because of him. It wasn't because of me. So I didn't have any qualms about them at all.

It was a very interesting tour, probably the most valuable tour for my subsequent job in Naval Reactors. It was a small staff. We had one captain, two commanders, and about, I think, eight lieutenant commanders. And we would select lieutenant commanders from the guys we'd given exams to, and we'd pick the top ones. I mean, guys like Rich Mies, you know.† We'd take him [chuckle]. "Yeah, we'll take him."

Paul Stillwell: Future four-star.

Admiral DeMars: Yes. So we had very, very successful staff. We'd go to New London, Charleston, Rota, La Maddalena, Holy Loch. We were gone about 50% of the time. So we didn't go out of our way to look for things to do when we were back except turn out the exams that we'd already done. That meant proofreading them and signing them out.

---

* LDO – limited duty officer, a former enlisted man or woman whose duties are limited to the area of his/her enlisted rating specialty.
† Lieutenant Commander Richard W. Mies, USN. As a four-star admiral, Mies served as Commander in Chief U.S. Strategic Command from 26 June 1998 to 30 November 2001.

For a sub we'd have about four members on the inspecting team. We had nuclear cruisers in those days; we'd take about six for those. And aircraft carriers take six or seven for those also. We'd inspect the spaces and the records, quiz the people, give exams, and do drills. Then we'd write up the whole thing. We'd closet ourselves in a little space on the submarine or the surface ship and write up the whole thing, and then debrief the CO, XO, engineer, reactor officer. The whole thing would take about 30 hours, maybe a little longer for a carrier. But it was exhausting work because you'd fly to Holy Loch. The next morning you were on a tugboat heading out to get aboard an SSBN. You'd work for 30 hours, you'd come back in, sleep for maybe two or three hours, and then get on a boat going back. Because we didn't want to mess around. It was time at home we wanted [chuckle]. And so we worked hard in order to have down time at home.

But it gave you a broad view of the program. Inventing the Propulsion Examining Boards was one of the most brilliant things that Rickover ever did, and then set it up so that they reported to the fleet commander. They didn't report to him. Reported to the fleet commander. So that dragged the operating forces into this business and the responsibility of it. They just couldn't fob it off on these EDs or this NR group.[*]

We gave grades that ranged from excellent to below average. Usually below average meant you failed and you had to have a re-exam. The squadron had to station safety observers aboard anytime the reactor was taken critical or you did drills or anything like that. And then they'd come back and they'd have a re-exam. About 5% of the ships per year failed. And we had no quota; it just kind of worked out that way.

Paul Stillwell: What kinds of things did you look for?

Admiral DeMars: Well, we were pretty rigorous in saying you could only fail if this was something that endangered reactor safety or the loss of radiological controls. Just because your ship was dirty, we wouldn't fail you. Just because your crew was dumb, we wouldn't fail you. But if we did find things where they weren't doing the trip point and calibration of the nuclear instrumentations correctly, that was probably a failure, even if it

---

[*] EDs – engineering duty officers.

was a wonderfully maintained ship. So we were very, very careful to be able to document why you failed, and it had to be because of reactor safety or radiological controls.

Paul Stillwell: How did your work tie in with ORSE, or was that part of it?

Admiral DeMars: No, this *was* the ORSE, operational reactors safeguards exam. Some called us the ORSE board. I always said that we were the NPEB, Nuclear Propulsion Examining Board, but ORSE board because it was operational reactor safeguards exam. And there were a couple of other kinds. If you were in the shipyard we did a pre-critical exam. We'd go aboard, and before you'd go critical we'd examine you and make sure you were safe to take the reactor critical.

Paul Stillwell: Any ships that you remember as being especially good or especially bad?

Admiral DeMars: No, I can't remember any of them, really, in detail. It was surprising in some. I mean, at least on two occasions—I was there three years—it was clear the CO was an alcoholic, and he wasn't functioning properly. Well, when we got back I took care of that by going to see—usually the deputy fleet commander was whom we reported to. He was generally a three-star aviator, so we got along well. And they would take care of that. Or we'd go to SubLant and tell them, "You've got to get rid of this guy." So some were very good, some were very bad and would get failed. But I don't remember the details.

I remember one case—can't remember the name of the submarine—but we were off of New London and we got into some kind of Catch-22 where they were shut down. And in order to start up they were going to have to violate a part of the Reactor Plant Manual. It was just some klugy thing. And this thing was dragging on, so I said, "Well, I'm going to lie down and take a little nap." We were on the diesel engine, and the reactor was shut down, so we were snorkeling. So I lay down for about three hours. I got up in three hours, and the diesel was still running. I thought, "Oh shit, they haven't figured out how to start up yet."

So I finally pulled the CO into the stateroom and said, "Look, what are you going to do? Are you going to snorkel forever till we run out of diesel fuel, and then have somebody come out and tow us? You're going to have to violate the Reactor Plant Manual in the greater good of safety. It's not that big a deal."

He looked at me and said, "Oh, yeah. I guess you're right." I mean, it was just common sense. You were violating, yes, but it wasn't a critical violation. And continuing to snorkel out there was dumb. I mean, the weather was bad, and on and on and on. So that stuck in my mind of how you really have to have common sense to run these things, not just follow all the rules.

Paul Stillwell: What proportion did you do ashore versus at sea?

Admiral DeMars: The only thing we did ashore, we would take back the handwritten report. We'd read the whole thing at the debrief, and the crew would be making notes. Then I'd go in and sit down with the captain and give him the grades personally. I'd say, "I think these will end up being the grades, but these are the grades now." Then we'd take the report back and we had two yeomen who would type the whole thing up. Somebody who was not doing an exam would proofread it. It wouldn't necessarily be one who gave the exam. And then sign it out, and that was it. So that's all we did in the off crew; we didn't do anything else off-crew.

That's all we did, we were giving exams, because we figured we were away half the time, we were taking this out of our body, so we were going to play golf, we were going to enjoy our families. And we held up on that. But nobody ever asked us to do anything, really, so that was good.

Paul Stillwell: Did these reports, then, go to Admiral Rickover?

Admiral DeMars: Yes. He would get them.

I got early selected to captain while I was on the Nuclear Propulsion Examining Board. After a year there, I became the head guy as the captain. It was interesting. In those days, when you got selected to captain you couldn't make captain until something, I forget what it was, you had to be serving in a billet, or it had to be approved, and this and that. Well, I had done one carrier exam under instruction with another head of the Nuclear Propulsion Examining Board, just to see what it was, when I first got there, and I saw how commanders were treated on the aircraft carrier. So I went to the yeoman, and I said, "Look, I've been selected for captain. I don't want you to make me up an ID card; that would be illegal. But I want you to type up my orders to the carrier for Captain DeMars, not Commander DeMars." He got a big smile on his face because he was an aviator. Typed them up. I went aboard as Captain DeMars. I took my new collar devices and put them on [chuckle]. I went aboard and got treated quite nicely as Captain DeMars. [Chuckle] And then when I came back I had a wetting-down party, and away it went.

While I was there, they kept advancing who they paid nuclear pay to. And I usually stayed one or two year groups ahead of that. I never got paid nuclear pay in my entire career. Eh, it didn't matter that much to me, and I never told Margaret about it. [Chuckle] But they came out with a new advancement and this and that. But because of the vagaries of the rules, all the JOs—you know, the eight lieutenant commanders—got paid it, and the head of the Nuclear Propulsion Examining Board got paid it, but not the two commanders. And so, my God. I made up a telegram and I sent it to Bob Long, who was either OP-02 or the Vice Chief, complaining about this and saying, "This is absolutely unfair, I don't know who made up these rules, etc., etc."[*] Never heard from Long. He was the kind of guy that wouldn't call you on something like that. But I heard from Ron Thunman, who was in BuPers at the time. He called me up and said, "Bruce, you know, if you have something like this you ought to come to us with it."

I said, "Well, who in the hell made up this effing rule, Ron?"

He said, "Well, probably us here." [Laughter] He said, "Yeah, we're going to fix that. You're not going to get any pay out of it; we just won't give it to the captain there." [Laughter] So, anyway, once again, I just have always spoken out on things that I didn't like.

---

[*] Vice Admiral Robert L. J. Long, USN, served as Deputy Chief of Naval Operations (Submarine Warfare) from 27 September 1974 to 5 July 1977. He served as Vice Chief of Naval Operations from 1977 to 1979. His oral history is in the Naval Institute collection.

Paul Stillwell: Who was the captain that you worked for initially?

Admiral DeMars: Stan Catola.[*] And just before that, very briefly, Walt Sullivan was the guy that hired my son to work for Stone and Webster. He was the president of Stone and Webster then. But they were all good guys. We all got along very well. We'd have parties to see somebody off. It was just a good time, and we worked our butts off. God, we worked. But in those days you flew on commercial airplanes. Nowadays they bum rides and they fly on reserve airplanes, because there's not enough money.

I actually thought about getting out then because of this new pay thing, and then it passed. I investigated what I could do. I was looking at being a commercial ship surveyor and that kind of stuff. But I let it go.

The detailer, Bill Smith, visited and asked me what I wanted to do.[†] I said I wanted to be the squadron commander of Submarine Squadron 12, because I'd served in that as an XO and a CO. And he said, "Oh, we can do that, but you're going to have to stay here an extra year. Instead of two years you'll have to do three years in the Nuclear Propulsion Examining Board; it's just the way it rolls."

I said, "Okay, why not?" So I was there for three years. I think it set a new record, 128 exams. Oh! And so I saw a lot while I was there, an awful lot.

Paul Stillwell: That averages almost one a week.

Admiral DeMars: Yes. And I was then ordered to Squadron 12 as CO. [Chuckle]

Paul Stillwell: So you actually got what you asked for.

Admiral DeMars: That was the only time I asked for something. But I'll shortly tell you why that was a mistake. And I was fortunate I never asked for anything prior to that.

---

[*] Captain Stanley G. Catola, USN.
[†] Captain William D. Smith, USN, later a four-star admiral.

So I got up there, Development Squadron 12. It was a good tour but too short, and I'll get into that in a minute. I was only there like 11 months.* I reorganized the staff to put more emphasis on publications and support for the seven or eight submarines that were in the squadron.

One of the interesting things we did there was a SinkEx, the ex-USS *Sealion*.† The poor fellow I relieved was Bob Fountain, whom I relieved three times in a row.‡ I relieved him here, then I relieved him down in OP-22B, and then I relieved him in Guam. So I always knew which drawer the pencils and papers were in, because he was a very orderly man. He had done all this work, and they had this USS *Sealion*, and it was rigged up inside a bunch of pontoons. The pontoons had air compressors and such on them, and they could submerge it to about 120 feet on pulleys and everything. Then if it didn't work, they could surface it and bring it back up. The idea was to have a submerged stationary target and see how the Mark 48 torpedo would operate. You did things like that in those days. With a war shot, it was to be. So, bless his heart, he towed that thing out there twice, and because of either weather or contacts in the area, they had to abort it and tow it back in. So within a month of my taking over we were going to try it again.

Everything lined up properly, the weather was good, no interlopers coming through the area. So they lowered it down, and we got all set to go. We were about, oh I'd say 10,000 yards off. Shot that baby hot, straight, and normal. Blew up. Boom. So that was kind of exciting. Everything worked right in the torpedo, so that was good.

Paul Stillwell: I think *Sealion* was the boat that Eli Reich commanded.§

Admiral DeMars: By the end it was an LPSS, a troop carrier. It had been converted.

Another thing I experimented with. Why couldn't we see if we could get the shore-based RDF stations, which run all up and down the East Coast, alerted and standing by so that intermittent RDF on submarine radio transmissions could be intercepted and

---

* Captain DeMars commanded the squadron from June 1978 to May 1979.
† The former *Sealion* (LPSS-315) was sunk as a target off Newport, Rhode Island, on 8 July 1978.
‡ Captain Robert R. Fountain Jr., USN.
§ Lieutenant Commander Eli T. Reich, USN, was the first commanding officer when the *Sealion* (SS-315) was commissioned in March 1943. While he was skipper, the boat sank the Japanese battleship *Kongo*, the destroyer *Urakaze*, and the prisoner of war ship *Rayuko Maru*. Reich eventually became a vice admiral and was instrumental in the development of Navy missile systems in the 1960s.

triangulated? So we got a diesel submarine out there and put up a random schedule, like once they'd communicate and then four hours later they'd communicate. Just very briefly for five minutes at a time. And these stations along the beach weren't alerted; they didn't know what that was. And it was interesting. We thought there might be something that could come out of that.

I fought with what was then NUSC Newport, the big weapons station there.* I really didn't think they were fleet sensitive. They were sensitive to their own needs, but with respect to properly designing both fire control systems and sonars I thought they were out to lunch. In order to shoot a Mark 48 torpedo you had a set of tables that were the size of the phone book. And so here you are, you're getting ready to go to war, and you're looking through this thing, you're making these settings. I talked with them several times: "Why can't you improve this, etc., etc.?"

Well, about that time—and I think this was a push by Joe Williams—we got the desktop computer installed, where you could put in a program.† I hired a company to take all this telephone book and get it in the desktop computer. I think the company was Applied Math, Bill Browning's group, a small shop that is up in Groton also.‡ Browning wrote the submarine search manual and other submarine operating pubs. As a result of this work, now you just dealt with that; it gave you the settings. You put that setting in, boom-boom-boom-boom-boom. So that really pissed off NUSC. They thought, "Oh, what are they doing? Why's he getting into this?" They tried to intercede, and Williams told them what to do, of course, in his own appropriate way. [Laughter]

Paul Stillwell: He doesn't suffer fools lightly.

Admiral DeMars: No. So I learned a lot, that aspect of it, while I was up there.

---

* NUSC – Naval Underwater Systems Center.
† Vice Admiral Joe Williams, Jr., USN, served as Commander Submarine Force Atlantic Fleet from 24 September 1974 to 20 June 1977. His oral history is in the Naval Institute collection.
‡ Dr. William J. Browning is founder and president of Applied Mathematics, Inc., Gales Ferry, Connecticut. His work principally deals with applications of mathematics to naval operations. He wrote the submarine search manual and other submarine operating publications.

Then, after I was up there about nine months I got a call from the then submarine detailer, Frank Kelso, who said they were bringing me to Washington in two more months.*

I said, "Wait a minute. I had this deal."

He said, "You didn't have that deal with me." [Laughter] So I got ordered back to Washington as OP-22B.† And that told me, well, DeMars, you should have been smarter than to ask for something, because who are you going to complain to now? They gave you what you wanted. You didn't ask to stay there two years, you just asked to be ordered there. And so, anyway, it makes a funny story now, but I was really whizzed off at the time.

Paul Stillwell: Well, you had the word "development" in your charter as squadron commander. Did you have a specific set of things you were supposed to pursue?

Admiral DeMars: Oh, yes. Yes. We were the tactical development agent for the submarine force. And we ran submarine ASW exercises where we drew up the whole thing, sent submarines out one on one, and barrier patrols and all that sort of stuff. We developed all the NWPs, naval warfare publications, for the submarine force. It was our job to do that, on weapons and sonars and tactics, and on and on. So it was quite interesting. That's why I liked it. It was quite interesting, and the ships that would do all the work for you. But they also deployed, so you had submarines in your squadron that would make regular deployments, and when they were back you used them in these exercises. And so we had quite a large staff that would analyze this, and on. We used some contractors, local, Sonalysts and Bill Browning's operation. So it was fascinating, very interesting work.

Paul Stillwell: Were there any specific innovations you recall, tactically?

---

* Captain Frank B. Kelso II, USN, later Chief of Naval Operations from 1990 to 1994.
† Captain DeMars reported in May 1979 as Deputy Director, Attack Submarine Division on the staff of the Chief of Naval Operations.

Admiral DeMars: No. In most cases you just turned the crank. Most things had been invented by then, I think. We had finally come to grips with how to deal with quieter Russian submarines—they were continuing to get quieter—and try and see what we could do with that. And with different kinds of plotting techniques. And experimenting with how you could use the Doppler signals off of incoming—not active, but noise from submarines, to put that into the target solution. I mean, if it's up-Doppler that means you're closing, if it's down-Doppler you're opening, but how could you use more fine tuning of that to help you make your passive sonar solution more accurate. So that was working at the time. But I was only there 11 months.

Paul Stillwell: Was it virtually all passive sonar?

Admiral DeMars: Yes. We just didn't feel that you wanted to lose your covertness, so we practiced passive. After a while, because of my fairly vast experience in spec ops, I don't think the Soviets had any intercept receivers. We could have pinged on them, and they would have never heard it. We had intercept receivers on board our submarines that could hear active ping and not only get a bearing on it but get a range off of it. So we knew that if they had that, that would just give you away. Just shoot a torpedo down that bearing line and they've got you. But they didn't use much active either.

Paul Stillwell: Were you able to take advantage of SOSUS in some of this work?*

Admiral DeMars: Yes. The submarine force worked closely with SOSUS, and with the VP community, how you can hand over a contact.† You know, VP finds it, you get a submarine out. Or SOSUS gets a sniff, send a VP out, they find it, send a submarine out, VP turns it over to the submarine, the submarine trails it. So we had fairly good tactics worked up to do that. Part of our charter was to write the NWPs that showed you how you coordinated with both VP aviation and SOSUS to prosecute. And then the TASS

---

* SOSUS – sound surveillance system, a seafloor network of listening devices used by the U.S. Navy to detect noises from transiting ships.
† VP – land-based antisubmarine patrol planes.

ships, the towed array ships, which belonged to the SOSUS business also.* We worked with them. That was very interesting work.

Paul Stillwell: What do you remember about the normal roles of the squadron commander—riding the submarines and so forth?

Admiral DeMars: Yes. Well, that's why I wanted to become the squadron commander. I changed it around a little bit, and I required all my staff to ride. By this time you didn't have to ride to get submarine pay, so a lot of people would hide in the corner. But I had a chief sonarman, I had a chief torpedoman, I had a bunch of very talented people, and I required everybody to ride. I required them to go down and talk to the XO before their ride and see where they could help the submarine: "What do you need? What are you working on that you just don't seem to have the smarts or the enthusiasm or the time to get done? I'm going to ride you in two weeks and, you know my commodore, he's a son of a bitch and he wants me to do something to help you. You've got to give me something to do." So that worked reasonably well. And I would have the analysts ride also. They were all military. And trying to help out the ships in a meaningful way, just not go out there and watch movies, which is what most riders do if you're not careful.

So I reorganized the staff to put one officer in charge. I had three branch heads: one publications, one was doing the tactics, and one was doing the squadron stuff. So you kept track of that. And I rode enough that I got to meet everybody. We had to work our boats up for special ops also, and pass the certification, so you were kept pretty busy.

Paul Stillwell: Well, I've heard that the good kind of staff is the one that provides support, not one that beats people.

Admiral DeMars: Yes, exactly. Exactly. Well, that's what I wanted it to be. The submarine crews had a harder job than we did. We had all had those jobs, so we knew how hard they are.

---

* T-AGOS is the designation for ocean surveillance ships operated by civil service mariners of the Military Sealift Command. They are equipped with the surveillance towed array sensor system (SURTASS), a submarine detection system.

Paul Stillwell: Did you have any diesels left at that point?

Admiral DeMars: No. No. In fact, there were very few left in the Navy at that point. But no. In fact I don't think there were any in SubLant at that point.

Paul Stillwell: I think *Bonita*, *Bonefish*, and *Barbel* were in the Pacific.

Admiral DeMars: Yes, that's right.

So I was ordered to OP-02 as 22B, which was the deputy director of the attack submarine division. OP-02 was organized so it had a strategic division, an attack submarine division, and a deep submergence division, and at least two of them were run by a two-star. I was the deputy for that.

We bought a house, this house we're sitting in now, in three days. This was my first tour in Washington. You know, I was a reasonably senior captain by then. I had avoided it that long. And so we were living in this crummy little housing at Bolling Air Force Base that was built, I think, in World War II. And we had two kids. My son was at Virginia Tech at that point, and my daughter was looking around for someplace to go to college in another year or so. So we got a realtor and we drove around for three days. I said to Margaret, "Okay, we've seen everything we can afford; pick the one you like the most."

She said, "I don't like any of them." Ah.

"Well, pick the one you dislike the least. [Chuckle] She said she liked this neighborhood, it was a nice neighborhood, but it was a crummy house. It was just a little raised ranch. We bought it and we lived in it for a couple years, and then got sent to Guam. But we had two kids in college shortly, no sub pay, and once again no nuclear pay.

OP-02 was Vice Admiral Chuck Griffiths, a real prince of a fellow.* Wonderful guy.

---

* Vice Admiral Charles H. Griffiths, USN, served as OP-02, Deputy Chief of Naval Operations (Submarine Warfare), from 8 August 1977 to 30 September 1980.

Paul Stillwell: I've heard that from everybody.

Admiral DeMars: Yes, just a wonderful guy. OP-02B was Rear Admiral Steve White, smart as a whip, tough as nails. But he liked me, and he was the guy that fingered me and brought me to Washington. I got to know him first when he was running the PCO school for Rickover at his headquarters.

Paul Stillwell: Any examples of his toughness?

Admiral DeMars: Yes, yanking me out of my squadron command after 11 months was one. [Laughter]

Paul Stillwell: The cardinal sin.

Admiral DeMars: Yes. He was tough, but he was sort of a Joe Williams type. I mean, always a smile, but he just got things done. And OP-22 was Rear Admiral Dickinson Smith, a very decent guy, a nice guy to deal with and I liked him.* We got along well.

It was a very confusing tour at first, because I'd never been in Washington. I don't know how many months it took me to realize we were working three different budgets. One had already been passed, and we were spending against that one. The second one we were defending in Congress. And the third one we were putting together. And I finally sorted that out. I said, "Well, God, no wonder I've been so friggin' confused here." Because it really was; I mean it was a big deal.

There were no word processors in those days. They did have a computer in the Pentagon that you could get time on, like after 6:00 o'clock at night. So sometimes we'd use that. But generally we just had secretaries that typed it out, and you proofread it, you made changes, and they typed it out again. They had electronic typewriters but no word processors.

I've always bragged that I was never an executive assistant or an admiral's aide or a military assistant to an important person. Well, I did get nominated to be the military

---

* Rear Admiral Dickinson M. Smith, USN.

assistant for the Secretary of the Navy during this tour. The Secretary of the Navy was Hidalgo, very courtly man.* I went down and interviewed with him. I didn't want the job, because I didn't think those were important jobs, just horse holders. So I went down, and he was very nice. "Well, Bruce, what do you do to relax?"

I said, "Well, I try and play golf if I have time."

He said, "Well, how do you get along with Admiral Rickover?"

I thought, "Ah, this is my chance." I said, "Well, we're very close," which was bullshit, of course. [Laughter]

Now, that set off an alarm in the back of his head: "This is the last guy I want on my staff; he's close to Rickover, he'll be telling everything I'm doing." So he went on pleasantly for another couple of minutes and then thanked me, and I left. I didn't get the job.

Paul Stillwell: Was that a deliberate land mine you threw out there?

Admiral DeMars: Absolutely. Absolutely. The last thing I wanted to do was be the military assistant to the Secretary of the Navy. You know, going around and holding his horses. So that worked well.

The big deal that happened during then, we had the big fight going on whether the 688 class was the right thing to do, or should we have something we called "Fat Albert," which was sort of a *Narwhal*-y sort of thing.† It went slower, wasn't as big, didn't carry as many weapons, wasn't as fast.

Paul Stillwell: And presumably didn't cost as much.

---

* Edward Hidalgo was Secretary of the Navy from 24 October 1979 to 20 January 1981.
† USS *Los Angeles* (SSN-688), a nuclear-powered attack submarine, was commissioned on 13 November 1976 as the lead ship of her class. She was 360 feet long, 33 feet in the beam, and had a maximum draft of 32½ feet. She displaced 6,000 tons standard and 6,900 tons submerged. Her maximum submerged speed was 30-plus knots. She was armed with four 21-inch torpedo tubes.
USS *Narwhal* (SSN-671), a fast-attack nuclear attack submarine, was the only ship of her class. She was commissioned 12 July 1969. She was 314 feet long, 38 feet in the beam. She displaced 4,450 tons standard and 5,350 tons submerged. She had a top speed on the surface around 20 knots and a speed in excess of 30 knots submerged. She was equipped with four 21-inch torpedo tubes.

Admiral DeMars: And *presumably* didn't cost as much, but it was in the round-off. They had gone twice to the CNO, Hayward, to continue the 688, and he had thrown them out and said. "No, go back and study it again."[*]

Well, we put together this brief for him, and I was chosen to be the briefer. Some sacrificial lamb: "You know, I've got this guy DeMars, he's only a captain." So I went in, and I was standing up in front. And it was an all three-star meeting. There must have been 12, 14 three-stars there, plus the Vice Chief. Hayward came in the end of the room, and there was smoke coming out his nostrils and ears. I mean, he was pissed. He was pissed. He sat down, and I started the brief. Then he said, "Goddamn it, I told you submariners I didn't like this. And you went away, you brought it back again. I sent you out again, you brought back the same thing again." I started the brief, and again he launched into something else. It happened three times.

I finally said, "Admiral, we've worked hard to look at this. We've done the best we could. I'm here to present it to you and to answer any questions you have." And I said it very forcefully. I thought the three-stars were going to fall over dead. [Laughter] Hayward looked at me and just shut up.

So I got through the whole thing. He didn't ask any questions, but then he launched into it at the end. And I was taken aback with the response of the three-stars, which was nonexistent, including the submarine three-stars. Nobody said a word, except Chuck Griffiths. He stood up for it, because it was his program. But nobody else said a word. And there were four or five other submarine three-stars there, and I kept looking: Why the hell aren't they weighing in? Well, I was getting my Washington education.

But it was the end of Chuck Griffiths. I mean, his last tour was OP-02, because of that. He had much more capability beyond that. But it taught me a big lesson, that you had to treat those things carefully. But it got no support from the other submarine three-stars, and I was amazed.

Paul Stillwell: I take it you didn't get any blowback personally.

---

[*] Admiral Thomas B. Hayward, USN, served as Chief of Naval Operations from 1 July 1978 to 30 June 1982. His oral history is in the Naval Institute collection.

Admiral DeMars: No. No. In fact, I got back and I was kind of sitting in my little office, which was about half the size of this room, wondering what the hell that was all about. My phone rang, and I picked it up. It was Rickover, who said, "I understand you stood up for the submarine force today."

I said, "Yes, sir."

He said, "Good." Click. Steve White evidently called him and said, "You should call this guy DeMars and tell him he did a good job." So that was good.

Paul Stillwell: What was the outcome after that?

Admiral DeMars: Oh, 688s. "Fat Albert" went away. I guess Hayward figured he just couldn't win.

We were doing pretty well then. We were getting three to four submarines a year authorized, and we were doing pretty well in the submarine force.

I thought the relations were good in those days between the CNO's staff and the SecNav staff. OSD was a minor player, which was good, because the farther away you are from the scene of the action, the less you know and the more hard line you are.*

After two years I made flag. There were about eight submariners selected, and Guam was always a submarine duty station. I'm not sure why, but it was. So I looked at who was selected. Three guys had already served in Guam. One or two guys had four or five kids, and they wouldn't send them to Guam. There was only me and one other guy. I said, "I'm going to go to Guam." Well, I got ordered to Guam.

I remember coming home, and I said, "Margaret, we've been ordered to Guam."

She said, "Oh, Guam. That's in the Pacific, isn't it?"

I said, "Yeah." And I went down and I got my big atlas from the Naval Academy. I opened it up to the Pacific, and I said, "There's Guam."

She said, "Ooh, that's not very big, is it?" [Laughter]

So, anyway, we rented this house. That was very interesting. We were at a Christmas party hosted by the captain who ran the British naval staff here. He was a submariner. It was up in his house in Bethesda, and it was a really crummy house and he

---

* OSD – Office of the Secretary of Defense.

was complaining. We were standing in the kitchen having a drink and he said, "God, I've got to find another place for my relief. I'm embarrassed at where he will have to live."

I said, "Well, I have a fairly decent house. It's a nice neighborhood." And so we shook hands right there in the kitchen. I didn't know what the Queen would pay, although she pays quite a nice rent, and he didn't know what the house was, but we made the deal. All told, we had five different sets of British naval officers live in this house. And so it was great continuity. They took good care of it, obviously.

Paul Stillwell: I have another question about OP-02. This was the period when the Carter administration was squeezing dollars to the point that some surface ships couldn't get under way or had very little maintenance.* Was there any effect from that in the submarine force?

Admiral DeMars: No, because we could always plead safety and that, so not the tremendous impact. There was an impact in the Pentagon. In response to this—Harold Brown was Secretary of Defense—they de-lamped like every second light in the passageways. Took the fluorescent tubes out. And they turned off all the hot water in the heads, so you only had cold water in the heads. That was their contribution to a reduced budget. I thought it was the dumbest goddamn thing I had ever seen, but I'd been in the Navy long enough by then to not be amazed, I guess. Yes, cold water and dim passageways. But no, the impact on the fleet was minimal, I think.

I had a number of very interesting titles for my Guam tour. I was the Commander Naval Forces Marianas. There *were* no naval forces in the Marianas. [Laughter] I was the Commander in Chief Pacific Rep for the Trust Territories and Commonwealth of Northern Marianas. And I was the Commander Naval Base Guam. So it was the absolutely great job. I mean, it was a superb job. Big fish in a small pond. I learned about the rest of the military, because there was a little bit of everything there. There was an Air Force base. There was a Navy magazine. They had a Marine barracks that

---

* James E. Carter Jr., who had graduated from the Naval Academy in the class of 1947, served as President of the United States from 20 January 1977 to 20 January 1981.

reported to me. There was a shipyard. There was a hospital, dental clinic, a SOSUS station, a submarine tender. So everything was there. I was El Supremo there.

There were lots of opportunities on Guam to do good and to have fun. I had two bosses: CinCPac and CinCPacFlt. They both were in Hawaii. Not only was it a different time, it was a different day, so I could go out and golf on Monday; it was Sunday in Hawaii, and nobody would call me. And I played lots of golf there because the Navy owned the only 18 holes on Guam. There was a small nine-hole golf course up at the Air Force base, but it wasn't worth very much. I had a barge, I had a band, I had an airplane. So I was living high on the hog from working in a small closet in the Pentagon to now, I was El Supremo.

We lived in Admiral Nimitz's house, the one that he had lived in for about a year when he was prosecuting the war.[*] It was really a BOQ.[†] Had a bunch of small bedrooms around a central kind of a courtyard, and a big screened-in porch—and then subsequently a glassed-in porch had been put on—looked out over the Philippine Sea. Gorgeous. Two-martini sunset every night. I mean, it was just wonderful.

I had a Filipino steward, Jose, and he was great. Margaret and he could put on great parties. Both CinCPac and CinCPacFlt gave me an entertainment allowance, and I went out of my way to make sure that my chief, who dealt with them, never let either one know that I got money from the other one. [Laughter] Near the end of the year, we would call and say, "Do you have any money you haven't spent yet?" And so we would have extra parties.

Paul Stillwell: Whom would you entertain?

Admiral DeMars: Well, you have the local Guam crowd, all the politicians, because they have a two-house legislature; they have a house and a senate there. And all the village commissioners, who were largely former chief petty officers and master sergeants in the Air Force and the Army, and they were kind of like the aldermen, ran all the villages.

---

[*] In late January 1945 Fleet Admiral Chester W. Nimitz, USN, moved the Pacific Fleet headquarters from Pearl Harbor to Guam. He took with him only a relatively small staff, leaving the remainder of the staff in Hawaii. He was relieved as Commander in Chief Pacific Fleet in November 1945 in Hawaii.
[†] BOQ – bachelor officers' quarters.

They were good to deal with. I liked them. And then we'd have people come through all the time—Secretaries of the Navy, Justices of the Supreme Court, so you have a lot of opportunities to do that sort of thing in addition to just the stuff you should do. Plus all the commands there. I mean, we had all these different things. They all had commanding officers, and so I had to make sure they understood who the boss was. Fortunately they were sharp. Their boss was usually in Hawaii or in some cases Washington, and I wrote a concurrent fitness report on them, so they knew who they had to please.

The big three on Guam were the governor, the bishop, and the admiral. I remember my first visit with Bishop Flores.[*] He had been interned in the Santo Tomas prison camp in the Philippines as a young teenager.[†] When the war was over, he was befriended by the Marines and the Navy and they sent him to college in the United States. Later he moved up and was our bishop, wonderful man. He had no illusions about how the world operated, what he should do, and this and that.

So I called on him. We were sitting there talking, and he said, "Admiral, I hope you don't get discouraged out here, it's so political on Guam. The politics are just fierce."

I said, "Well, Bishop, I grew up in Chicago, Cook County."

He slammed the table and said, "You're not going to have any problem at all." [Laughter]

But he was a wonderful guy. I spent more time behind the rail. Every time they'd have the big services for Easter, Christmas, or that, they always had me behind the rail wearing my whites doing something. Reading something or leading something. And I finally told the bishop, I said, "The Methodists are going to lift my tickets if I keep doing this." He liked that story.

But there was lots of political-military, pol-mil, interface there, because of the Northern Marianas and the Free Association we were going into. And I would have my aide check the airplane manifests for Pan Am flights that would stop there for a layover

---

[*] Archbishop Felixberto Flores was the first Chamorro bishop in Guam.
[†] The Japanese used the Santo Tomas camp in Manila, Philippine Islands, for internment of enemy civilians, mostly Americans, during World War II.

of three or four hours.* If there was somebody I was really interested in, I would send my aide out to the airport. He'd find the guy, the Prime Minister of Tonga or something, and invite him to the house for lunch. We'd have him out for lunch and talks. I met an awful lot of people. I just enjoyed doing that. And we'd have a lot of people come through, and they'd either stop at the Navy station there and refuel, usually at 2:00 in the morning, or at the Air Force base, and they'd always invite me to go up there and meet the people. And so it was a very interesting tour.

Paul Stillwell: Did you see any vestiges still from World War II?

Admiral DeMars: Oh, yes. All over. And when I'd get out and walk around, talk to the villagers and that, which I'd do a lot, they would talk about World War II. They'd say, "You know, the Japanese weren't all bad. They were bad if you were a Jesuit priest, but they'd bring us extra rice because they knew we had a family," and on and on. It was very interesting.

I really saw most of the vestiges of World War II out in the islands in Micronesia. Dug-in tanks on Saipan, and Jap Zeroes broken down on one wing in Yap, and all over the place. Because I visited Saipan, Tinian, Palau, Bloody Nose Ridge, and on and on and on. So there's a lot still there. Old Japanese BOQs and ammunition depots. It was a fascinating place.

Paul Stillwell: Well, I think especially in Peleliu it's very much the same as it was during the war.†

Admiral DeMars: Yes, yes. I climbed Bloody Nose Ridge. It's hard enough climbing it without somebody shooting at you. But it was a fascinating place. That was an interesting time to be out there.

---

* PanAm – Pan American World Airways, a commercial carrier that pioneered transpacific flights in the 1930s and set up way stations on various islands. It was the primary U.S. international airline until it went out of business in 1991.
† U.S. Marines made an amphibious assault on the island of Peleliu in the Palau group in September 1944. The U.S.-Japanese fighting produced many casualties.

Micronesia, which is where I had sort of suzerainty, is very large. If you look at it, it's the size of the United States. You push it all together, and the landmass is the size of Rhode Island. So it really is a strange place. They had a new High Commissioner at that point. A woman, Jan McCoy, was commissioned by Reagan.* Wonderful lady from California. She lived up on Saipan, in the High Commissioner's house. And I met her on the way out. I stopped in Hawaii for some briefings and that and met her there. Fred Zeder was the Assistant Secretary of the Interior for something or other, and this stuff fell under him.† He was a very rich guy from Texas, oilman. He was a friend of hers, and so I got to know her.

So we got out there, and I was about to make my first tour to all the islands. So I called her up and said, "Jan, I'm going to tour all the islands. I've got an airplane." She didn't have an airplane. "Would you like to come with me, and meet everybody and kind of get you into it?" We became close friends after that. She was the kind of woman you can do that with and enjoy being with. I mean, she was very straightforward, very nice to deal with.

Paul Stillwell: What were the issues during those visits?

Admiral DeMars: Well, one was the whole issue of Free Association was undergoing. All these landmasses, such as they are, were part of the United Nations Trust Territories, except for the Northern Marianas Islands who elected to become a commonwealth of the United States. The rest of them were going to go into Free Association with the United States, which meant that we would protect their defense, and they would run their internal business. We'd given them, I don't know, $20 million a year or something for 15 years to try and let them wean themselves into a new future. So that was an issue.

But more importantly, the Navy was in charge of infrastructure projects throughout Micronesia. The Department of the Interior had been doing it, and they did a

---

* Janet Jenkins McCoy was the last High Commissioner of the Trust Territory of the Pacific. She served in that position from December 1981 to July 1987, when she became Assistant Secretary of the Interior for Territorial and International Affairs. During World War II she was among the first officer candidates in the Women's Army Auxiliary Corps.
† Fred Monroe Zeder II in 1982 became the President's Personal Representative for Micronesian Status Negotiations.

terrible job. So they got kicked out, and the Navy got brought in, the Navy Civil Engineer Corps. So we were building airports and harbors, roads, all over. In each one of the capitals of Yap, Truk, Tinian, Palau, Saipan there was a lieutenant and a small staff overseeing the construction of this going on. Plus there were five civic action teams, three Navy team, one Air Force team, and one Army team, which was usually headed up by a jaygee or a lieutenant and then a number of chiefs and senior petty officers, equipment operators and that. They were building roads and doing minor infrastructure work to help out the islands. I had to worry about them, so I'd visit them and see what they were doing, and visit the civic action teams and that.

Paul Stillwell: Was there any concern that they would take work away from the locals?

Admiral DeMars: No, no. Not for that. Most of the locals that wanted work could work on these civic action things, the infrastructure stuff.

My other big issue that I got to know an awful lot about were the Jesuits. I'd only been there several months and this tract came across my desk. You know, "United States ripping off the natives in this Free Association move," etc., etc. What the hell is this? I read it, and down at the bottom was "Brother Henry Schwalbenberg. S.J." So I went down to see the bishop. I thought, "I've got to sit down with this guy and square him away. And Bishop Flores said, "Oh, I'm sorry, Admiral, but that's not in my diocese, my jurisdiction. That's Bishop Neylon, who lives on Truk."[*]

I said, "I can get in touch with him."

I had a guy on my staff sort of responsible for all the islands, and so he got me in touch with Bishop Neylon. We got together in Palau one time. And he was a typical Jesuit. He was wearing a Hawaiian shirt, [chuckle] and we both had a Scotch and we talked. "Well," he said, "I'll set you up a meeting with Brother Henry. You should talk with him." I said okay.

About two months later—things pass slowly out there—I was back in Truk meeting with Brother Henry. He was about 25 years old, Boston College graduate, smart

---

[*] Bishop Martin Joseph Neylon, Society of Jesus, an American. He served in the Marshall and Caroline Islands from 1969 until his retirement in 1995.

as a whip, speaks Japanese. And so we had a big discussion about this, and I said, "Look, you're embarrassing yourself with your lack of knowledge." [Laughter]

He looked at me and he said, "What do you mean, Admiral?"

I said, "Look, read two books on World War II and tell me islands aren't important."

He said, "Oh. Oh."

I said, "Look, I'll have a deal with you. You draw up your paper, stamp 'Draft' on it, send it to me, just addressed to me, 'Personal.' I'll just open it, I'll get out my red pen, and I'll write stuff on it. 'BS,' and this and that. 'That's a good point,' etc., etc. I'll send it back to you. Just between the two of us. Nobody else is going to know it."

He said, "Would you do that?"

I said, "Sure. Be fun."

So we struck up a very close relationship. A couple of times he came to Guam. Margaret loved him like a son. A nice young man. And so we did that. I changed him a little bit, he changed me a little bit. So that was fun.

Paul Stillwell: I read your end-of-tour report from Guam.

Admiral DeMars: Oh, yes.

Paul Stillwell: You really emphasized the value of getting around and visiting.

Admiral DeMars: Yes. Absolutely. Very, very important to get around and to meet with everybody.

I took Margaret on lots of trips. My predecessor, Bob Fountain, had not taken his wife anywhere.* And part of it is the Navy has squirrelly rules about who can fly on military aircraft. So I always made sure when I got invited, like the new president of Yap was having, the Yap state was having his inauguration, make sure the invitation is addressed to Admiral and Mrs. DeMars. Then it was no problem.

---

* Rear Admiral Robert R. Fountain Jr., USN, served in the various Guam-based billets from April 1979 to August 1981.

I remember two great trips. Traditionally the admiral spoke at the Yap Outer Islands High School graduation, which was on Ulithi Atoll. My dad was there on a destroyer when it was a big fleet anchorage for us in World War II. There's an Outer Islands High School there where kids would go there and they had teachers there, but they'd have to bring like an aunt or a grandmother there to cook, and their own food and everything. I mean, it was a very austere sort of thing. So we would go down there. I went down one year by myself in my little airplane, made a speech, and got kind of the lay of the land.

So the next year I said, "We're going to do this right. I'm going to take my band down. They need music." But of course I just had this little Sky King airplane, two engines, held six people. So we had to get an airplane. So I had my staff work on that, and we got the Marines in Okinawa to fly a C-120 down, propeller-driven cargo plane. So they came down, and I put out the word I was going to take only enlisted people with me, to round this out. And your ticket to go is you bring a case of beer or a case of Cokes, and then you can get on the airplane. I said I wanted people who were Sailor of the Quarter, Airman of the Year, those sorts. I put that out to all my commands. The commanding officers were whizzed off because they couldn't go, but I said, "That's just the way it is."

So this plane showed up, and the guy flying it was a colonel. He was the head of the squadron. I said, "Oh, jeez, I didn't expect the CO. Do you want to see Ulithi?"

He said, "No. The airfield's a little under spec, so I thought I'd better do it myself."

I said, "What do you mean, under spec?"

He said, "Oh, it's shorter than we're allowed to land on, but we can manage that."

So we got on, got all loaded up and strapped in, and we were heading down there. He came back and asked Margaret if she'd like to sit up in back of him when they landed. So she went up. She's great for that sort of stuff. We flew over this thing, and it was a ground coral runway. He banged that thing down on the end of the runway, brakes on, reversed the engines whoowhoowhoowhoowhoo. We ended up with our nose sticking out over the other end of the runway. [Chuckle] Then he taxied up, went around, backed up, so our tail was sticking out now, so he had it way out. We all got off. Margaret's eyes were like saucers now. [Laughter]

We had a great time. We had the ceremony. It was topless. It's a topless society. They wear a lot of greenery, but it's topless. And so I gave a great speech, as usual. Then we went through the receiving line and they presented a beautiful thing, I'll show you later, a big banner that they had stitched out. It's a thu, which is what the men wear, but they'd stitched on it, "Long Live the U.S. Navy," and presented that to us. I thought that was very sweet.

Then they had a big luau, but no utensils. You had a big pandanus leaf, and you put poi in that, and you had like a piece of fish and a mangrove crab in there and all sorts of stuff. Then you just kind of squatted down on the ground and ate that. We weren't overly dressed up. I was wearing just tropical whites and Margaret was wearing just a nice blouse and skirt, but she looked around and said, she said, "Bruce, we're the only ones perspiring here. The ones that are visiting."

I said, "Well, Margaret, none of the rest of them have any real clothes on." [Laughter]

So that was a great tour. And the band played. They loved the band. The band just went over really big. So then we got back aboard. The pilot just was: wwrrrwwrrr. Margaret didn't go up forward this time. And we leaped off that island and came back.

The other trip that I took that was really something. All the communications came through the broadcast station there on Guam. And so I'd have my aide go down and monitor things and keep me up with what was going on. He came up and said, "I think you'll be interested in this, Admiral." The naval attaché in New Zealand had sent a message to the Seventh Fleet commander asking if his band would be available on a certain date for the 20th anniversary of the establishment of the Cook Islands as a country.* So I said, "Oh, that's interesting." About three or four days later, back from the Seventh Fleet, "Sorry, my band's not available on that date."

I said, "Okay, now, time to strike. We'll go do that."

---

* The Cook Islands form a self-governing democracy. They are in the South Pacific, northeast of New Zealand—between French Polynesia and American Samoa.

So I sent a message down to the naval attaché and said, "I have a band, and if I can arrange air transportation, we'd love to come down." So, okay. Now, how do you do that?

We would have VP airplanes, P-3s, come out to Guam for four months at a time and fly missions out of there.* They were based in Hawaii. So I called the CO in, and I said, "How'd you like to go to the Cook Islands?" Rarotonga was the capital.

He said, "Why, Admiral?"

I said, "Well, there's this celebration. I'd like to take my band down there and my wife, and we'll go down. We'll have a good time."

He said, "Okay. Now, this has to be very carefully done." This was a sharp guy. He was an aviator. He said, "We're only allowed to fly operational missions or training missions. We can do that, but on an operational or training mission you're not allowed to have civilians on board."

I said, "Well, the only civilian's going to be my wife. I mean, my band, they're in the military."

He said, "You're right. You're right. Okay. We'll do it."

So here we had two P-3s. We got aboard, loaded up. Here were all these panel operators sitting there operating their sonars and all of that sort of stuff, MAD gear, and my band.† We took off. We had to land in Pago Pago, American Samoa, and refuel, and then we flew on down there and landed in Roratonga.

It is the most beautiful place Margaret and I have ever been in our life, just a wonderful place. My band was a big hit, obviously, because they don't have bands like that down there. It was a big celebration. All the outer Cook Islands had come in to the capital. They had singing competitions, dancing competitions going on. My band led a parade through town. And on and on. We were there three days. It was a great trip. And that's all, we just boondoggled it. It was a great trip.

Paul Stillwell: But a lot of goodwill in the process.

---

* The Lockheed P-3 Orion is a high-performance land-based patrol plane.
† MAD – magnetic anomaly detection. The idea is that a metal submarine is an anomaly in the water around it, and the MAD gear can detect it.

Admiral DeMars: Oh, yes. Absolutely. Absolutely.

Quarterly CinCPacFlt would have a meeting just to get everybody together, Seventh Fleet and all his operational people. We had it once in Guam, thank God only once. Guam's not that much. We usually have it in the Philippines, Japan, or Korea, which is where the other sort of landlords like me were.

Paul Stillwell: Who was CinCPacFlt?

Admiral DeMars: It was Sylvester Foley.[*] And I'll always remember at one meeting, after he'd been there a little while and got to know me, we were all sitting around this big table. He said, "You know, Bruce, you might have made a good aviator." [Laughter] And everybody started laughing.

I said, "Admiral, I think that's a compliment, but I'm not sure." Now everybody was really laughing. He's a good man. He just got made a Distinguished Graduate of the Naval Academy. A very fine man.

We were engaged in the final stages of the Commonwealth of the Northern Marianas treaty. It hadn't been inked yet to make them a commonwealth. They were still a trust territory. I had the only safe, I think, in the government there. I had two checks in there worth 30 million bucks that they were going to get once they signed. This thing wasn't moving along, wasn't moving along. Some Navy JAG captain was kind of running it, and he was doing the best he could, but it was way over his head.[†] So I got myself involved in it.

To go from Guam to Saipan it's a 20-minute airplane ride. So I got in my airplane. It's like a chip shot, and you're up there. So I went up there and started to get involved in it. I spoke before the legislature a couple of times. There was a big argument about were they getting the land rights properly, and it was kind of just a lot of bureaucracy at the end. I think I finally pulled it off by explaining in one of my sessions before the congress up there how much money they were passing up, interest per day, on $30 million. Their eyes just—oh, oh.

---

[*] Admiral Sylvester Robert Foley Jr., USN, served as Commander in Chief Pacific Fleet, 28 May 1982 to September 1985.
[†] Navy lawyers are members of the Judge Advocate General's Corps.

There are two sorts of groups in the Northern Marianas. One are the Chamorros in northern Marianas, same as on Guam. And the others were people that came up from Yap, and they're sort of second-class citizens. They're shorter, they're darker, more heavyset. But the speaker of the house was one of the Yapees. I got to know him quite well. And so he said, "Admiral, I think we're there. I'll call a session of congress, we'll vote this thing in, and we'll do it this Saturday night." On Sunday the governor was going to have the State of the Commonwealth address. He said, "We'll get it all done."

I said, "Well, how are you going to find the people?"

He said, "I know where they're all on Saturday night. Where they're playing cards, where they're drinking. I'll have the police go out and tell them there's an emergency meeting of the government and they'll come in." And he did. And he said, "I'll only pick the right ones." So he always picked the right ones. [Laughter] This is like Chicago again—only pick the right ones. He got them all, brought them in, they voted it in, bang. The next day—I have a great picture downstairs, I'm wearing one of those marmars, flowered headdresses, and we're all signing this thing and passing checks, and so on and so forth. But it was a great caper. You can do those sorts of things there.

Palau was kind of interesting. That's a different place, a lot of Japanese influence there in Palau ever since pre-World War II, and post-World War II. Some undercurrent of the Japanese Mafia there, the Yakuza, and all of that. I used to go visit with the high chief there, called the reklai. He must have been 80 years old, and I'd sit in this little hut he had, we'd drink tea. On one wall there was a picture of Nimitz, on another wall there was a picture of Admiral Yamamoto.* I mean, this guy is playing all sides. He gave me a beautiful piece of women's money, which is a big thing made out of tortoise shell, just gave it to me once.

After I'd been there about a year, on Guam, the governor of Palau got assassinated.† So you wonder what the hell you do. So I told my JAG, who was a captain, "Put your whites on." I got my fellow who was in charge of all the politics of

---

* Admiral Isoroku Yamamoto, IJN, was Commander in Chief of the Japanese Combined Fleet during World War II.
† Haruo Ignacio Remeliik served as first President of Palau from 2 March 1981 until he was assassinated on 30 June 1985.

the outer islands: "Put your whites on." I put my whites on. We flew to Palau to sense what the hell was going on. I had no authority. I interviewed a number of the people there, who were all very helpful except this one guy who pretended he didn't speak English, but he did, and he was mostly Japanese, Japanese-Palau. I was pretty much convinced he had been part of it. But anyway, that kind of passed on.

For the farmers I visited all the places and that. A big farm on Guam was ten acres. So I asked the head of the commissary there, the head Supply Corps guy, why we didn't buy more local produce, why we had it all flown in or shipped in from Hawaii, old and stale. And he said, "Well, they don't meet mil specs. Their tomatoes aren't exactly the right size and they don't have enough bushel baskets."

I said, "Hey, what do you think about a pilot program to buy local?" His boss was in Washington, and I said, "I don't want you to tell your boss about this. We're going to run it as a pilot program, and if it's successful we'll see when we'll announce it." So he was a sharp guy, too, and he knew I wrote a fitness report on him.

So he said, "Yeah, we can do that."

So we started buying. We went up to where we were putting about, I forget, $250,000, $300,000, that kind, $400,000, into the economy per year buying local produce. I was a hero with all the farmers. They gave me a big plaque that's down below.

Then I thought, "Well, let's try to do the same thing with the fishermen, because in Guam you kept your boat one place, you bought your gas another place, you bought your ice another place, you bought your bait another place, you sold your fish another place. The Seabee battalion rotates to Guam from Mississippi or somewhere, once a year.[*] We'd get a different Seabee battalion for like ten months, and they were supposed to do certain projects. So I called in the head Seabee, and I said, "How about we build a fishermen's co-op? You know, a little cinderblock thing down there."

He said, "Oh, we're not supposed to do those sort of things, Admiral. We're supposed to do big things that are in the plan," etc., etc.

I said, "Well, how about you just get your guys to volunteer to do it on their spare time? I'm sure there'll be a lot of beer there and they're going to get training."

---

[*] Seabees is the nickname applied to members of the Navy's mobile construction battalions (CBs).

He said, "We can do that. We can do that." [Laughter] I mean, people were so good out there because they were so far away from the bureaucracy.

So I went down, saw the governor. He gave me some land, beautiful land, right down in Agana Harbor, and we built a beautiful fishermen's co-op down there with storage, ice-making machines, and all that sort of stuff. Piers, on and on and on. So I was a hero with the fishermen, and they gave me a wonderful plaque, a carving thing I have downstairs. But you could do stuff like that out there. It was like the Navy used to be many, many years ago.

Then I got ordered back to OP-02 after two years there. Margaret and I were ready to leave, because there's not a lot of cultural stimulation out there [chuckle]. But we had a good time, and I think we're well remembered there. Had a wonderful time.

Paul Stillwell: Well, before World War II the governor of Guam was a U.S. naval officer.

Admiral DeMars: Yes, exactly. Exactly.

Paul Stillwell: So you were kind of reverting to that.

Admiral DeMars: Yep. And they recognized that.

Paul Stillwell: I wonder if this would be a convenient place to break, just for the sake of your voice.

Admiral DeMars: Yes, it might be a good place to break.

Paul Stillwell: Well, I look forward to the next one. This has been most interesting.

Admiral DeMars: Thank you.

[Pause]

Paul Stillwell: One more little postscript about Guam, please.

Admiral DeMars: Yes. I would travel around a lot and talk to the locals. Two things. One, they always spoke very highly of Admiral Nimitz, when he was there. Because he would do the same thing. He'd go out and meet with people, and he told them, "You need to get more chickens here because you need to get civilized, and one way to do it is to get a bunch of chickens." He also was very instrumental in dealing with Cardinal Spellman, who was the vicar general of the Catholic Church.[*] Cardinal Spellman was the one that sent the Jesuits out to Micronesia following World War II to help educate and do those Jesuitical things that they do quite well.

The other thing in my traveling around and talking to those local Guamanians out in the villages, one of them told me that—you recall the Japanese fellow that was hiding in the jungles there for up until the '60s, I think?

Paul Stillwell: I think it was even into the '70s.[†]

Admiral DeMars: And they said, "We knew he was there; we used to leave food out for him." I thought, they're such kind people, such kind people.

Paul Stillwell: An interesting note to end on.

---

[*] Francis J. Spellman became Archbishop of New York and military vicar of the armed forces in 1939. He was created a cardinal in 1946 and served in that additional capacity until his death in 1967. In 1951, during the Korean War, he began the practice of spending Christmas with U.S. troops overseas.

[†] Sergeant Shoichi Yokoi, Japanese Army, was one of the last three holdouts who remained on Guam after hostilities ended in 1945. He was found in the jungle of Guam in 1972.

Interview Number 4 with Admiral Bruce DeMars, U.S. Navy (Retired)

Place: Admiral DeMars's home in Alexandria, Virginia

Date: Thursday, 24 May 2012

Paul Stillwell: Good morning, Admiral, on a very pleasant day.

Admiral DeMars: Good morning, Paul.

Paul Stillwell: We are ready to proceed now. We talked last time about your service in Guam, your only non-submarine assignment for many, many years. And then you came back to serve in OP-02 under Admiral Thunman. If you could resume there, please.

Admiral DeMars: Yes. And this was a little better move into the Pentagon, because I had already served there two years as the deputy in the attack submarine division. Now I was going to be the deputy for the entire submarine directorate. And my boss was Ron Thunman.[*] Of course, as we said earlier, he had been my executive officer on *Snook*. And the CNO was Jim Watkins, who had been the CO of *Snook*.[†] So I sort of felt at home.

I was the deputy to what we called the barons. There were three barons.[‡] The submarine baron was us, and there was the surface baron and the aviation baron. They were very powerful and I thought very useful. Obviously, you'd know I'd think that way having served there. Why were they powerful and useful? Because they controlled all the budget for their part of the Navy. All of it. Personnel, R&D, maintenance, new construction.[§] I mean, it was very, very powerful. They had the ability to pull together and coordinate things. In other words, you wouldn't build a weapon system without training the sailors that were going to operate it. You wouldn't launch off on new construction without having the ports available. On and on and on. I mean, it was just a coordinating spot.

---

[*] Vice Admiral Nils R. Thunman, USN, served as Deputy Chief of Naval Operations (Submarine Warfare), OP-02, from 1 July 1981 to November 1985. Admiral DeMars reported in July 1983.
[†] Admiral James D. Watkins, USN, was Chief of Naval Operations from 1 July 1982 to 30 June 1986.
[‡] The "barons" were the three-star Deputy Chiefs of Naval Operations for air, surface, and submarines.
[§] R&D – research and development.

It also was a tremendous bridge between the technical side of the Navy, NavSea, and the operational side of the Navy, which no longer exists, for a number of other reasons, and we'll talk about that later probably.*

Paul Stillwell: Do you think it's a shortcoming that the baron system no longer exists as powerfully as it did?

Admiral DeMars: Absolutely. It doesn't exist at all now. I mean, they keep trying to regenerate it. But the baron was a three-star, and his deputy was a two-star. Now the baron might be a one-star, and he's buried somewhere in the organization, and on and on and on.

Paul Stillwell: Well, and he was sort of the pope for the community.

Admiral DeMars: Yes, absolutely. I mean, he was very important in who got selected on selection boards and that, just by the force of his personality and that sort of stuff. With the testimony in Congress, Congress looked to that person to speak for his part of the service. But the position had enemies. It was largely people who weren't barons [laughter]. These were three-stars on the OpNav staff who didn't have as much power and didn't have as much influence. So they kept trying to chip away. OP-95, I remember, got all the electronic warfare money once, and it was a horrible failure because they weren't into training, they weren't into people, on and on and on.† So it did have enemies.

Paul Stillwell: OP-95 was one of my questions. Did that office serve a useful role?

Admiral DeMars: Well, you're asking the wrong guy. I think no. I think most of that stuff that's done like that in the Pentagon is far better off done out in the fleet. Trying to

---

* In 1974 the Naval Ordnance Systems Command (NavOrd) was merged with the Naval Ship Systems Command to form the Naval Sea Systems Command (NavSea), which exists to the present.
† OP-95 was the designation for Director, Naval Warfare on the OpNav staff. The codes for the organization of OpNav have since been changed.

figure out new tactics, new ways of doing things, new organizations. I think the purpose of the OpNav staff is to supply the stuff, the stuff being equipment and weapons and trained people and make sure that all fit together. The last thing you want to do is develop your operational approach in Washington. I think that is stupid. I still think it's stupid, and it's gotten greater and greater. Now, I had good friends that became OP-95 and we dealt with them and worked with them. But no, I don't think much of that. But they did have enemies.

Paul Stillwell: I think Admiral McKee was in that job for a while.[*]

Admiral DeMars: Yes, he was. He was. He would probably agree with me. I *know* he would agree with me. So they always had good people in there, but it was just the organization. I mean, they just didn't have any sway.

They had the usual baron stuff. And the three of us always got along well irrespective of who the barons were, because we felt we were the most important ones there [chuckle]. We supported each other at the meetings. Even if we didn't know anything about the other programs being discussed, we always supported each other. And so it was a good relationship. Because we felt we were doing the most important thing in Washington. Maybe BuPers was equally important, but they had to come through us also.[†]

Paul Stillwell: But wouldn't it become a zero-sum game in that if one baron got more money, then another one would get less?

Admiral DeMars: Yes, but there was the horse-trading. I mean, we weren't *totally* altruistic. [Chuckle]

I remember one quick story. When I was the baron, the OP-02, we were trying to field the SubACS weapon system, and it was horribly behind.[‡] IBM was building it out

---

[*] Vice Admiral Kinnaird R. McKee, USN, served as Director, Naval Warfare, OP-95, from 1979 to 1982.
[†] BuPers – Bureau of Naval Personnel.
[‡] Admiral DeMars served as Deputy Chief of Naval Operations (Submarine Warfare), OP-02, from November 1985 to October 1988. SubACS – submarine advanced combat system.

in Manassas, and it was terrible.* It was overrun, it was behind schedule. And it had to meet a new-construction submarine. There was SubACS A, Alfa, which was to meet a 688-class submarine, and SubACS Bravo was going to be for the *Seawolf*.† We were way behind. So we were going to have a submarine that wouldn't have a combat system. I fired, in essence, the guy who was running it and brought in a two-star, J. Guy Reynolds, a good friend of mine, fellow Chicagoan, and put him in charge of it.‡ He worked it hard for about a year and a half. Then he came to me and said, "Okay, Bruce, we need $60 million more [this was like March] to finish it out, and we'll get there."

I said, "Okay, how do we get that?"

He said, "Why don't we go talk to Mel Paisley?" Mel Paisley was Lehman's RDA guy that went to jail later and got religion, and on and on.§

So we made an appointment and went in to see Paisley. We sat down, J. Guy and I. And the only other fellow there was a two-star who was the comptroller. Aviator. So we laid it all out. Paisley asked all the right questions: "Have you skimmed all your own programs?"

"Yes."

"Have you beat up on the contractor?"

"Yes."

"Have you struck a deal with Congress not to take any of the money away?"

"Yes."

So after about 15 minutes of this, he turned to the comptroller and said, "Okay. Skim the aviation programs and the surface programs for $60 million; give it to OP-02."

We said, "Thank you very much," and left.

---

* IBM – International Business Machines.
† USS *Seawolf* (SSN-21), the first of a three-ship class of nuclear-powered attack submarines, was commissioned 19 July 1997 after construction at the General Dynamics shipyard in Groton, Connecticut. She displaces 7,460 tons surfaced and 9,137 tons submerged. The ship is 353 feet long, 40 feet in the beam, and has a maximum draft of 36 feet. Her top speed on the surface is 15 knots; top speed submerged is 35 knots. The submarine is armed with Tomahawk missiles and has eight 26½-inch torpedo tubes.
‡ Rear Admiral James Guy Reynolds, USN, served from 1985 to 1987 as Director, Submarine Combat Systems Project in the Naval Sea Systems Command.
§ Melvyn R. Paisley served from December 1981 to March 1987 as Assistant Secretary of the Navy (Research, Engineering, and Systems). In October 1991, a federal judge sentenced Paisley to four years in prison and fined him $50,000. Paisley admitted receiving more than $3.3 million in kickbacks from various corporations for steering Navy contracts their way during his time in office. John F. Lehman Jr. was Secretary of the Navy from 1981 to 1987.

I got back to my office. I had barely compressed the seat in my chair and the phone was ringing off the hook from Bob Dunn, the aviation guy, who of course knew because the comptroller was an aviation guy.[*] I never heard from Joe Metcalf.[†] I don't even think he knew what happened. But that was typical. The surface guys rarely had a plug in to anything that was going on.

So there were occasional times. No, I didn't ask him to skim them. I just thought he'd come up with magic money from somewhere. He did. So that was an example where we worried about ourselves. *But* we did deliver SubACS on time to that 688, the *San Juan*, and also to the first *Seawolf*.[‡] So it all worked out.

Paul Stillwell: What do you remember about Admiral Thunman in the role of OP-02?

Admiral DeMars: He was good. He was a hard worker, very dedicated, and a good guy to work for. I knew him quite well, obviously; he had been my XO for almost two years on the *Snook*. And so I liked working with him. He and I got along very well. We were very frank with each other and open, and we sort of shared the same approach.

That leads to another interesting story. We were fighting for submarine construction. And he would go to everything. If they had a cockfight in D.C. and congressmen were going to be at it, he'd go and lobby them for support. Of course, they didn't have those things, at least as far as I know. But he came back one morning and said, "Bruce, the strangest thing happened last night. I went down to this reception on Capitol Hill and this fellow came up to me, an older guy, his name was Gray Armistead, and said, 'You guys are doing a terrible job in how you're going after these new submarines, and trying to get them and that.' He said, 'I'd like to come in and talk to you about it.'"[§]

---

[*] Vice Admiral Robert F. Dunn, USN, served as Deputy Chief of Naval Operations (Air Warfare) from 15 January 1987 to 25 May 1989. The title changed from Deputy to Chief to Assistant Chief on 1 October 1987. His oral history is in the Naval Institute collection.
[†] Vice Admiral Joseph Metcalf III, USN, served as Deputy Chief of Naval Operations (Surface Warfare) from September 1984 to December 1987.
[‡] In 1986 SubACS was redesignated BSY-1. Late that same year the first set was installed in the *Los Angeles*-class attack submarine *San Juan* (SSN-751). The system became operational in 1989.
[§] Reginald Gray Armistead, born in 1921, was a World War II naval aviator who remained in the Naval Reserve after the war. He subsequently served on congressional staffs and still later was a consultant for Grumman Corporation, General Electric Corporation, and Newport News Shipbuilding.

Ron said, "Sure. Come on in." And he said to me, "I want you to sit in on this, Bruce. [Chuckle] This is different."

I said, "Well, who do they work for?"

He said, "Newport News Shipbuilding." Okay, fine.

So we sat there. It started off, these three guys showed up. Gray Armistead, who worked for Newport News, had been an aviator in World War II, a wonderful guy. He had also worked on the Hill. He was a very nice guy. I still stay in touch with him. He raises cattle out in Sperryville now.[*] Ed Braswell, who had been the staff director for the Senate Armed Services Committee.[†] And Frank Slatinshek, who I think had had the same job for the House Armed Services Committee.[‡] So these were powerful guys. But they showed up, and it was wintertime, they were wearing big overcoats and fedora hats. I thought, "Oh, this is interesting." [Chuckle]. So we got all that, and they sat down on the couch. I sat behind a table we had in Thunman's office. Thunman sat behind his desk.

They said, "Okay, well, you guys aren't doing a very good job. You're working very hard, but you're not getting anywhere, not getting the message out." They sort of said, "You need a point man to do all this for you."

Thunman said, "Well, we've got one." He mentioned some captain who was doing that.

"Nah, nobody knows him."

And I'll always remember, Armistead said, "Why can't Bruce be the point man? Why can't he be the program coordinator for the program?" We were trying to get the *Seawolf* through also.

Ron said, "Well, he's my deputy."

"Well, can't he do both jobs? Does he get along with the CNO?"

"Yeah, he gets along with the CNO."

"Okay, he can do both jobs." So we agreed on that, on and on and on. It was only about a half-hour meeting.

---

[*] Armistead died 26 June 2012, a few weeks after this interview.
[†] T. Edward Braswell Jr., chief counsel and staff director for the Senate Armed Services Committee.
[‡] Frank Slatinshek was chief counsel for the House Armed Services Committee.

They got up and left, and Ron and I looked at each other and decided, "Well, hell, we couldn't do any worse than we were doing." [Laughter]

But it was the beginning of a very fine association. It helped us out immensely. And they weren't particularly parochial toward Newport News. They knew if you got more submarines it would be shared between EB and Newport News, because there really was no competition; you were just trying to keep both guys working.

Paul Stillwell: So Pascagoula was out of it as a building yard at that point?

Admiral DeMars: Oh yes, yes. They'd been kicked out of it. At one point there were six shipyards building nuclear submarines. One of them they towed the submarine out of, New York Shipbuilding.* Pascagoula got kicked out. They built the *Snook*, and they did a terrible job. I mean, it was poor workmanship, etc., etc. They built submarines at Mare Island Naval Shipyard and Portsmouth Naval Shipyard. So they built them all over. But that was the 41 for Freedom, and 637 class, on and on.

So it was lots of very hard work, and those guys helped us out immensely with access and entrée. I remember going to lunches they'd put on at Mr. K's, a place on K Street that is no longer there. We'd have a couple of senators there and the Chief of Naval Operations, Watkins. Can you imagine doing that these days? Well, Watkins liked Armistead—they knew each other—and trusted him. That was the way things were done in those days, and it got done well.

Paul Stillwell: Well, it was certainly in his interest to get more submarines in the fleet.

Admiral DeMars: Yes, of course. Of course.

So it was a lot of hard work.

Paul Stillwell: Did Admiral Thunman pick you for that spot?

---

* The attack submarine *Pogy* (SSN-647) was under construction as business dwindled at New York Shipbuilding Corporation in Camden, New Jersey. Soon after she was launched on 3 June 1967, her contract was cancelled and the unfinished ship was towed to Philadelphia for temporary berthing. She was subsequently assigned to Ingalls Shipbuilding, Pascagoula, Mississippi, for completion.

Admiral DeMars: Yes, I think he did.

So then I was there two years, and Thunman moved on to be Chief of Naval Technical Training or something.

Paul Stillwell: I think he was CNET.

Admiral DeMars: Yes, Chief of Naval Education and Training.* And I moved up to relieve him. I didn't understand at the time. Most people, once again, would have gone off to be a fleet commander or something if they were going to have a future in the Navy, but they kept me there. Later on, it became apparent why they were doing it. But I was happy with that. I had made a mistake once in picking where I wanted to go—that was DevRon 12—and I wasn't about to do that again. I always thought, "Hey, if I don't like it, I can get out." I was approaching 30 years in the Navy. But I was happy. I felt I was doing something important and I liked it. I liked the business of being a Washington weenie.

So now I was OP-02, working still for Watkins, although he moved on after that. It wasn't much different from 02B. Because I became three stars then, we rated quarters on the Washington Navy Yard and one steward, and that was kind of fun because it was different. On Guam we had quarters and one steward. But this was in Washington.

The baron system was still working well for the Navy. As I said before, it worked well because they were the bridge between the technical side and the personnel side and the construction side, and the power had not shifted. Goldwater-Nichols came in later and shifted the power to the Secretariat and the program managers.† So they ended up with having all the money, and the technical codes didn't have the money. So if there was a problem they had to tin-cup the program managers to fix it, which is exactly the opposite of the way things should work. I mean, I feel that the technical codes should have all the money to do things right, and the program manager should have a very small staff but with power to direct.

---

* Vice Admiral Thunman served as Chief of Naval Education and Training from November 1985 to October 1988.
† The Goldwater-Nichols Defense Reorganization Act of 1986 went into effect on 1 October of that year. It mandated a good deal more in the way of joint-service relationships than had been the case up to then. For details, see "DoD Reorganization," *U.S. Naval Institute Proceedings*, May 1987, pages 136-145.

Paul Stillwell: And the CinCs got more power in the acquisition business.

Admiral DeMars: Yes, not a lot, though. And they weren't prepared to do it. Unfortunately it was the OSD that got more power in the acquisition business, and they made all the acquisition decisions and in essence cut out the service secretaries. So it was really OSD, and dealing with them was, oh, you talk about the Kremlin.* OSD is so out of touch and so far away from things. I mean, there was some sort of feeling that the farther you could move decisions away from where they were executed, the better you had the decision, whether it was tactics or manufacturing [chuckle]. So you moved all the decisions to the Pentagon, and more staff, more bureaucracy, more reports, more meetings.

Anyway, while I was there as OP-02 I started arctic trips. We did arctic trips in those days. A submarine would go up and do some stuff up in the Arctic, including even in one trip firing Mark 48 torpedoes and recovery. I would take every year a group of people who were very important to the submarine programs, mostly Congress, General Accounting Office. That's how I got to become good friends with Chuck Bowsher.† Once I took Congressman Murtha and the entire Defense Appropriations Committee up, eight guys.‡ So it was very powerful.

We would fly up to either the northwest slope of Alaska or Iceland, Greenland, and then get aboard a helicopter. Go out, land on the ice. The helicopter would take off and leave, and you were kind of standing there hoping that all the navigation had been done properly. About half an hour later this submarine would crack through the ice, guys would climb out the sail, come down with chainsaws and cut away the ice from the hatch. We'd go down below, have steak and lobster for lunch or something, and spend the whole day on the submarine going through things, doing things. Then the next day the submarine would crack through again, and we'd meet up with the helicopter and go back. So it was a wonderful trip. It was a great opportunity to get people to really know what the business is all about.

---

* OSD – Office of the Secretary of Defense.
† Charles A. Bowsher was Assistant Secretary of the Navy (Financial Management and Comptroller) from 1967 to 1971. From 1981 to 1996 he was Comptroller General of the United States.
‡ John P. Murtha Jr., Democrat-Pennsylvania, served in the House of Representatives from 5 February 1974 until his death on 8 February 2010. He was on active duty in the Marine Corps in the 1950s and 1960s.

We always made them Blue Noses, which meant there was a little ceremony, which they all partook in gladly.* You had to sit in a bucket of ice cubes and get your nose painted blue, and on and on. But they all willingly took part in it and loved it. So that was important.

Another funny story on that. One trip I was going up, and I had Senator Al Gore aboard.† He was a little standoffish; he was a young guy. He was working on one of the first laptops I ever saw, just a little one, and I was talking to him about that. He said, "Admiral, I'm really so happy to do this. You know, I've been to the South Pole, but I've never been to the North Pole."

I said, "Ooh, Senator, I don't know what your staff told you. We're not going to the North Pole. We're going about 90 miles away, but you can't tell the difference." So he was just crestfallen.

Anyway, we went, we came back, and I talked to my one guy that did all that and I said, "Talk to the Arctic Submarine Lab," which is in San Diego. [Chuckle]

Paul Stillwell: Of all places.

Admiral DeMars: Of all places, but University of Washington did most of the work. I said, "See if we could *go* to the North Pole." They loved it, because that was great for their budget. So we did, we worked it out. And the staff asked me, "Should we invite Senator Gore?"

I said, "Yeah, as a courtesy. He obviously won't."

He said, "Are you really going?"

"Yes." He came! And bless him, when he was on those trips he would talk to the sonarman, "How do you know what's the thickness of the ice?" and "How do you know where you are?" Then he'd buttonhole me and say, "Can I get all this ice thickness data and location data?"

---

* The Order of the Blue Nose is a Navy category for those who have been north of the Arctic Circle.
† Albert A. Gore Jr., a Democrat from Tennessee, served in the House of Representatives from 1977 to 1985, in the Senate from 1985 to 1993, and as Vice President from 1993 to 2001. He was the unsuccessful Democratic candidate for President in 2000.

I said, "Yeah, we can put all that together and give it to you. It would be mildly classified, but we can do that." So we became sort of close friends out of that.

Paul Stillwell: I wonder if he invented the Internet on one of those trips.[*] [Laughter]

Admiral DeMars: He already had. [Laughter] I liked the guy. He was kind of a different kind of guy, but I liked him. I got along well with him.

Paul Stillwell: Well, he comes across as kind of stiff.

Admiral DeMars: Yes, he is, he was. He was very stiff, hard to deal with. But on the submarines he got along very well. I mean, he sat down, he would talk to the sonarmen very close and candidly. When you were in his field that he liked, he wasn't stiff at all.

Paul Stillwell: Did you have any dealings with Waldo Lyon?[†]

Admiral DeMars: Not very much, because he was kind of getting up in years in those days. Not very much, but we did some.

We got a good submarine building program traction then while I was OP-02, not because of me but just because everything was going well. We were building three to four submarines a year in those days.

Paul Stillwell: Mostly *Los Angeles* class?

Admiral DeMars: Yes, *Los Angeles*, and we'd started the *Seawolf* program, but mostly

---

[*] Former Vice President Gore has been widely mocked for his claim that he invented the Internet.
[†] Dr. Waldo K. Lyon (1914-1998), a civilian employee of the Navy, was founder and director of the Arctic Submarine Laboratory. He did pioneering development work that made possible submarine operations under the arctic icecap. He retired in 1996 after 55 years of government service. His oral history is in the Naval Institute collection.

Los Angeles and Trident. We were banging out one Trident a year.*

We enjoyed continued undersea superiority vis-à-vis the Soviets. We watched that very closely in OP-02. They built good boats, because they had world-class metallurgists, chemists, physicists, mathematicians, and they'd build pretty good boats. They'd be quiet, but a year later they'd be noisier than hell. They didn't know how to maintain things. They didn't have that culture of taking care of what they had. They didn't know how to do that. And their sonars were terrible; they were bad.

Paul Stillwell: Did you as the baron have a say in operations, or exert an overall philosophy?

Admiral DeMars: No. Only that I got all the briefs on all the special operations from the COs, so I learned all the new stuff. We did have a couple of times we had very dicey operations, and I would inspect all the communication facilities we were going to have to communicate with the boat during this time. And then I got called over by Dick Cheney, who was the chairman of the intelligence committee, I think, or something in the House, and he wanted a brief on it, so I went over with Bill Studeman, the head of Naval Intelligence.† We thought it would be half an hour. We were over there three hours, and I was glad I had checked everything. He asked all good questions. He was very interested. He said, "Okay, it sounds like you guys are ready to pull this off, so go ahead; I don't have any problems."

Paul Stillwell: What was your reaction when the book *Blind Man's Bluff* came out?‡

---

* USS *Ohio* (SSBN-726), the first of a class of nuclear powered submarines armed with the Trident ballistic missile, was commissioned 11 November 1981. All told, the class comprised 18 ships, the last being the USS *Louisiana* (SSBN-743), commissioned in 1997. The first four ships of the class have since been converted to fire conventional warhead guided missiles rather than nuclear ballistic missiles.
† Richard B. Cheney, a Republican from Wyoming, served in the House of Representatives from 3 December 1979 until he resigned on 17 March 1989 to become Secretary of Defense. Rear Admiral William O. Studeman, USN, served as Director of Naval Intelligence from September 1985 to July 1988.
‡ Sherry Sontag and Christopher Drew, with Annette Lawrence Drew, *Blind Man's Bluff: the Untold Story of American Submarine Espionage* (New York: Public Affairs, 1998).

Admiral DeMars: I thought it was trash. Many of those things in the book came from people who were in their cups and just mouthed off too much when they talked to the author. Then he milked that for all it was worth. So I didn't think very much of that. I think he extended his knowledge far beyond his experience.

Paul Stillwell: Chuck Larson said he was proud that none of his people talked to the authors.*

Admiral DeMars: Yes, yes. I mean, most people didn't. That's the amazing thing. Most submariners didn't. They just really understood it. And they knew what was going on; they knew where we were. In fact, most boats that were good, a lot of the sailors had access up in the control room during the most sensitive operations.

But the Soviets had a strange philosophy. They thought the way to get undersea superiority was to go fast and deep and have many compartments in your submarine. Like a tank or something. They didn't realize it was quieting and sonar. Because you could defeat fast and deep by engineering your torpedoes deeper and faster, and if one compartment fills on a submarine you have more problems than just buoyancy.

But we were having a big problem with—once again OP-02—senior officer promotions. It was kind of the tyranny of percentages. Ten per cent of the people in the Navy were submariners, 50% were naval aviators, and the rest were surface and the other corps. So if you laid a flat-out percentage on everybody, you never got enough people to run your submarine force.

So I had a dust-up with Secretary of the Navy Lehman on that.† This was late '86. I was concerned by the shortages, and I was working with BuPers. I had put together a briefing which I had given to Trost, who was the Chief of Naval Operations—a submariner, obviously—and he liked it.‡ I was scheduled to give it to Lehman, but we never quite got there. Then I was made the president of the captain selection board. And

---
* Admiral Charles R. Larson, USN (Ret.). From 1973 to 1976, as a commander, Larson was commanding officer of the submarine *Halibut* (SSN-587) during intelligence-collecting operations.
† John F. Lehman Jr., served as Secretary of the Navy from 5 February 1981 to 10 April 1987.
‡ Admiral Carlisle A. H. Trost, USN, was Chief of Naval Operations from 1 July 1986 to 29 June 1990.

I had gotten along well with Lehman. I took him on an arctic trip, and on and on, and he and I got along well. I first got to know him when he came through Guam.

So, anyway, I'm sure you know how a selection board works. The Secretary of the Navy signs out a precept: "We need so many, you know, left-handed engineers, and guys under 5-foot-5, and on and on and on—females, minorities, specialties." So he came out with that, and I had read that and understood it. I went and saw Trost, and he just said, "Yeah, do a good job."

I went to see Lehman, and he started telling me specific guys I should select: "Okay, I want this guy"—by name. And on and on and on. And he didn't realize I wasn't writing anything down. [Laughter]

Paul Stillwell: And that was well beyond the precept.

Admiral DeMars: Oh, you're not allowed to do that. You're supposed to follow the precept. And, in fact, when you start a selection board, everybody takes an oath to follow the precept and all the rules. We had nine officers on the board, all admirals—and when you sign it you take another oath that you followed the precept. So this was way outside. But he had been doing that before. But he didn't notice I wasn't writing these names down, so that was interesting.

The results came out, and I went to see Trost. He said, "Okay, fine." I went to see Lehman. He was livid: "You didn't follow me. You selected too many submariners, you didn't select those I wanted." In a selection board it's a blind vote on everything, and you consult and you talk and stuff. I was pretty sure that at least one or two of the members on the board were talking to Lehman or his office. Later I divined that. I was too naïve to think that was going on when the board was going on, but that was true. That's why he was so spun up when I got there.

I saw him two or three times. The first time he said, "Okay, I want you to deselect four officers and select four different ones."

Paul Stillwell: His list.

Admiral DeMars: Well, he didn't say that exactly, but that obviously was what he meant. I said, "No, sir, I can't do that. That's illegal. We've signed the board, everybody's taken an oath, all these admirals are spread around the world now." I mean, one was Boorda; he was back with his ships.[*] And I refused. So he sent me away. Came back a second time. And usually when I'd meet with him he'd have, like, 15 people in the room. He'd have his JAG, he'd have his general counsel, on and on and on.[†] There was just me, and he never asked me to sit down. In one meeting Jim Webb was there.[‡] He was getting ready to relieve Lehman. And Webb told me later he was so embarrassed by the whole thing he never came to another one of those, and he moved out of the SecNav offices back down to OSD. He was just embarrassed by the whole thing.

So, anyway, I got a lot of support. I got a phone call from Bob Schaefer, who was on the HASC staff, who said the committee was concerned about me.[§] They had looked at the issue, and they felt I was correct and was legal in the proceedings. So the third time I had a meeting with Lehman he said, "Okay, I'm going to have to form a new board."

I said, "Yes, sir." So I went back to my office—this was about 6:00 o'clock at night—and dictated a letter to my secretary. It was very formulaic: "I was appointed in accordance with umpty-ump, we convened the board in accordance with the precept, everybody agreed, signed the thing; you did not like the results and said you were going to form a new board; I hereby resign as president of this board." Ah, the next morning somehow that was in *The Washington Post*.[**] [Laughter]

Paul Stillwell: Somehow.

Admiral DeMars: Somehow. Well, I had it rushed down, and I delivered it to Lehman's office—he wasn't there—and the CNO's office, and somehow it got in the *Washington*

---

[*] Rear Admiral Jeremy M. Boorda, USN, served from 1986 to 1988 as ComCruDesGru 8 and part of that time was Commander Battle Force Sixth Fleet.
[†] JAG – an officer in the Judge Advocate General's Corps, that is, a uniformed lawyer.
[‡] James H. Webb served as Secretary of the Navy from 1 May 1987 to 23 February 1988.
[§] Robert E. Schaefer was a member of the professional staff of the House Armed Services Committee.
[**] George C. Wilson, "Navy Secretary Causes Fury Over Promotions: Admiral Calls Order 'Illegal,'" *The Washington Post*, 3 March 1987, Page A1. George C. Wilson, "Lehman Says Admiral Defied Authority," *The Washington Post*, 4 March 1987, page A3.

Post. Then it really hit the fan. I mean, oh, man. Arnold Punaro, who was on the SASC staff, called me and said he was concerned, something bad was going to happen to me.[*] He told Senator Nunn that Lehman could not have picked on a worse person in the Navy [chuckle].[†] And he also said that I couldn't appreciate the significance of what was going on. They didn't understand that till later, and I'll tell you that in a minute.

There was a letter from Senators Nunn, Warner, Glenn, and Wilson to the Secretary of Defense expressing concern about this whole thing.[‡] So I had tremendous support, and I didn't do anything to garner this; I just had a lot of friends and associates in Congress on the Hill, mostly staffers.

Paul Stillwell: Where was Admiral Trost on this?

Admiral DeMars: Oh, he was with me. But he just let it play out. He didn't take an active part, which was the right thing to do, because it was playing out in the right direction, I thought. And I was ready to leave. I was ready to say, "Okay, fine, I'll get out and do something else. This is not going to kill me in life." I've already told you that, that was my sort of thing.

Well, the Secretary of Defense's Inspector General, IG, was called in. They called all these other board members back from all over the world [chuckle]. Re-interviewed them, and they interviewed me. They came up with a big report. While this was going on, Lehman had the Navy's Office of Legislative Affairs actively trying to work Congress, but they wouldn't see him. Senator Warner, Glenn, etc., they all refused. OLA, Office of Legislative Affairs, asked Gray Armistead to help. Of course, he refused [chuckle]. On and on.

The Navy JAG told me long after this that when Lehman had a press conference on it, he had advised Lehman before the press conference that he was in the wrong on

---

[*] Arnold L. Punaro was staff director for the Senate Armed Services Committee.
[†] Samuel A. Nunn, a Democrat from Georgia, served in the Senate from 8 November 1972 to 3 January 1997. He was chairman of the Senate Armed Services Committee from 1987 to 1994.
[‡] John W. Warner, a Republican from Virginia, has served in the Senate from 2 January 1979 to 3 January 2009. He had previously been Secretary of the Navy from 4 May 1972 to 9 April 1974.
John H. Glenn Jr., a Democrat from Ohio, served in the Senate from 24 December 1974 to 3 January 1999. In 1962, while serving in the Marine Corps, he was the first American astronaut to orbit the earth.
Pete Wilson, a Republican from California, served in the Senate from 3 January 1983 to 7 January 1991.

this; what he was trying to do was illegal. Lehman told him to shut up and stand behind him at the press conference and smile. That guy should have retired. Give me a break.

So the IG report came out. It totally said we did the right thing, sustained the board's position, on and on. About two weeks later Lehman announced his retirement. It wasn't because of this, because he was scheduled to go anyway, but he didn't leave on a happy note.[*]

Paul Stillwell: Well, I think part of the reason for his departure was that he realized he was not going to get his 600-ship Navy.

Admiral DeMars: Well, but he came awful close. We had like 598 or something. And he did a good job in that regard. But it was the whole tenor of the country. He tended to take credit for everything that happened, whether it was Rickover's firing or 600-ship Navy.[†] He was just part of it, but he could never understand that he was just part of it.

But what was going on was—the year before there was an undercurrent that two Marines had been selected for brigadier under the same sort of circumstances I just related here. And I got this from Punaro.

Paul Stillwell: Punaro was a Marine Reserve.

Admiral DeMars: Yes, he was a Marine Reservist, and so he was plugged in. And they were wrestling with that, and so they held up the promotion of both of these guys. They didn't get promoted. The next year, after my thing broke and all that, one guy got promoted, the other guy didn't. So that was going on. That's what Punaro had said, that

---

[*] Secretary Lehman left office as Secretary of the Navy on 10 April 1987. The new Secretary, James Webb, took office on 1 May. Webb upheld the results of the selection board chaired by Admiral DeMars. See "Webb Overrules Lehman Decision; Selected Officers to be Promoted," *The Washington Post*, 16 April 1987, page A5.

[†] In March 1982, Admiral Kinnaird R. McKee, USN, succeeded Admiral Rickover as Director of the Naval Nuclear Propulsion Program. For a detailed account of the Rickover firing, see John F. Lehman Jr., *Command of the Seas* (New York: Scribner's Sons, 1988).

this made some other things much clearer. So, anyway, the fallout of this is that Lehman has never forgiven me to this day.*

Then I was nominated shortly thereafter to head NR, Naval Reactors, and Lehman started working behind the scenes. He called the Secretary of the Navy, who was Ball then, and told them that both Bush and Tower were against DeMars's nomination.† Well, Gray Armistead knew Tower, and Tower was in Paris at the air show.‡ Armistead called him up and he said, "Who's DeMars?" So that went away. [Chuckle] But that's what Lehman was doing. I mean, he was so vindictive in the whole thing.

I'll always remember that I knew I'd been nominated to be Naval Reactors—and they were discussing it on the Hill—long before anybody told me in the Navy. So one day Trost called me in and said, "Bruce, we're going to nominate you to be Naval Reactors." I just smiled, and he said, "You know, don't you?"

"Yeah."

He said, "How do you know?"

I said, "Ah, my friends in Congress told me."

He said, "That's probably why we've given you the job."

So anyway, after three years as OP-02, I was getting ready to get out and sell insurance or something. Instead, I got shifted to Naval Reactors.

Paul Stillwell: I'm guessing you felt a sense of vindication that the selection board results held up.

Admiral DeMars: Oh, yes, yes, I did. But I knew they had to. I mean, I knew they had to, because we'd done everything right. You get several BuPers staffers, captains usually, maybe a commander, that help you run the board, and I dealt very closely with them and consulted with them. Didn't do anything they didn't think was right. And every day we'd get a readout of what percentage of officers we'd selected, and here and there and on and on and on. So I knew we had it made. Plus the fact that you take an

---

* In his memoir *Command of the Seas*, Lehman recounted his version of the selection board incident in detail. Admiral DeMars addressed Lehman's assertions point by point in an appendix to this oral history.
† William L. Ball served as Secretary of the Navy from 28 March 1988 to 15 May 1989. George H. W. Bush was Vice President of the United States from 20 January 1981 to 20 January 1989.
‡ John G. Tower, a Republican from Texas, served in the Senate from 15 June 1961 to 3 January 1985.

oath before you start the board and an oath when you finish the board. If anybody was friggin' in the riggin' then they'd violated their oath. So I was pretty sure we were going to make it. But, you know, politics is politics. But I was prepared to do something else if I had to, but I didn't, so I felt good about it.

Paul Stillwell: You've got a note here about social demands. What was involved in that?

Admiral DeMars: Oh, when I became Naval Reactors? You had no social demands unless you wanted them. And so having been in the Navy so long and done so much, particularly in my 02B and 02 jobs, to kind of further the submarine force and the Navy, and on and on and on, I was just tired of all that bullshit, and so was my wife. So when we went to Naval Reactors we were very happy, because you did whatever you wanted there, and let it be.

Paul Stillwell: What would be examples of these social demands?

Admiral DeMars: Oh, oh. I mean, they always wanted you to speak. I didn't mind testifying before Congress; that's part of the job. But speaking to the AFCEA conference and the Navy League conference and all that kind of stuff.* Things on Capitol Hill and receptions. They're all a waste of time, attended largely by staffers who want to go there to eat, junior staffers that go there for a free meal and booze. Didn't want to do any of that stuff. And give speeches to Navy Leagues in Chattanooga, Tennessee, or something. So it was mostly that.

Paul Stillwell: Please talk about the process of testifying before Congress to sell your program.

Admiral DeMars: Well, that was an interesting process and it's a very good process. Sometimes it's a little vexing. You study, you study, study, study, because the last thing you want to do is have them ask you a question: "Well, how fast does that submarine go,

---

* AFCEA – Armed Forces Communications and Electronics Association.

Admiral." And you've forgotten. I used to always go and take only one fellow with me, either when I was OP-02 testifying or when I was Naval Reactors. Take one guy who sat behind me, and I told him, "Never, never pass me a note or whisper anything in my ear. You're just there in case somebody tries to assassinate me or something. You jump in the way." Because you see these vast groups of people that follow in the speaker, and it must be very disconcerting to Congress that this guy doesn't know his stuff, he's got all these people with him. So I purposely did that.

But it was very good. Usually the way to do it is you make up a detailed statement that goes in the record of what you want to say. And then you say, "I'd like to submit this statement for the record, but I have a few remarks if you'll permit me to give you that at the start." And they always say yes. And then you say very quickly the things you want to say, like seven, eight minutes. And then open it up for questions. They like that, because it doesn't bog things down.

I liked testifying before Congress. I thought it was important, and I knew—that was Rickover's view also—that Congress was the most important entity, and you had to keep them on your side.

Paul Stillwell: Did you go through the murder board drills beforehand?

Admiral DeMars: No. No, I never did that. I thought I knew how to do that. That was for guys that weren't comfortable with what they were doing. I didn't do that. I would have my staff make up a set of what I called "dirty questions," and I'd look over all those. If I wasn't comfortable with some of the answers, I'd call in specific people on my staff and say, "Okay, what's the answer to this one?" But I think if you do it that way you're more comfortable in your mind with what you're doing, rather than having all these voluminous papers, a big, thick notebook in front of you, and whipping through that to get the answer and then reading the answer. It should come off very easily. And certainly you know more than the person asking the question. [Laughter]

Paul Stillwell: No, but sometimes the congressman or staffer asks the "gotcha" question to try to embarrass somebody. Did you encounter that?

Admiral DeMars: No, not that much, really. Not that much. Occasionally, when I got in the middle of a fight between Newport News and Electric Boat over who got the submarine and who didn't—and that always went on—that would happen. But you just sort of deflect it. You don't get angry, you don't get upset, you just fall back on some sort of monosyllabic answer. And that satisfied the congressmen, too, because they're only asking it because their constituents wanted them to ask it. Sometimes I'm not really sure they cared about the answer. You never let it get to a point where people get heated. That's bad.

Paul Stillwell: Well, and I would guess after a while that you achieved a comfort level.

Admiral DeMars: Yes, and vice versa. I remember I used to testify when I was at Naval Reactors before the House Energy and Water Committee, and there was this one lady on there from Louisiana. Her husband had died in an airplane accident in Alaska.

Paul Stillwell: Boggs.

Admiral DeMars: Boggs, Lindy Boggs.[*] And [chuckle] since she was from the South she would always call me "General." [Laughter] There I was in my blues. She'd say, "Well, General, that was very interesting. Let me ask a follow-up question on that." All the rest of the guys would smile broadly. I wouldn't break a smile or anything; I'd just go on about it. And I found that fun and humorous. "General."

Paul Stillwell: How much did you travel in that job?

Admiral DeMars: Oh, a lot. A lot at Naval Reactors. I tried to visit every place that was important at least twice a year. I had two private and six government shipyards, two big Department of Energy laboratories—one run by GE, the other one run by

---

[*] Thomas Hale Boggs Sr., a Democrat from Louisiana, served in the House of Representatives from 3 January 1947 until his death in an airplane crash in Alaska on 16 September 1972. His widow, Corinne Claiborne "Lindy" Boggs, a Democrat from Louisiana, served in the House from 20 March 1973 to 3 January 1991.

Westinghouse—and a lot of homeports that had reactor-driven ships in them. And so I traveled a lot. I thought it was important to see what was going on.

But I had certain rules when I traveled. I'd go down to Norfolk or San Diego, and I'd walk through every submarine, every cruiser, and every aircraft carrier, nuclear powered, that was there. But I would only go through the engineering plants. And it used to drive the submariners mad. "We've got this new thing forward, Admiral, I'm sure you want to see it."

I said, "No, I just want to look at the engineering plant." I was trying to make a point that that was my responsibility, and that's all I was doing. I wasn't OP-02 anymore. And particularly when I went to, like, San Diego and there were two aircraft carriers in port and three submarines, that's a lot of walking up and down and decks and this and that. So, yes, I did a lot of traveling.

Paul Stillwell: But as OP-02 you'd visit the front end of the boat also.

Admiral DeMars: Oh, yes. As OP-02 I'd do the whole thing, obviously. But as Naval Reactors I said, "Hey, I'm just the nuc here."

Paul Stillwell: What can you say about your staff, both in OP-02 and later?

Admiral DeMars: Oh, they were good. Obviously, in OP-02 you get to pick whom you want to work for you, and every one of my executive assistants made four stars, so I made good picks.

Paul Stillwell: Who were they?

Admiral DeMars: Archie Clemins, Rich Mies, Skip Bowman.* That's it, I think. So I picked the right people.

---

* All three were captains at the time they were executive assistants to OP-02. Admiral Archie Clemins, USN, served as Commander in Chief Pacific Fleet from 1996 to 1999. Admiral Richard W. Mies, USN, served as Commander in Chief U.S. Strategic Command from 1998 to 2001. Admiral Frank Bowman, USN, served as Director, Naval Nuclear Propulsion, 1996-2004.

Paul Stillwell: That's impressive.

Admiral DeMars: Yes, yes. You pick the right people. And Naval Reactors, superb staff. I mean, these were very good. For the most part they had come into the Navy, interviewed by Rickover and his staff, as ensigns. And then most of them, at the point where they could do it, converted to civil servants. We had a few ED officers but most of them were civil servants. Superb staff.

It was an interesting setup—a flatline organization. I had 19 direct reports.

Paul Stillwell: Wow.

Admiral DeMars: And most people will tell you that won't work, that won't work.

Paul Stillwell: It's a huge span of control.

Admiral DeMars: Yes. But it's a big organization. And, really, it was a brilliant organization set up by Rickover. He really was a brilliant man. Two hats, and two budgets for R&D, one from DoE, one from the Navy.* And quite frankly, the Navy got more R&D money from DoE than DoE gave the Navy. But you never let either one of them know. And you had to be careful what you spent the DoE money for. You couldn't spend it on torpedo tubes or something like that.

Paul Stillwell: What did you spend it on?

Admiral DeMars: Oh, you'd spend it on reactors. But a lot of it went into quieting, a lot of it went into developing a life-of-the-ship reactor core, 30 years. Things like that. I mean, it's pretty amazing stuff. Done in these civilian labs run by Naval Reactors.

It was a lean headquarters staff, about 300. And, as I said, superb people. The philosophy was: Have the work done in the field and oversee it very closely. You did very little work in the headquarters, but we got voluminous reports and telephone calls.

---

* R&D – research and development. DoE – Department of Energy.

And then if there was a problem they'd go out in the field and look at it. But you're not there designing a reactor in headquarters. You task either Bettis or KAPL, the two DoE labs, or one of the shipbuilders to do something, and then you oversee that.* It was a very interesting approach to how things get done. In so much of the rest of the Navy they try and do it all in Washington. It doesn't work that way.

Paul Stillwell: You said in one of your speeches I read that when you were in the OP-02 organization you were a mole for NR. What did you mean by that?

Admiral DeMars: Well, I think that was tongue in cheek. And everybody knew that the OP-02 guy was a mole for Naval Reactors, and if something was said at a meeting that NR should know about, it usually got back there. But it was more tongue in cheek than anything.

Paul Stillwell: What was your relationship with Admiral McKee when you were still OP-02?†

Admiral DeMars: Oh, very close. Very close. He knew that I was the mouthpiece over there for what he was trying to do, and so we stayed pretty close together. And obviously, we were as important as he was in getting more submarines every year. He would testify every year and so would we, so we had to be together on things, we had to have the same approach. And fortunately he's an easy guy to get along with, once you agree with him. [Laughter] No, no, he's a wonderful guy. A very close friend of mine now, and has been for a long time. So we had a good relationship.

But we had the largest operating reactor system in the world, 176 reactors on about 150 ships and shore-based reactors. I say "operating" because that rules out the Soviets [chuckle]. Half of theirs didn't operate.

But the philosophy also, at least that I had, was that you needed to establish yourself, as head of NR, as a serious technocrat, and you needed to do that with your NR

---

* Bettis is the name of a nuclear laboratory in West Mifflin, Pennsylvania, not far from Pittsburgh. KAPL – Knolls Atomic Power Laboratory has two sites in upstate New York, at Niskayuna and at West Milton.
† Admiral Kinnaird R. McKee, USN, served as Director, Naval Nuclear Propulsion, 1982-88.

staff. They had to look at you as not the tactical guy but as a serious technical guy—with your NR labs, and with the shipyards. You had to establish yourself as a different kind of admiral with the CNO, Secretary of the Navy, the OpNav staff, OSD staff, and DoE. This guy's a different guy. He doesn't give speeches; he won't serve on selection boards. And you establish yourself both as a technocrat and as a different admiral with the Congress and the fleet. And that was the persona I tried to project. Because I think it's what Rickover did, purposefully, and what McKee did also, although he was a different kind of personality, obviously, thank God. So I thought I was just going to do that.

It was different on my first lab visit up to—I think it was Bettis, near Pittsburgh, run by Westinghouse. It was usually a full-day visit. You get some briefs, then you toured, then you got more briefs, and everybody wanted to lay things out for the admiral because he only came twice a year. We got into the first brief, and it went on for about 20 minutes. It was some esoteric thing, I forget what the hell it was. And I said, "Wait, stop. Stop. I don't understand anything you're saying." Dead silence in the room. [Laughter] Dead silence. Some of the people on my staff smiled, but everybody at Bettis was just: "What the hell?"

I said, "Look, I think things are understandable, but I like to go at things from first principles. And first principles are the math and the physics and the chemistry that I learned in high school. That's the way I'd like to approach. Now, why don't we go take the tour now? You can redo your talks and we'll come back and do it."

So on the tour other guys at Bettis and my staff said, "Admiral, we don't understand that stuff either." [Laughter] So I brought a different approach to it, I think. Maybe Rickover understood it, I don't know, or didn't care.

Paul Stillwell: To whom did you report in this role as technocrat? Who was you boss?

Admiral DeMars: The Secretary of the Navy, really, and I made it the CNO also, as did my predecessors. And the Secretary of Energy. Now, the Secretary of Energy thing was easy at the beginning because it was Watkins for four years.[*] And then the second four

---

[*] Admiral James D. Watkins, USN, whom DeMars had known personally for more than 20 years, served as Secretary of Energy from 1989 to 1993.

years it was Hazel O'Leary, who was an absolute disaster.[*] We both sort of mutually agreed never to see each other again. And so [chuckle] I dealt with her deputy, Bill White, who I'm good friends with today.[†] He's from Texas, mayor of Houston three times and almost made governor. And Tom Grumbly, who was the Under Secretary, I dealt with him, and everything was fine, we got things done.[‡] But Hazel O'Leary was, ahh, unbelievable.

Paul Stillwell: What was the problem with her?

Admiral DeMars: She was a lightweight, she was very political, and she spent money inappropriately. She'd go to Africa on a trip, for what reason? Who knows what? There's a whole big staff, entourage, and on. I think she was an embarrassment to the administration also. Anyway, that was their problem, not mine.

And out of all that, what are you trying to do? Never forget that Congress is your most important long-term supporter. They are. Administrations come and go. Watkins is replaced by an O'Leary and Trost is replaced by a whatever, and on and on and on. But it's Congress that keeps the thing going. So you always tell the truth with them, always be frank. If you made a mistake, fess up and get on with it.

Paul Stillwell: Well, Trost was replaced by Frank Kelso.[§] What do you remember about him and your relationship?

Admiral DeMars: Oh, it was a very close relationship, obviously, because he was a submariner. He and I went to the land-based reactor site together on initial training up in West Milton, New York, so he and I got along very well. He liked to golf, I liked to golf, so that was good. He was very supportive when, later on I'll talk about getting the *Virginia* class started, protecting the funding for that, because he knew it was very

---

[*] Hazel R. O'Leary served as Secretary of Energy from 1993 to 1997.
[†] William H. White served as Deputy Secretary of Energy from 1993 to 1995. He was subsequently Mayor of Houston, Texas, from 2004 to 2010.
[‡] Thomas P. Grumbly was Under Secretary of Energy in 1996-97.
[§] Admiral Frank B. Kelso III, USN, served as Chief of Naval Operations from 29 June 1990 to 23 April 1994. His oral history is in the Naval Institute collection.

important after we had shut down submarine construction for so long.* So we got along very well.

Paul Stillwell: And he had run the Nuclear Power School.

Admiral DeMars: Right. Yes. So he was a dyed-in-the-wool nuc.

I had some sort of management rules—maybe I'll bore you with them now, just put them down very quickly—to run that Naval Reactors thing. I thought:

- The boss must be involved in the details. I mean, the top guy has got to be involved in the details, and if you are, the other bosses that report to you are going to have to be.
- Most of the money should go to the technical efforts. So it's what I spoke about before, keep the project offices small, keep the technical offices large.
- Beware of success-oriented programs. There will be serious problems, and if you just want success you're going to get it, but it's all going to crash on you.
- Control of the contractors is absolutely vital. Use all means available—contractual, political, ego, threats.
- Keep the top company guy involved. The top guy in each company has got to be involved. He's got to know what's going on with what he does for Naval Reactors.
- There can't be too much communication from the bottom up to the very top, and it must primarily convey problems, not status. You don't want the status, you want problems.

Paul Stillwell: Admiral Kelso was pushing the TQL at the time.† Did any of that permeate into NR?

---

* The fast attack nuclear submarine *Virginia* (SSN-774) is a lower-cost alternative to the *Seawolf* (SSN-21) class. The *Virginia*, which was commissioned 23 October 2004, is 377 feet long, 34 feet in the beam, maximum draft of 32 feet, and displacement of 7,800 tons. She has 12 vertical-launch system tubes and four torpedo tubes.
† TQM – total quality leadership is a method by which management and employees can become involved in the continuous improvement of the production of goods and services. It involves soliciting inputs from employees and acting on them.

Admiral DeMars: No. We had a firewall against that. [Laughter] I didn't think it was a good idea. I think every time you get something like that where you have balloons with it on it, and buttons, and all of that, it just deflects you from real leadership and real work. I thought that was a big mistake. And those things come and go, so you just ride them out. That's why when you project "I'm a different admiral," you just say, "No, I'm not going to do it." They don't know what to do. They absolutely don't know. "No, I'm not going to do that. We're not going to have TQL sessions." Oh, okay. And they go away.

Here are some more guidelines:

- You should have a headquarters rep at each contractor site. That's very vital, so you've got your man there. And he writes you regularly, writes you once a week and calls you once a week.

- Testing must be prototypical because the product tests are performed in the real world.

- The boss must have regular meetings that get into painful technical details.

- Look at first principles.

- Tend the political base.

- Always tell the truth, don't oversell.

- This is kind of a humorous one—any product that has real worth to the country will be over budget, behind schedule, and have exquisite quality in the final product. Because that's the system; the system never gives you enough money. And everybody else sucks their teeth—oh, it's overrun, blah-blah-blah-blah-blah-blah. And sometimes there's vast mismanagement, but even if there isn't, still, you don't have enough money. But you want the end result. It's like when you redo your kitchen; it's going to be over budget, it's going to be late, but you want you wife to be happy when you get done.

Naval Reactors was different, and it took me about three years to figure out what it was all about. Most places in the Navy, when you become a department head you've been a division officer so you know what department heads do. You become an XO you've been a department head. On and on. When you become CO, you've been an XO so it shouldn't be a great—for some people it is—it shouldn't be a great thing. You learn it very quickly. But Naval Reactors—I thought about this a lot after I kind of divined what was going on. It took about three years out of the eight to figure out I really had a handle on this job.

Paul Stillwell: What are some of the things you learned? Or is that what you've just enumerated?

Admiral DeMars: Just what I enumerated, I think. Well, the vastness of the organization, and also how to deal with civilians. All of a sudden I was dealing with civilians, largely. I didn't find that that much of a problem but, at the same time, I found out that the people working at the two DoE labs, they were more Naval Reactors people than they were GE and Westinghouse people. They were proud to be part of that, they worked their whole life at that, they would retire from that. And so you had to maintain that. The shipyards were proud of what they did, and on and on and on.

Paul Stillwell: Admiral Rickover, like you, had the representatives in the various manufacturers. Did you also communicate directly with the ships?

Admiral DeMars: Yes, they had to write me. We had a system where everybody wrote me either once a week or once a month or once every two months. The ships wrote me a letter once every two months and told me what was going on, what the problems were, and what they were doing about it. If they were in the shipyard it was once a month. My reps at all the places, and the head of the labs and the head of the shipyards would write me once a week, and call me on the phone once a week to elaborate on what they put in the letter. So you have a tremendous flow of information, tremendous flow of information. And that keeps you up with what's going on.

And there was an open-door policy there—it was with Rickover, it was with McKee, and it was with me. None of my 19 direct reports had to make an appointment to see me. They just came up, asked the secretary, "Is he free?" Yes. They'd walk in, start telling me something.

Usually I had an inkling what it was about because of this tremendous flow of information. I'd say, "Okay, why are you here?"

"Well, I need the decision, should we do this or should we do that?"

I'd say, "Okay, do that," and away they'd go.

If we had some differences out in something we were trying to do between one of these direct reports, the electrical guy and the heavy equipment guy, or something like that, I required each side to send me a one-page piece of paper listing their side of the issue. I'd get that and read it, and say, "Okay, we'll have the meeting." They'd all come in. A would sit on one side of the table, B would sit on another side. They'd go back and forth, shouting at each other, and sometimes vituperously. I mean, it was really heated.

Then, after about 20 minutes (decreasing sound), all quiet down, they'd all look at me and say, "Okay, Admiral, you've got to make a decision."

I'd say, "Okay, I go with B." Then they'd all get up and leave and execute B! I mean, it was a remarkable process, as compared to meetings that last two hours in the Pentagon and you never get a decision.

So it was a great, dedicated staff, smart, industrious. Of my 19 direct reports they were all engineers save one, who was a former Supply Corps lieutenant, Tim Foster, and he did all the liberal arts stuff.* He initially worked for NR as an active duty officer, then resigned and continued to work for NR as a civilian. Congressional relations, budgets, PR, and did a superb job at it. That was a very important part. He was the guy that arranged the arctic trips and all that sort of stuff. So it was a good operation. Great staff.

Paul Stillwell: It sounds as if you just perpetuated the Rickover model.

Admiral DeMars: Absolutely.

Paul Stillwell: If it's not broken, don't fix it.

Admiral DeMars: Absolutely. No, and so did McKee for that matter. Unfortunately my relief didn't. He changed it.

---

* Thomas L. Foster worked in the Naval Nuclear Propulsion Program from 1963 to 1994, serving from 1972 to 1994 as Director of Resource Management.

Paul Stillwell: Skip Bowman.*

Admiral DeMars: Yes. He changed it, and I think for the worse. He got an executive assistant, a captain. He got an aide. No more open-door policy; you had to make an appointment to see him. Staff did not like it, did not like it. Anyway, but life goes on.

Paul Stillwell: You talked about public relations. It seems to me you had a lower public profile than Admiral Rickover did.

Admiral DeMars: Yes, because I wasn't as smart as him. [Laughter] And he was there 30 years. I'm sure the first eight years he wasn't that high a profile. And he was different. I mean, the boat COs used to call him "Rick" in the days because they'd all been World War II heroes and he wasn't. And so he matured and changed as he was there.

No, my big profile came from my fight with Lehman and that was about it, and getting the *Seawolf* stuff.

Paul Stillwell: But Admiral Rickover liked to be provocative, as least from my reading about him.

Admiral DeMars: Oh, yes, yes, no doubt about it. That was part of his enjoyment in life. And if you'd served there for 30 years you had to get enjoyment somewhere. I mean, that was a very grueling job. I don't know how he did it for 30 years [chuckle].

Paul Stillwell: Did you follow his practice of sending out souvenirs of stamped envelopes?

Admiral DeMars: Yes. Oh, yes, yes, yes.

Paul Stillwell: And key chains?

---

* Admiral Frank Bowman, USN, served as Director, Naval Nuclear Propulsion, 1996-2004.

Admiral DeMars: No, no, not that. The only thing we sent out were letters on every initial sea trials to everybody in Congress plus the President, the Vice President, other people. No, I didn't do that other stuff because we just didn't collect it. And that was good. In fact, I found out they had a whole bunch of it still in the headquarters, so I had Tim Foster get a bunch of bags and fill the stuff in bags and give them to members of the staff: "Let's get this stuff out of here; I want to get out of this business." Which is good, because nowadays you couldn't do any of that because of ethics rules.

So all was going great for about two years when I got there, and then the wall came down, the Soviets became Russians, and all submarine construction was stopped.* Just stopped. We're not going to build any more. We were going to build 30 *Seawolf* class; we had built two. The third one got canceled. We were going to build 68 688 class; we stopped at 62. Just stopped construction of it. Tridents, we never said how many we were going to build, and that was purposeful, but we stopped at the 18th one. So all of a sudden, boom, there was no more work for the shipbuilders. I mean, we went from three to four per year to zero. And that multiplies down through the suppliers and on and on. So I led the battle to get the third *Seawolf* authorized. I thought we needed that to bridge us over while we were trying to figure out what really to do because the world had fundamentally changed.

Paul Stillwell: And *Seawolf*s cost a whole lot.

Admiral DeMars: Yes, yes. Well, every first of a kind costs a lot. Not as much as a carrier, not as much as a big cruiser, on and on and on. You get what you pay for.

Tim Foster and I worked together on big thick report on this whole thing, and I signed it out to Gerry Cann, who was Assistant Secretary of the Navy for Research, Development, and Acquisition, and it sort of laid it all out.† Oh, that hit like a turd in the

---

* In 1961 the East German regime built a wall that separated the Soviet- and NATO-controlled sectors of the city of Berlin. It was a symbolic gesture at the height of the Cold War. A number of East Germans were killed in subsequent escape attempts. On the night of 9 November 1989 the East German government suddenly and unexpectedly opened the wall to permit free transit. The wall was subsequently torn down, this time a symbol of the easing of relations between the superpowers.
On 26 December 1991 the Supreme Soviet, the highest governmental body of the Soviet Union, recognized the collapse of the Soviet Union and dissolved itself.
† Gerald A. Cann served in that position from 1990 to 1993.

punchbowl. Oh. So they came back and said, "Well, you've only given one side of how you can rescue the submarine building process. You've got to figure out how you can rescue it without building submarines." So we went back and forth with that sort of BS.

I briefed everyone. I had problems with the SecNav, Sean O'Keefe, because I was a little forward leaning.* I got ahead of him several times, like setting up a briefing for the Secretary of Defense without him knowing about it [chuckle]. I mean, I was really working hard, and that was a mistake, and on and on and on. He was new and was just in the job, and I got some word back from somebody in the Congress that said, "Hey Bruce, there's another Secretary of the Navy after firing you." [Laughter] He was frustrated in my hard-charging efforts, usually without his permission, to restart submarine construction. But that effort to get rid of me never went very far.

Paul Stillwell: Did the tactical missiles get on board submarines during your watch, the Tomahawks?†

Admiral DeMars: Yes, that was when I was OP-02.

Paul Stillwell: Could you talk about that, please?

Admiral DeMars: Well, yes, it was an interesting thing. It just started off very low key. Stephen Hostetler, I think, was the program manager for the Tomahawk. They came to town and briefed the barons, and we all thought, "Gee, that's kind of interesting." And in those days they didn't have the GPS, they had the terrain monitoring where you had to kind of terrain monitor the entire world, which was kind of a drawback.‡ And we saw some problems with the nuclear version, because we thought this would get really tough in arms control and that sort of stuff. But it turned out great, and we embraced it heavily in submarines, obviously. And so that was a great invention. I think the Navy did a good

---
* Sean O'Keefe served as Secretary of the Navy from 2 October 1992 to 20 January 1993.
† Tomahawk is a long-range cruise missile that entered the fleet in the early 1980s, capable of delivering either conventional or nuclear warheads. Originally conceived to have both antiship and land-attack versions, the antiship type is no longer in service. The original guidance system relied on the missile matching its course with the terrain below its path. Navigation now is guided by satellite.
‡ GPS – Global Positioning System, a satellite-based navigation system that provides terminals on earth with their geographic positions.

job in bringing that and then converting it from terrain tracking to GPS, and converting the warheads to different kinds of warheads, and on and on.

Paul Stillwell: And they got used in Desert Storm.*

Admiral DeMars: Yes. Desert Storm, and in Libya. In Libya something like 120 cruise missiles were fired; nearly 100 were shot from that one Trident submarine converted to a cruise missile submarine.†

Paul Stillwell: That's a lot.

Admiral DeMars: It's a lot.

We finally got the third *Seawolf* authorized after four years of hard work, so that kind of gave us some breathing room.‡ I also, during this period, was working on rationalizing the industrial base, and that meant calling in each one of my major suppliers, like the three guys that built pumps, the four guys that built valves, the two guys that built reactor cores, and just sitting down one group at a time and saying, "Look, we can't afford to have competition anymore. We're trying to make it gracious for one of you to get out of the business, or two of you to get out of the business. And we will use money up to the ceiling in the contracts to help you get out and not punish you. But if somebody doesn't want to stay in, this is your way out."

It was amazing who wanted to get out. The second guy that built cores, up in Connecticut, said he wanted out, so we zeroed up on B&W down in Lynchburg.§ We had 28 cores at various stages of construction up north, and we built a new facility down in

---

* In January 1991 U.S. and Allied Coalition forces attacked Iraq to get it to retreat following its August 1990 invasion of neighboring Kuwait. The holding action in the meantime was Operation Desert Shield. The conflict itself became known variously as Operation Desert Storm and the Gulf War. Coalition forces won the war in February 1991.
† During Operation Odyssey Dawn in March 2011, U.S. warships fired cruise missiles at Libyan air defenses. The guided missile submarine *Florida* (SSBN-728) fired 93 of them during the operation.
‡ The third and final submarine of the *Seawolf* class is the USS *Jimmy Carter* (SSN-23), which was ordered in 1996 and commissioned in 2005.
§ B&W – Babcock and Wilcox.

Lynchburg to store them, we completed those cores to a certain degree, moved them all down there. Did all of that within budget.

So essentially we moved to a monopoly in the entire program. I didn't ask permission to do that with the Secretary of the Navy. I didn't let OSD know it was going on. We just did it. There was so much other turmoil going on with everybody trying to figure out how they were going to survive the end of the Cold War that this was a minor offense [chuckle].

Paul Stillwell: Well, and it was the opposite of what Lehman had pushed for, which was second sourcing.

Admiral DeMars: Yes, exactly. The only one that I drew a vehement "Goddamn it, no!" on was the two shipyards, obviously, EB and Newport News, and I was pretty sure that was going to be the answer.[*] Although later they tried to get together, and it was blocked by Trent Lott because he thought that would put too much pressure on his yards down South if you had this big behemoth up here that did all the nuclear work and could also do conventional ships[†]. I couldn't get them to do it, but that was okay. If we hadn't done that we'd have been out of business, we'd have been bankrupt. So we did that.

Then we started work in my headquarters, without any direction, on a post-Cold War submarine, which ultimately became the *Virginia* class. I got my section heads that were relevant to this together and said, "Okay, we're going to start the design of a new class of submarine. It has to be cheaper than *Seawolf*, have adequate quiet speed, have cruise missiles on board, have a special operations capability, a lockout thing, on and on." Laid down all these things. And I said, "There aren't going to be a lot of new submarines authorized from now on. We're going to have to do something different in Naval Reactors, reach as far ahead as we think we can grasp in new developments. This is going to be the newest operating research and development submarine that's ever been put out by Naval Reactors."

---

[*] Two shipyards build nuclear submarines for the U.S. Navy: Electric Boat Division of General Dynamics in Groton, Connecticut, and Newport News Shipbuilding, a division of Huntington Ingalls Industries.
[†] Chester Trent Lott, a Republican from Mississippi, served in the Senate from 3 January 1989 to 18 December 2007. He was Senate majority leader from 1996 to 2001. The Huntington Ingalls shipyard in Pascagoula, Mississippi, builds conventionally powered ships for the Navy.

So they all set to work, and they then factored that down into the labs and to Electric Boat, who was the design agent for it, and we started work on it. After about a year, I went over and saw Kelso and told him what we were doing, and he supported me fully and protected my budget during the process. But Naval Reactors started that, and it's always held up now as the premier building program in the Navy, because we did a very careful job. And the cost projections now, 20 years later, are still right on with that submarine cost.

Paul Stillwell: Whose job was it to match the personnel resources with this fluctuating number of submarines?

Admiral DeMars: Bureau of Naval Personnel. When I said Naval Reactors had people in the field do things and then they oversaw it, very close working relationship between BuPers and Naval Reactors. So it was them that had to keep things on track with people.

Paul Stillwell: Would that also tie in with OP-02?

Admiral DeMars: Yes, but I think by this time OP-02 had gone away.

Paul Stillwell: Okay.

Admiral DeMars: Yes, it was during this period it had gone away. It went away under Kelso's regime, that's right. The second team, the OP-95s and the OP-whatevers got control. They said there's too much controversy raised by this system. That's what you *want* in an organization, you *want* controversy. You *want* to have the decisions made at the CNO/SecNav level. Because the decisions were always made at the top. You had a two-star meeting that laid things out and you voted, and then a three-star meeting that laid the same things out and the three-stars voted. And there was a SecNav guy on each one of those. So it was a wonderful system. They didn't like it. Anyway, that had gone away by then.

Paul Stillwell: And Admiral Kelso also brought in Admiral Owens as the resource king.[*] Did you work with him as well?

You have a sly grin. [Laughter]

Admiral DeMars: No. No. In fact, he came over once. He and Admiral Oliver, who was his deputy.[†] They said they'd like to come over and brief me and the senior members of my staff on the budget, and I said fine. So he came over, we sat down in my conference room, and he started off and said, "Well, we're going to have to take a 10% cut here in Naval Reactors budget."

I said, "Oop, wait a minute." I said, "Bill, would you come in my office?" He came in my office, he sat down, and I said, "We're not going to take a 10% cut in the budget. I have a handshake with the CNO that protects my budget. Do you want me to get him on the phone right now, and we'll solve this and sort it?"

"Oh, no, no, no, no."

I said, "Okay, fine. Why don't you go back, and take Admiral Oliver? We don't need the brief." [Laughter] So he's still a little frosty with me to this day.

But I knew I had Kelso's support, and that was when Kelso wasn't feeling good. I mean, he was in terrible physical shape. So he was being taken advantage of by some people, I think.

I'll give you a couple of examples of how revolutionary this submarine was. The 688 had three reactor coolant pumps per reactor loop, and each reactor coolant pump had three speeds. The new submarine had one pump per loop at one speed. When you back that out through the circuit breakers and the controllers and this and that, tremendous savings.

We went with what I call solid-state motor-generator sets. Those are the devices where you put AC in one end, and DC comes out the other, or vice versa.[‡] We discovered that there were solid-state ones being built now that don't turn. The motor-generator sets have motors in them and generators and carbon brushes and they're a

---

[*] Vice Admiral William A. Owens, USN, served as Deputy Chief of Naval Operations for Resources, Warfare Requirements, and Assessments from 1991 to 1993.
[†] Rear Admiral David R. Oliver Jr., USN, Director, Programming Division, N80, OpNav staff.
[‡] AC/DC – alternating current and direct current.

maintenance nightmare. This thing, just electricity comes in one end of one kind and goes out the other end. You can make it whatever you want. So that was good.

Flat-screen displays in the maneuvering room. No more gauges and dials. Flat screens.

A DC electric plant, was AC before that. Now we have big turbo-generators that produce DC, it gets rectified there and sent around.

Magnetic bearings on the turbo-generators, where the bearings are levitated in the turbine generator by magnetism, so you do away with a lube oil system and all of that.

Paul Stillwell: And friction, obviously.

Admiral DeMars: Yes. And noise.

A life-of-the-ship reactor core, 30-year reactor core. On and on and on.

This was a revolutionary submarine, really. There were only two things that I was really concerned about, and I demanded that we go to sea, once again because we couldn't do prototypical testing. One was the evaporators. We were going to replace the evaporators with the reverse-osmosis units, which were in commercial use throughout the world, to make pure water. So we put the half a unit on a 688 class, and it worked fine. Worked beautifully, no problem.

The other thing I was worried about was the magnetic bearings. So we found a Trident that was undergoing its one-month refit in Kings Bay before it went out on patrol again.* I talked SP, Special Projects, into letting us put magnetic bearings on one turbo-generator of the two. Would take them to sea and find the problems. So we put it on, put all the controllers on, this and that, and we lit it off. And when they lit off the main engines, all the rumbling and this and that, bam, it crashed. So in came the technicians again, and they fixed that. Meanwhile, this thing was supposed to be going off on patrol, so I was under intense pressure now. "What the hell's DeMars doing?" blah-blah-blah blah-blah-blah? So we went to sea. When it dove it was rocking and rolling, crashed again. Back into port. Got that fixed. Went out about, like six weeks late. But had you

---

* Since 1979 Kings Bay, Georgia, has been the East Coast base for nuclear-powered ballistic missile submarines.

done all that in new construction, the bill would have been astronomical, astronomical. So it was the right thing to do, but I had to take a lot of heat for that.

So those were the only two things that I thought that really merited a very prototypical test at sea. The rest of it worked fine. There were some bugs as we went ahead.

The front end of the ship did the same thing. Under my encouragement we went away from periscopes to electronic periscopes. You just come down, you've got a big screen there that, you just stick it up, boom, bring it down, see whatever you want. Lot of stuff like that.

In order to get the thing inculcated and moving properly, I told Electric Boat, "I'm very serious about costs, so I want you to design a submarine with cost in mind. So you have to know why it costs to build a submarine. What are the costs of building a submarine?"

They said, "Oh, yeah. We can do that." EB always says that.

So I said, "Okay, I want you to have three or four people from the waterfront that actually build the submarine on your design team."

They looked at me and said, "These guys up here, in the headquarters?"

I said, "Yes." And so, well, I've got a couple of examples that really proved that out.

There is a shield tank that holds the water around the reactor vessel, and one of these waterfront guys said, "Why does it have to be seven-eighths of an inch?"

And a designer said, "Well, we've engineered the amount of water and the pressure, and this and that; why do you ask?"

He said, "Well, we buy one-inch blade plate steel, and we grind an eighth of an inch off. That costs money."

They said, "Oh, I think we can use one-inch."

Another guy said, "We put in a pipe support for all the pipes, for lube oil, condensate, feed, every three feet, irrespective of what it's carrying, how big the pipe is. It's a sound fitting on it; it goes over to the bulkhead, and it's welded into the bulkhead, a lot of touch labor. What if you engineered that and only put in what you needed?" We cut pipe hangars by 60%--tremendous cost saving there.

So that went on and on and on. Then they began to believe that this was really something, they had to listen to these guys. And other things were: "Why do I have to lay on my back and weld this thing, when at Quonset Point it's sitting there and you can tilt it any way you want?"* So on and on and on.

Paul Stillwell: This is modular construction.

Admiral DeMars: Yes, there was all modular construction.

And then we went to the government shipyards that overhaul and maintain submarines and did the same thing: "How do you spend your money overhauling?" Got a lot of good ideas from that that could factor back into the design. So we worked hard. That's why today the cost of these things is still holding up.

As Naval Reactors, one of the fun things was initial sea trials, and I did about 45 of those while I was there for the eight years. It was the point where we were initial sea-trialing all the submarines and carriers that had been started before the Cold War ended, so we had a lot of them. It's the first time the ship goes to sea. For submarines it's the first time it submerges. The first time the ship goes to full power. Many of the sailors on board had never been to sea. So it's a very interesting process. They do dock trials in port, which means they run all the equipment with shipyard people aboard. Then they do what's called a fast cruise, where you kick all the shipyard people off and for two days you run through the routine of starting up the reactor, starting up the forward end, as if you're getting under way, and you run the whole ship for two days.

Paul Stillwell: The ship is fast to the pier.

Admiral DeMars: Fast to the pier, fast cruise. And the CO called me once a day and told me what was going on, what was working and wasn't working. And if it was absolutely necessary to allow some shipyard worker to go down and adjust a widget that was not working he would do that, but that it was very rare.

---

* Sub-assemblies for the Electric Boat submarines are built at Quonset Point, Rhode Island.

Paul Stillwell: Any particularly memorable trials?

Admiral DeMars: Well, there are some problems, but usually it all went well. One Trident—I think it was the *Maryland*, but I can't remember—we were coming out of Groton, Connecticut, and we got out just beyond Block Island and turned south into the heavy swells.* The CO hadn't been careful enough in running the low-pressure blower to keep the water out of the ballast tanks, and they slowly filled up in heavy seas and that. So we were rocking and rolling down there; all of a sudden we took a big deep down angle and up angle, and water started coming down, almost solid, down the bridge hatch right into the control room, down into the torpedo room [chuckle].

So they went to shut the lower hatch. You have a ring that you keep on the hatches when you're in port. It's metal and it has plastisol on it. It's to keep from nicking up the seating surface. That had been left on, and shouldn't be left on when you get under way, so you couldn't shut the hatch. They finally got that shut, they pushed it up, some brave sailor got up there, took that off with water rushing down, they shut that. They had shut the upper hatch by then on the bridge, so we had now guys on the bridge that we couldn't talk to because everything was flooded out. So we started draining down the upper and lower hatch, filling up the torpedo room with water and pumping that overboard. We finally got it all done and got it out. But the chairman of General Dynamics—I can't remember his name right now, a very, very decent guy—he never came on another sea trial. [Laughter] He would always send the president of EB; he was very frightened.

Paul Stillwell: I bet that was not a good day for the skipper, either.

Admiral DeMars: No, no. We had a few words about, "Why is that thing still on, and isn't it on your check-off list?" and on and on and on, with them and with the shipyard also.

---

* The nuclear-powered ballistic missile submarine *Maryland* (SSBN-738) was launched 10 August 1991 at the General Dynamics shipyard in Groton, Connecticut. She was commissioned 13 June 1992.

One from Newport News, we got under way, and the evaporators that make water wouldn't work. It was a steam process in those days. The ship couldn't make it work. The shipyard had special people aboard for initial sea trials, a certain number, and they couldn't make it work. One of my engineers, who was an electrical engineer, said, "Let me take a go at this; give me the tech manual." Sat down with the tech manual, sat down in front of the thing, went through the whole thing. Three hours later we were making water. I had a very smart staff.

But when we got back in, coming alongside and I first went over the brow, and there was the president of the shipyard. The president of the shipyard didn't ride on that one, I don't know why; the ops guy did, which was fine. The president was standing on the end of the pier because he had been off doing something else. I lit into him when I got to the end of the pier: "Goddamn it, you're supposed to have people out there that know how to operate this thing. Don't you know how to operate it? Did you build it right?" Boom boom-boom-boom-boom-boom. Then I just turned away, got in my car, and left. I just tore his hide off [chuckle]. But that's what the initial sea trials were for. So the shipyard knew, God, if something goes bad out there, the head of the shipyard's going to get really tanned by the head of Naval Reactors, and he will tan us for that. So that's one of the side effects, why Rickover started riding and all of that, to focus everything on a very, very chancy operation if everything isn't done right.

One of the things I felt very proud about was figuring out the angle problem. On all submarines, including mine, at the end of the four-hour full power run you do a back emergency drill. As you start getting slower and slower in speed, the ship takes a very large angle. Well, you're sort of just hanging there. You're going like half a knot, so it's not dangerous. But Rickover used to kind of go hermantile. Yahyahyahwhy, etc., etc. So when I did my first sea trials I'd forgotten about it, but it happened again. And so I called up the David Taylor Model Basin.* I said, "I'd like to have one or two guys at the next ride on initial sea trials and I'd like instrumentation on speed, angle, and course. We're going to figure out why this happens."

---

* The David Taylor Model Basin at Carderock, Maryland, has a large towing tank in which models of ships' hulls are subjected to various conditions to determine how they will react.

So they came, and it took about three sea trials, but it turned out there's something called rotating torque, that the propeller when it's rotating puts a torque on the ship. Well, we all know that because your rudder's offset a little bit and that. But as you slow down, you still have that on there. And so as you're going slower and slower through the water, which there's no effect from the rudder and that, it starts to take over and it will slew the ship and it will also cant it up or down, depending upon where it kicks in. That's what was causing it. So I felt very proud that Rickover put up with this goddamn stuff for 30 years, and I had solved it in about a year [chuckle]. It was one of my prouder moments.

The CVNs, the carriers, were very interesting but very tiring. I mean, to go from the bridge down to the bottom of the engine room is like a 14-story building. The elevators never worked on those things. But they were very interesting because there was a lot going on.

One of the things I learned from them later played into the design of the *Virginia* class. I went down in the space where the shipyard monitors the engineering plant for the sea trials, trying to figure out what was going on. On a carrier they have two reactors, two maneuvering rooms, one control room, and I mean everything is, ahh, very confusing. In there they had built a flat-screen-panel system that told you what was going on with feed, condensate, unloader operation, steam flow, and everything. You could look at it, and I said, "Explain this to me." Fifteen minutes later I understood what was going on, so I said: "Well, why don't we design instrumentation for that?"

"Admiral, that's your job, not ours." [Laughter]

So when we started the design of the *Virginia* class, I said, "I want us to go do something like that." We did, and it works wonderfully.

I invented one thing—well, I invented a lot of things at Naval Reactors, but one of them was what I called "cumbersome work procedures." I said we do a lot of stuff that's hard, too hard or unnecessary in our business; I would like to start a program, called "cumbersome work procedures." Now, I said, "I never want to see that in capitals, I don't want to see any badges, no balloons, but I want you to get the word out to my organization—the shipyards, the land-based reactor sites, and the labs—and every time I visit I want a briefing on what they've figured out on something."

And it was very remarkable. We went to one land-based reactor, and this sailor showed me how it used to be done. All the log readings he had to take were by equipment, irrespective of the three levels in the engine room. You know, first of all you took the lube oil system, and there were three things on this level, and that level, and that level. So you either had to be careful as you went down or you had to go up and down. He went and took all of those and mapped them out so that as you walked along the upper level of the engine room you could take all the right readings; walk down to the middle level. Very simple and straightforward but a lot of work. I lauded him: That's great. Stuff like that. It was pretty remarkable what people came up with. And I also let them hit us. We had procedures out that didn't make sense, didn't really work.

I remember one of the things that I convinced the shipyards that they were doing wrong. We have a sample sink, where you draw a primary sample from the reactor plant. And it's radioactive, so you have to be careful. You wear a facemask, and some little valves in there. To replace one of those valves if it's leaking at sea, the engineering laboratory technician, who's a specially trained machinist's mate, goes, draws the valve, puts on some rubber gloves, shuts some valves, goes in, wrenches off this valve, takes it off, puts the new valve in, hooks it up, opens up, leak tests it, it's all fine. Boom, that's done. It takes maybe an hour. I said, "I'd like you to tell me how long it takes in the shipyard to replace that valve, when you have to write a work procedure, you have to do this, you have to go draw the spare, you have to boom-boom-boom, retest it, etc., etc., etc." It took three days. There was something fundamentally wrong here. So we tried to spread that out to how do you streamline processes for jobs that aren't that critical, and get on with it. So that worked out well, and I was very proud.

And then Hank Chiles, who was SubLant, picked up that idea, and he pushed it throughout the submarine force.[*] So whenever I'd visit a submarine, they'd be very proud to show me what they were doing different. And Hank did a very fine job of doing that and doing it very, very well too.

---

[*] Vice Admiral Henry B. Chiles, USN, served as Commander Submarine Force Atlantic Fleet, 1990-93.

During the time I was there we had the unfortunate death of Mike Boorda.[*] He was CNO, suicide, very tragic. I think I was his closest friend in the flag ranks. In fact, Gray Armistead had sort of adopted me and him. We used to go out to Gray's cattle ranch up in Sperryville and spend the night with him and help him herd cattle, and on and on and on. So Mike was a very good friend of mine.

Paul Stillwell: How would you explain that closeness?

Admiral DeMars: Well, I don't think he was accepted by the surface Navy because he was a mustang.[†] I don't know. He'd been an enlisted man, a chief I think, and then he must have gone to college.[‡] But he was not a typical surface Navy guy, and nobody was warm and fuzzy with him. He was from Illinois, as I was from Illinois. My dad was a mailman; his dad ran a post office down in a small town in central Illinois. So we just sort of hit it off together. But it was largely through Gray Armistead that we got to know each other. And I really liked the guy. I thought he was trying to do the best thing he could. He was astute, and on and on and on. But I think he was kind of an outlier in the surface Navy.

Then he got into that totally unnecessary dustup on whether one of his ribbons from Vietnam merited a "V" on it or not for being in combat. It was all bullshit, but he tried to take it too personally. I used to go over and see him. But, anyway, that was bad.

We had a meeting with the Secretary of the Navy. All the three- and four-stars came to town and we had a meeting with the Secretary of the Navy.[§] Before the SecNav came in and his senior staff, I sort of either got elected or volunteered to be the spokesman. I said, "Look, I may be the only one here that doesn't want to be CNO."

---

[*] Admiral Jeremy M. Boorda, USN, committed suicide on 16 May 1996 while serving as Chief of Naval Operations. Among the several reasons cited as possible causes was that he was about to be interviewed by news media representatives about whether he was entitled to combat devices on his service ribbons received during the Vietnam War. See Nick Kotz, "What Really Happened to Admiral Boorda," *Washingtonian*, December 1996.

[†] "Mustang" is Navy slang for a former enlisted man who has risen through the ranks to become an officer.

[‡] Boorda was commissioned in 1962. He earned a bachelor of arts degree from the University of Rhode Island in 1971.

[§] John H. Dalton III served as Secretary of the Navy from 22 July 1993 to 16 November 1998.

Paul Stillwell: This is after he killed himself.

Admiral DeMars: After he'd killed himself and we had the funeral, and the Secretary of the Navy said we should sit down with all the flags, which was a very nice thing, and so did the Secretary of Defense. So I said, "I'll be the spokesman. Anybody else want to be the spokesman?" Nobody wanted to be because there were several people there that wanted to be CNO [chuckle], several that didn't care, and me, who didn't want to. And so we had a good meeting. We talked a little bit and said, "You know, maybe better communications would have helped, and on and on." It was a nice meeting simply because it was thoughtful of them to want to do it. Then the Secretary of Defense came in, sat down, we sort of went through the same thing with him.* But the whole thing was very tragic and totally unnecessary.

Paul Stillwell: Well, and beyond the issue of the "V"s on the ribbons, he was getting beat up in print. There was an anonymous letter in *Navy Times* that was really disrespectful and said, essentially to Admiral Boorda, "You should go for the good of your Navy."

Admiral DeMars: Yes. No, the whole thing was terrible. He was a more sensitive guy than most people realized, than I certainly realized.

Paul Stillwell: What was the upshot of the meeting?

Admiral DeMars: Nothing. Nothing. It was just a feel-good meeting. And I think, because of my personality, we had a good discussion with the Secretary of the Navy and his staff. When the Secretary of Defense came down, I said, "Oh, we've really had a great meeting with the Secretary of the Navy and his staff, and I think we've talked over a few things. There's really nothing we think you can do for us." Because I didn't like OSD. I never liked OSD. I thought they were an unnecessary, overly large appendage. I said it in a very nice, polite way, but that was: "Thank you very much for coming; we

---

* William J. Perry served as Secretary of Defense from 3 February 1994 to 23 January 1997.

know that this is a very nice thing you're doing, but we don't need anything." And he understood. A decent guy.

Paul Stillwell: What was Dalton's role in all this? He was SecNav.

Admiral DeMars: Just sort of watching everything, wondering what he would do. He was very supportive, though.

Paul Stillwell: Were you involved in all in the process by which Admiral Johnson got the job?[*]

Admiral DeMars: No, not at all. Not at all.

The interview process in Naval Reactors—I probably did about 5,000-plus interviews in eight years. And actually it was, once again, fun and a relaxation from what you normally had to do in that job. Here you had some of the smartest young people in this country coming in, wanting to be in your organization. And so I thought it was a significant thing, once again, Rickover started. Because where else do you go in the Navy where you come in and talk to the top guy? And so it forms a sort of bonding experience right from the beginning, and makes you appreciate and understand that the guy at the top really is interested in everything.

The things weren't very long. You know, ten minutes would be a long interview. And at least I tried to ask questions that would sort of probe how the person thought. "How'd you pick your major? Have you ever had a job in life? Are the people who teach you professors or teaching assistants? And if they're teaching assistants, do your parents know they're paying for that?" You know, questions like that. Or: "You're from Susquehanna; how did your town get its name?" That always threw people. That always threw people. [Laughter] You just want to see how they think. Well, bubbubbubbub.

The process was that they'd get two interviews by people on my staff talking about their major, and three if they were going to *come* on my staff. Then I'd get the

---

[*] Admiral Jay L. Johnson, USN, was acting Chief of Naval Operations from May to August 1996 and Chief of Naval Operations from August 1996 to July 2000.

transcript of their college grades and a write-up of those interviews, and I'd look at that, and I would either write yes or no on it. I never told them I was going to take them or not; I thought let somebody else handle that angst.

Also, I was maybe a little more liberal with certain people that I thought had potential because they were hard workers. Like me. And I would put a "T" on it with a circle: "Track." That meant, "I'm taking this person, but I want to know how he does at Nuclear Power School and the land-based reactor site." Usually I batted like 98%; they all made it through. We would pick about 85% of the people who came.

Paul Stillwell: Well, the Rickover interviews were legendary, including the humiliations. Did you include some of the humiliation in it?

Admiral DeMars: No, no. I never thought so, but in the individual's mind, probably it was. He thought the questions were humiliating because he didn't know the answers. But no, I didn't believe in that.

Paul Stillwell: No sitting in the little room?

Admiral DeMars: No, no. No sitting in the little room, no smoking cigars and writing reports on it, on and on. I thought that was childish. And I think McKee did also; he didn't do that.

Paul Stillwell: Was there any advantage in the candidate having come from the Naval Academy?

Admiral DeMars: No, absolutely not. Absolutely not. In fact [chuckle], I always felt that probably the ones that weren't from the Naval Academy had maybe a better total technical education in their narrow field.

The funniest part, to end it up, the last interview I gave was the last week I was there and the last group. And the last guy, I got in the pieces of paper and it was a physics major from Cal Poly, kind of a foreign name. All straight A's. I thought, "God, why am I even worrying about this?" When the guy came in, he was wearing a turban. There was nothing about that in the report from my staff who interviewed him. I thought, "My goddamn staff, they're doing this on purpose." So we had a straightforward interview. I asked him the usual questions and that. And then at the end I said, "Well, you know, that turban, is that cultural or religious? If I accept you and you come in the Navy, you can't wear that."

The young man said, "Admiral, if you accept me, it goes off tomorrow." [Laughter] I thought, "This guy is going to do well."

Paul Stillwell: Are there any other especially memorable ones?

Admiral DeMars: No, they all sort of meld together. That was the most memorable one. None even came close to that. Nobody got up and stormed out, and nobody pounded on the desk. Most of them were very nervous, as you can imagine. And they wanted it badly.

Paul Stillwell: Well, the ones that you had the "T" on for tracking, did you then get reports on what they did?

Admiral DeMars: Yes. At the end of their training for nuclear power—Nuclear Power School and the land-based reactor—I would get a report on how they had stood. I was just interested, did they get through or not? Just about all of them made it through.

Paul Stillwell: Did you have a role in picking COs for individual ships?

Admiral DeMars: No. I left that to the Bureau of Personnel. COs, XOs, engineers. The interviews that were very interesting were the candidates for command of a carrier, because they were all commanders and had spent a lot of time at sea, and wanted to do it.

Usually pretty good guys. I was surprised. The sine qua non for naval aviation is still command of a carrier. You know, Lehman tried to invent this air group command.*

Paul Stillwell: Super CAG.

Admiral DeMars: Super CAG, and that never went anywhere. They wanted to do it, they were all very smart. Many of them were test pilots. And so they had good backgrounds. I didn't change Nuclear Power School, but I changed the prototype around a little bit, because these guys know how to operate things, to get them through there quicker. But those were very interesting. They were good. Usually took most of them; only turned down one or two.

Paul Stillwell: I think Jay Johnson was a Super CAG who made it as a flag officer.

Admiral DeMars: Yes, a number of them make it. Joe Prueher, same way.† But they all are very sensitive when you talk about that, rightly so. "Well, I didn't have a carrier."

My outer office—just once again how Naval Reactors is—all I had were a secretary and two sailors. I would change those sailors out every two or three years. I'd ask Atlantic Fleet and Pacific Fleet submarine force: "Send me your best guy." And I always had one yeoman and one nuc—electrician, machinist's mate. And I'd have my secretary interview them and then tell me whom she recommend. And I'd interview each one of them because they came all the way from the fleet. I would have my secretary tell me what she thought, and then I'd pick that guy. They did great. They wore civilian clothes. Once one of them came in and said, "Admiral, I probably don't have to tell you this, but as long as you don't tell other people we're sailors we can get a lot done for

---

* John F. Lehman, Jr., served as Secretary of the Navy from 5 February 1981 to 10 April 1987. Until 1983 the air wing commander was a department head under the carrier's commanding officer. In 1983 Lehman changed that by creating the post of "Super CAG," which would have equal status with the ship's commanding officer.

† Admiral Joseph W. Prueher, USN, served as Commander in Chief Pacific from 31 January 1996 to 20 February 1999. He was later U.S. ambassador to the People's Republic of China from 1999 to 2001.

you." [Laughter] "We wear civilian clothes, and they think we're GS-15s or something."*

Paul Stillwell: Did you have senior civilians who did the pre-interviews with the candidates for nuclear power?

Admiral DeMars: Yes, but just people on my staff. Senior people that had been on my staff for quite a while would interview them. Either, if they're a physics major, some guy that had majored close to physics or electrical engineering, mechanical engineering, so on and so forth. Yes. And they would ask pointed questions in their discipline and write up whether this person's grades were merited by what he seemed to know or not know.

Paul Stillwell: Did you ever get any liberal arts candidates?

Admiral DeMars: Oh, yes. Once we had an English major from the Naval Academy stand first at Nuclear Power School. I think the Naval Academy gives you a good education; I really do. The thing you have to keep you eye on there is, as you know, the liberal arts guys have to take some engineering and the engineers have to take some liberal arts. You've got to be careful they don't dumb down the engineering for the liberal arts guys, that they get good professors that are very demanding. That's the only thing I think we have to keep an eye on. But, hell, I ran the largest nuclear power program in the world with a bachelor of science from the Naval Academy. I never went to PG school. I didn't want to go to PG school. So it's a good education.

In my relations with the Navy, I would go over and meet with the SecNav and the CNO monthly, separately. And I'd write out a whole bunch of things I wanted to discuss. We'd sit at a table and talk. No briefings. That kept them up with what I was doing, what my concerns were, and this and that. That worked very well. They liked it; I liked it. In fact, with the Secretary of the Navy the Under would always come in and sit there and listen.

---

* GS, for government service, designates a pay grade level within the U.S. Civil Service.

Paul Stillwell: Was Admiral Boorda as supportive as Admiral Kelso was?

Admiral DeMars: Yes, oh yes. Very, very much so.

Paul Stillwell: Well, and I would think there'd be some value in just having you autonomous, because that's a going concern doing well.

Admiral DeMars: Yes, yes. Absolutely. And they'd ask me other things. Well, what about this, and bumbumbumbumbum.

Relations with DoE: With Watkins they were very good, with O'Leary, as I said, not very good. In fact, when I retired they had a nice ceremony for me in the SecNav's office when I went over there. SubLant gave me a golf driver, and SubPac gave me a wedge. And Steve Honigman, who was the general counsel, was there.* I said, "Well, I really probably shouldn't accept these, but with you here, Steve, I guess it's okay." [Laughter] We got a big laugh out of that. It was very pleasant. I got a medal from them. I didn't want a parade or a ceremony when I retired. I think those are overdone. People say things they may not even believe, and a lot of people hear them believing—"Was I that good?" So I didn't want to do that. I'd had enough time in the Navy. I was ready to leave. So they did a very nice thing.

But, interestingly enough, DoE didn't do anything, except Grumbly, who was the Under Secretary of Energy, came over to the SecNav event. I got along very well with him, and he gave me a very nice plaque, said very nice stuff on it. It was signed by him, not Hazel O'Leary. [Chuckle]

Paul Stillwell: Well, how was it ascertained that this was the time to terminate your job?

Admiral DeMars: Eight years. It's an eight-year tour by federal statute. When Rickover retired they big-dealed through—and a lot of people take credit for that, but it was largely Jim Watkins, I think—put through a bunch of rules in a presidential directive that Reagan

---

* Steven S. Honigman, a civilian, served as general counsel of the Navy from 1993 to 1998.

signed.* It said, okay, here, it should be eight years, he should have control of the assignment of COs and engineers, he had two hats—Department of Energy, Department of Defense—and all that. And then a year later it was passed into federal law. So it's an eight-year tour.

Paul Stillwell: Well, it was six for Admiral McKee.

Admiral DeMars: Well, he left early. That was because of me. I don't think I'd have stayed and done four and a half years as OP-02. That's why they were keeping me around, to be his relief.

So we had a nice office affair, and a very nice affair in my office where all my staff was there and my family and all of us and that, and we had a big chili cookout. So it was a fun thing. I made a few nice remarks, and they lampooned me a little bit.

But one of the things that was the nicest—it was through Tim Foster's interdiction—both houses of Congress passed a proclamation.

Paul Stillwell: I read them.

Admiral DeMars: Yes. For me that means more than almost anything else. I mean, it takes a lot of work to do that, and maybe I'd made a few enemies in Congress but not enough to block that. So I thought it was very nice.

As I said, my relief changed things. He got an executive assistant and an aide, no open-door policy, closer to the CNO. Staff didn't like the changes, but that's life.

After I left I spent two weeks golfing. Developed golf elbow, so I went out and bought a computer and started my new life.

Paul Stillwell: Well, before we get to your new life, if you've got the patience, I have some more questions.

Admiral DeMars: Absolutely. Absolutely.

---

* Ronald W. Reagan served as President of the United States from 20 January 1981 to 20 January 1989.

Paul Stillwell: There were a couple of nuclear submarine movies that came out in that era: *Hunt for Red October* and *Crimson Tide*.* I wondered what your reaction was to those.

Admiral DeMars: I thought *Hunt for Red October* was superb. *Crimson Tide* I didn't like as much because that's not the way submarines work.

Paul Stillwell: Artificial conflict.

Admiral DeMars: Yes, artificial conflict. But *Hunt for Red October* I thought was good. It was good for the submarine force. It was a little over-dramatized, but I thought that was good. *Crimson Tide* I didn't like as much. My favorite is still *Run Silent, Run Deep*.†

Paul Stillwell: Which Ned Beach hated.

Admiral DeMars: Right. [Laughter] He made a lot of money off of it.

Paul Stillwell: What was your relationship with Admiral Shellman when he was at EB?‡

Admiral DeMars: Oh, very close, because they had responsibility for the West Milton land-based reactor site; they did all the maintenance up there and that. And so a couple of times we had problems up there and we'd have a big meeting up there and he'd come up and we'd sit across the table. And I remember once him saying, "Look, you guys,

---

* *The Hunt for Red October*, a movie released in 1990, starred Sean Connery as the commanding officer of a Soviet submarine crew that attempted to defect to the West. The film also includes scenes on board a U.S. submarine. *Crimson Tide*, released in 1995, starred Gene Hackman as commanding officer of a U.S. ballistic missile submarine and Denzel Washington as exec. The two had a confrontation over the skipper's desire to fire missiles without confirmation of the legitimacy of the order.
† Commander Edward Latimer "Ned" Beach Jr., USN, wrote a number of books, most notably the World War II submarine novel *Run Silent, Run Deep*, published in 1955. It became the basis for the 1958 movie of the same name, which starred Clark Gable and Burt Lancaster.
‡ Rear Admiral Curtis B. Shellman Jr., USN (Ret.).

Admiral DeMars is being very fair with us on this. We've got to get working on this and fix it." So it was that kind of a guy. He and I were close anyway.

Paul Stillwell: Well, you'd been shipmates.

Admiral DeMars: Yes, we'd been shipmates. Twice. Both on *Sturgeon* and in Squadron Ten. So I really liked the guy. Unfortunately, he died of a heart attack at EB walking up between two of those big buildings that are on the way from the waterfront. Otherwise he'd have been president of EB. He was just very good.

Paul Stillwell: What do you remember about the decommissionings of the *Sturgeon* and the *Cavalla*?*

Admiral DeMars: I gave great speeches. Just superb speeches. [Chuckle] The *Sturgeon* was good because Bo Bohannan was there and a lot of the early guys were there. And Bohannan was much more important to the sailors than me because he had been the CO and a real swashbuckler. The *Cavalla* was out in Hawaii. Mike Barr, who remember I told you earlier was I thought the smartest guy on *Snook* as a young jaygee. In a wardroom with a lot of kind of dim bulbs he was just brilliant; he was SubPac at the time.† We had a good time out there. But I didn't choke up or anything. I'm not that sort of person. I don't know what I am, but I like to work and I like to do new things. Other things and that, that's fine. But both of them were very nice. It was very nice of them to ask me, and I enjoyed it.

Paul Stillwell: When you were discussing OP-02, you touched briefly on your fellow barons. They were Admiral Martin and Admiral Dunn in aviation, and Admiral Metcalf

---

* USS *Sturgeon* (SSN-637) was decommissioned 1 August 1994. USS *Cavalla* (SSN-684) was decommissioned 30 March 1998.
† Rear Admiral Jon Michael Barr, USN, Commanded Submarine Force Pacific Fleet from July 1993 to February 1996.

and Admiral Nyquist in the surface.* What do you recall about working with them?

Admiral DeMars: Right. All of them were good friends and are good friends to this day. We got along well together. For another month, Dunn is now the president of the Naval Historical Foundation and I'm the chairman, so we're even closer now.† And he's finally, I think, forgiven me for stealing $30 million from him for the SubACS. But I got along well with all of them. Probably the closest with Dunn and Nyquist. Metcalf was a little more distant. But we all got along well together. We all really thought we were the most important ones [chuckle] in the Pentagon and doing the most important stuff for the Navy, and we tried to help each other out as much as we could. It's a good relationship.

Paul Stillwell: When you were OP-02, what do you recall about your relationship with the submarine type commanders?

Admiral DeMars: Very close. We knew our place, and they knew their place. It's a full-time job running the submarine force. I mean, you've got nuclear reactors, you've got nuclear weapons, you got deep submergence, it's a big deal, and so we tried to do all the Washington stuff for them and support them as much as possible. We always had good people in those jobs. I had no complaints about any of them. Very good people.

Paul Stillwell: Any more to say on deep submergence?

Admiral DeMars: No, only that one of the branches in OP-02 was deep submergence, and Dwaine Griffith was head of that when I was 02B.‡ Dwaine and I had gone to Rickover's school together, and he was brilliant. Dwaine was brilliant, University of

---

* Vice Admiral Edward H. Martin, USN, served as Deputy Chief of Naval Operations (Air Warfare) from 25 February 1985 to 14 January 1987. Vice Admiral Robert F. Dunn, USN, served as Deputy Chief of Naval Operations (Air Warfare) from 15 January 1987 to 25 May 1989. The title changed from Deputy to Chief to Assistant Chief on 1 October 1987. His oral history is in the Naval Institute collection.
Vice Admiral Joseph Metcalf III, USN, served as Deputy Chief of Naval Operations (Surface Warfare) from September 1984 to December 1987. Vice Admiral John W. Nyquist, USN, served as Assistant Chief of Naval Operations (Surface Warfare) from December 1987 to January 1991.
† In June 2012, Rear Admiral John Mitchell, USN (Ret.), replaced Vice Admiral Dunn as president of the Naval Historical Foundation.
‡ Captain Dwaine O. Griffith, USN.

Idaho graduate. And so he ran good stuff, but I didn't have to worry about that. He was on top of that all the time.

Paul Stillwell: When Admiral Rickover was running NR he had all sorts of hassles with the shipyards, particularly EB and Takis Veliotis.[*] Was there any lingering animosity by the time you got the job?

Admiral DeMars: No, I don't think so. Veliotis, of course, had fled to Greece [chuckle]. When you met him and shook hands with him you always wanted to check if you still had your watch and ring. [Laughter] He really was a scoundrel.

I never had any trouble—the two shipyards were totally different. If you told EB you wanted something done, they'd say, "Oh, yes, sir. Yes, sir," and you'd get a bill the next day. If you told Newport News, they'd start arguing with you about why exactly what you wanted done wasn't what you wanted done. That's why the NR staff loved EB more than Newport News. After I'd been there a couple years and, as I said, I began to figure out the job, I liked the Newport News approach better. I think you *should* be challenged, and they knew more about the shipyards than we did, though we pretended we knew more than they did. And so they were both different, they're both good yards.

I wish the government hadn't missed that opportunity to put them together way back when. That would have been a very powerful yard. Would put all the nuclear under one thing and would have been a lot better. But they both do well now. They share the *Virginia*-class submarine program, which is good for the country. We'll see where all that goes as the next round of budgets takes place here. But no, there was no lingering animosity.

Paul Stillwell: What do you recall of your relations with InSurv and OpTEvFor?[†]

---

[*] Panagiotis Takis Veliotis was born and educated in Greece. He was with Davie Shipbuilding in Quebec, Canada, from 1953 to 1972. From 1973 to 1977 he was general manager of the General Dynamics shipbuilding yard in Quincy, Massachusetts, then was general manager of the Electric Boat Division of General Dynamics from 1977 to 1982. He was involved in taking kickbacks and left the United States.
[†] InSurv – the Board of Inspection and Survey. OpTEvFor – Operational Test and Evaluation Force.

Admiral DeMars: Nothing at all. They just didn't fall within my purview or concern. I thought they both had their missions to do. We didn't intersect. We've never had any controversy, either when I was in OP-02 or in NR. NR, not at all, and OP-02, we just read the reports and got on with it.

Paul Stillwell: Several of the nuclear cruisers went away during your time in NR, and I'm guessing that was mostly because they didn't have Aegis.*

Admiral DeMars: Well, all of them went away. I had done several initial sea trials in them after refueling, and I used to ride them and try and support that part of the Navy. The surface Navy in general didn't like nuclear power. They didn't appreciate the endurance and the speed. I had a little trepidation about nuclear-powered surface ships because I thought they were very vulnerable. And if you looked at the *Cole* accident in Yemen, if that had been nuclear powered that would have been a big deal.† So I had mixed thoughts when we decommissioned them.

Paul Stillwell: What was the procedure for handling reactors when ships were decommissioned?

Admiral DeMars: Well, it's been worked out to a fare-thee-well. The ships are normally stripped down of other stuff on it and towed into Puget Sound Naval Shipyard. They're defueled, generally, at a different shipyard if they've got that job. They're defueled at Norfolk or Hawaii, or at Puget Sound. You get the fuel out. And then you cut out the reactor compartment, which has the radioactive components still in it. You seal up both ends. You take out all the lead and you take out all the PCBs, hazardous material, seal up both ends, and then it's barged from Puget Sound out into the Pacific Ocean, up the

---

* The Aegis air defense system, which involves the use of computers and phased-array radars, is installed in the cruisers of the *Ticonderoga* (CG-47) class and destroyers of the *Arleigh Burke* (DDG-51) class.
† On 12 October 2000 the destroyer *Cole* (DDG-67) was in the port of Aden, Yemen, for a refueling stop when a small boat laden with explosives was detonated beside the ship. The explosion blew a hole in the side of the ship, killing 17 sailors and injuring 39. The ship subsequently returned to the United States and was repaired. She returned to service in April 2002.

Columbia River, to the Hanford reservation.* And then it's put on a crawler truck and taken to this big shallow trench about 100 feet deep, where they're stacked up there on cement pylons. There must be over a 100 there now. It's a very nice process. It's the nicest thing at Hanford, which most things are contaminated and look bad.

My staff told me, "Okay, Admiral, when we get this filled at a certain event the plan is to fill in the trench and cover everything up.

I said, "Why? It's harder to see it. This way you go down, you can look at it. If something looks like it's rusting you can fix that. If the concrete is spalling on one of the foundations you can fix that. And besides, we ought to be proud of it." So we didn't. We're not going to cover that over; we're just going to leave it out there in the rain. That doesn't hurt it.

So they're very well taken care of. As for the rest of the submarine, there's a lot of things in there that are scrapped and sold to other people: diesel engines, some nonnuclear pumps and valves, watertight doors. There were dams buying them for a while [chuckle], to be able to use in dams. And all the steel is resold. You may have shaved with a nuclear submarine this morning. [Laughter] And so it's a good recycling program. It's very well received.

Paul Stillwell: I remember once being out at Bremerton 20 years ago and there were a bunch of former boomers that had the missile compartments taken out, and then the front and back welded back together. And I heard that was so the Soviets could use their satellites and see they were in fact demilitarized.

Admiral DeMars: I don't remember that, but it's probably true. We did some crazy things for that arms control stuff.

Paul Stillwell: And once I saw the *Sam Rayburn*, just the bow and the stern used for training. She was down near the mouth of the Chesapeake Bay. What was her role?

---

* The Hanford Nuclear Reservation is on the Columbia River in the state of Washington.

Admiral DeMars: That's the moored training ship down in Charleston. We built two moored training ships, as we called them. We took Polaris submarines and we put extra equipment in there so you could run a reactor plant that wasn't for military purposes. Extra equipment, largely extra diesel generators and extra fill system in case you had to fill the reactor. Because we had shut down all the training reactors in Idaho during the time I was at Naval Reactors, so we had to have somewhere to train. So we built these moored training ships, and sailors and officers go there now in addition to going up to the two reactors in upstate New York.

Paul Stillwell: Maybe she was just being moved from one place to another.

Admiral DeMars: It could have been. Because I think we did—you're probably right—we did that conversion, I believe, at Norfolk Naval Shipyard, so she was probably being towed down to Charleston.

Paul Stillwell: What do you remember about your relations with the basing facilities—Bangor, Kings Bay, New London, etc.?

Admiral DeMars: Not much. The Navy did a pretty good job about doing that. I did weigh in on that when the Navy put up the Sub Base New London on the BRAC list.[*] That was during the reign of Clark, the CNO that hated submariners. He was CNO for five years, never had a three-star submariner on the OpNav staff during that period.[†] He was an unthoughtful person. He invented the LCS![‡] Anyway, he put Sub Base New London—it was just punishment—on the list. So I wrote a little, not even op-ed piece, a little article about three paragraphs long and got it on the front page of the *New London Day*. And I also sent it to the head of the BRAC committee. And it got taken off the BRAC list. [Laughter] Not because of me but just was a dumb thing to do.

---

[*] BRAC – base realignment and closure, a process for reducing the number of U.S. military bases.
[†] Admiral Vernon E. Clark, USN, served as Chief of Naval Operations from 21 July 2000 to 22 July 2005.
[‡] The Navy is testing different configurations for follow-on production of littoral combat ships, designed for warfare close to shore. The test ships are the USS *Freedom* (LCS-1), commissioned 8 November 2008, and the *Independence* (LCS-2), commissioned 16 January 2010. The latter has a trimaran hull.

Paul Stillwell: At the 50th anniversary of NR you described yourself as naturally obstinate. How did that manifest itself?

Admiral DeMars: Is that what I said? Well, I might have just been affecting that guise because that's the way that makes Naval Reactors work best, if the top guy [chuckle] is naturally obstinate. No, I think I'm more just—I question a lot of things. I always like to know what are we doing that, and why is—etc., etc., etc. So it's more of a questioning attitude than it is an obstinate attitude. I've only had two Secretaries of the Navy want to fire me, so I can't be that obstinate. [Laughter] Lehman was one, and the other one was Sean O'Keefe.

Paul Stillwell: What's the record? [Laughter]

In one of the speeches, you said you saved *NR-1* and the *Enterprise* from premature decommissioning.* What was involved in those?

Admiral DeMars: Well, I just thought that, for *NR-1*—now it *is* decommissioned, unfortunately, with no follow-on for it. One of my obstinate things, I think we spend too damned much money trying to go out into outer space and not enough trying to go down into inner space at the bottom of the ocean. We know more about from here to Mars than we do from the surface to the floor of the ocean. I thought losing *NR-1* was a bad thing, so I went out of my way to protect it. I rode on its initial sea trials after it got refueled and that was quite interesting.

The other one was *Enterprise*. I just didn't want to decommission carriers early because I thought we needed them. And *Enterprise* worked reasonably well. I remember once [chuckle] I went over to see Frank Kelso and he brought that up. We were refueling *Enterprise* at the time. He said, "Bruce, don't you think we should decommission *Enterprise*?"

NR-1, a nuclear-powered, deep-submergence research and ocean-engineering vehicle was launched 25 January 1969 by the Electric Boat Division and delivered to the Navy on 27 October 1969. She was 140 feet long, had a beam of 12 feet, and displaced 400 tons submerged. She was taken out of service in 2008. USS *Enterprise* (CVAN-65) was commissioned 25 November 1961 as the world's first nuclear-powered aircraft carrier. She was reclassified CVN-65 in 1975. She is the only ship of her class. She is due to begin inactivation in the autumn of 2012.

I said, "Well, Frank, I don't know if your staff's keeping you up to date, but we've already got half the reactors refueled, and we've got reactors for the other half, so we'd be wasting an awful lot of money." The Navy's going to start that process in about a year. Very expensive to decommission a ship with eight reactors on it.

Paul Stillwell: She's just now on her last deployment.

Admiral DeMars: Yes, and still doing well. A hell of a ship. Hard one to run, but a great ship.

Paul Stillwell: You had a note in some of the papers you showed me about Jay Johnson and the Navy Exchange inquiry.[*]

Admiral DeMars: Oh, yes. I didn't realize it was Jay Johnson at the time. I was Naval Reactors and, as I said, I didn't go out of my way to do other things. But I got a request from Steve Honigman, who was the Navy general counsel. He was kind of a close friend of mine, for some strange reason. He had been a JAG lieutenant and he was from New York City, and he was a good guy, a very smart guy. He came over one day and said they had had this minor dustup in Norfolk because the head of the Navy Exchange was giving out free Christmas trees to admirals, delivering them to the houses and setting them up. Somebody had done a little quick investigation of that down there, and would I take a look at that and advise the Secretary of the Navy what should be done? I said sure.

So he gave me this report, which was quite voluminous, a 20-, 30-page report. Somebody down there had investigated it. So I said, "Well, let me just get this out of the way." So two days later [chuckle] I made up a report, had it typed up, and sent it over to the Secretary of the Navy. I said, "I've read that, I think it's a very fine report of the incident, and here's what I think you ought to do. You ought to have non-judicial letters of reprimand issued to the CO of the Navy Exchange, and two or three people involved in

---

[*] Admiral Jay L. Johnson, USN, was acting Chief of Naval Operations from May to August 1996 and Chief of Naval Operations from August 1996 to July 2000.

it." A couple of them were admirals that had gotten the trees. But I don't think Johnson was one of them.

Then all of a sudden the Under Secretary of the Navy, Danzig, sent me a message or something that said cease and desist.* Well, everybody was upset that I had done this so quickly, and I didn't know why. I thought they wanted it done. So then I found out why. They were trying to keep a lid on things because Jay Johnson was up for confirmation for CNO, and maybe he had gotten a tree, I don't know. So I just blew my stack. I went over to see Danzig, and I said, "Don't ever ask me to do anything again of this nature, I'm not going to do it; you hired me under false pretenses." I was really mad, and he knew I was mad. He apologized profusely. And that was the end of that.

See, I'd violated my rules: Be a different admiral and don't do that kind of crap. Violated one of my rules, and it bounced on me.

Paul Stillwell: You mean you violated it by accepting that charter.

Admiral DeMars: Yes, exactly, by accepting. I just thought I was doing a favor for somebody. What they were really hoping was that I would take a while to do it. It wasn't that hard; you read this report and say, punish these guys, let's get on with life. Anyway, that was that.

Paul Stillwell: Well, we're ready to go now to your list of your post-retirement activities.

Admiral DeMars: Yes, I was fortunate. I got on two great boards right away, one within a week of retiring, the other within a month.

One was Commonwealth Edison in Chicago, later Exelon. It's the largest nuclear utility in the country, had 19 reactors. I was chair of the generation oversight committee, I was on the audit committee, I was on the transmission committee and on the governance committee. I was also brought on to J. Ray McDermott, in New Orleans and then

---

* Richard J. Danzig served as Under Secretary of the Navy from 29 November 1993 to 30 May 1997. He was later Secretary of the Navy from 16 November 1998 to 20 January 2001.

Houston, board. They built offshore oil and gas rigs and nuclear plant components. I was the lead director on that one, and the audit committee and the governance committee.

I didn't know my butt from third base about corporate matters. I was used to dealing with civilians because I did that in Naval Reactors, but it was really on-the-job training. So it was a tremendous education because we had good people on those boards. Tom Shievelbein, I brought him aboard, the former head of Newport News, former chairman of Sears, and on and on and on. I learned a lot of stuff, and I helped out because I'd ask questions that nobody else would ask, that weren't dumb questions, but nobody else wanted to ask them so I did that. So it was really on-the-job training.

I had other minor efforts, a number of unsuccessful ones. RSD Associates, which was a little thing with two other friends of mine and we tried to make money out of it. It was unsuccessful. The Nonproliferation Trust, which was a large scheme to get commercial nuclear waste from other countries outside the United States and store it in Russia, make money off of that. Well, that didn't go anywhere, obviously. The Hitachi Foundation I was on for about a year, and I got off that because I didn't like it.

But I had some very successful things. I was the chairman of the Naval Submarine League, and I enjoyed doing that. I passed that on to Rich Mies; he has that job now. On the board of the Yellow Ribbon Fund, the board of Draper Laboratories, Newport News, later Huntington Ingalls Industries, senior advisory board, OceanWorks International, which is in Vancouver and Houston, an offshore oil and gas business. And I'm the chairman of the Naval Historical Foundation; Holloway had me relieve him, brought me into that.[*]

And so I've been trying to turn down a number of these because I ought to play more golf. I'm a member of the Burning Tree Club; Chuck Bowsher got me in there. That's the one that doesn't have women, out there in Bethesda. It's a golf club just for men. It's a wonderful place.

Paul Stillwell: Do you have any memories of the substance of things you dealt with on these boards?

---

[*] Admiral James L. Holloway III, USN (Ret.), former Chief of Naval Operations.

Admiral DeMars: Well, the Naval Submarine League, we put together the 100th anniversary of the submarine force, a display at the Smithsonian.[*] And then later we put $50 million into the Naval Historical Foundation to store that material, and now a large portion of it is in the Cold War Gallery in the Washington Navy Yard. So that was a fairly important thing.

The Yellow Ribbon Fund I like. It raises good money for mostly the families of injured servicemen that are at Bethesda hospital or Fort Belvoir hospital, and gets them cars and apartments while they're here. The fellow that owns CarMax, I think it is—you hear them on TV—he gives us cars for five dollars a day. We pay for that, we give them to the people. So it's people come in from out of town; they've never lived here. So we try and make life easier for them.

Paul Stillwell: How did you get involved in the book *Making Faces*?

Admiral DeMars: Oh, that was interesting. The CFO of OceanWorks International was a Canadian from Vancouver, and he and his wife had a young child, a girl, who had a cleft palate.[†] And she went through a number of operations, and by the time she was 15 it was all solved and it was wonderful. And they had recorded that with pictures and things and that, and were trying to put together a book and get it published, specifically aimed at families that had this horrible malady. So I said, "Well, hell, I can raise money for you to do that." So I gave him some money and I put the arm on OceanWorks, we got some money from them, and the book was published and it's a very great thing. I feel very proud of that, that we got that done. And it's for people who are all of a sudden faced with that. It walks them through what you have to do and how you have to do it, and on and on and on.

The Draper Laboratory board, just a lot of stuff there. They do a lot of work for the Navy. And I always feel smarter when I come back from there because it's up in Cambridge, Massachusetts.

---

[*] The centennial of the U.S. Navy's submarine service was in 2000.
[†] CFO – chief financial officer.

The Newport News advisory board's a very interesting one. There are five flag officers on there—three aviators, two submariners, and a Marine, four-star. And we meet with them three times a year. They present us all their programs, and then we try and help them. It's a very nice organization and they're very gracious.

Paul Stillwell: What are the objectives with the Naval Historical Foundation?

Admiral DeMars: Preserve, educate, and commemorate, basically, naval history. We do a number of things. Right now we're trying to assist in building a Cold War Gallery as an adjunct to the main museum on the Washington Navy Yard. And because we can't get enough money to do that as quickly as we can we started a STEM program—science, technology, engineering, and math. And bring in school children and use the exhibits that we have in there to facilitate teaching those technical curricula. It works quite well. We got a little blowback from our board that said, "Hey, we're supposed to be in history, not STEM." So we changed the name to STEM-H; that appeared to work. [Laughter] Well, the history of the Navy *is* STEM. I mean, you know, science, technology, engineering, and math. If you look at navigation and propulsion and weapons, it's a history of technical things. So it's worked out quite well. Very successful. It's a good organization. I like it.

Paul Stillwell: Well, can we get up to date on your family, please?

Admiral DeMars: Yes, I'm proudest of my family. I think of everything and what we've talked about here and that, my proudest thing really is my family. I have two children, Bruce and Margaret. That's easy to remember. They never complained about Navy moves; it was never an issue. And we moved 28 times in 40 years. I mean, we just kind of, oh, oh, oh—time to go. I have a great son-in-law, Jamie Troup, and a great daughter-in-law, Patty. My son and daughter are happily married, been married quite a while. And three grandchildren that I'm very proud of.

Paul Stillwell: Their names?

Admiral DeMars: Oh, yes. Bruce's children are Rebecca, who is 24, and Bruce, who is 21. And Margaret has an 18-year-old daughter named Catherine. They're all doing very well, maturing in life. I'm still very much in love with my wife of 55 years. We went to high school together, so we had about a six-year engagement when the Naval Academy wouldn't let us get married [chuckle]. But we were married graduation day from the Naval Academy, so we've been married 55 years. She did it all. Never complained, all the moves, raising the kids, my going away. And when you're away on a submarine there is no communication. So she's a tremendous supporter and a very sage adviser, and she still is to this day. We're mostly working at staying healthy, staying busy, and enjoying life. For me, that's Naval Historical Foundation, and golf.

And that is the end.

Paul Stillwell: Is there any question I should have asked but didn't?

Admiral DeMars: No, I don't think so. That was a good list you came out with. Did we cover most of your list?

Paul Stillwell: Yes, we did.

Admiral DeMars: No, I'm amazed we got through it all here. I thought we might have to bop into another one.

No, and I put in a lot of advertisements too, for the way that Naval Reactors works, because I thought that was interesting. I don't think anybody has ever really done that. And the only other person that could do it would be McKee.

No, I've had a great life, a great career. I think I had the attitude that it was going to be good or I'd do something else. [Chuckle] And so I think that's a good way to live. I never was put off by things.

Paul Stillwell: Well, I've certainly been grateful for you cooperation and all the preparation you did for each of these interviews.

Admiral DeMars: Well, I wanted to do it right. You're going to have to do all the work. What are the next steps now?

Paul Stillwell: Well, the next step will be to get it transcribed and edited, annotated, and then back to you for any further changes.

Admiral DeMars: Oh, God, I have to read the stuff?

Paul Stillwell: [Laughter] Well, I can do it for you.

Admiral DeMars: I may pass on that. Well, we'll see.*

Paul Stillwell: But obviously this is an additional legacy, in addition to your service. So I thank you.

Admiral DeMars: That's very nice. I debated a long time about whether to do it or not. Then I finally say, oh, hell, I'll do it.

Paul Stillwell: I'm glad you did.

Admiral DeMars: Well, I am too. I got to meet you, too, so even all the better.

Paul Stillwell: Thank you.

---

* This was a tongue-in-cheek remark. Admiral DeMars did review the transcripts and made a number of useful changes.

Appendix – Admiral DeMars's Response to a portion of John Lehman's memoir:

Secretary Lehman wrote a book, *Command of the Seas*, which contains his version of the selection board matter.

I thought I should get something on the record, particularly since I was correct in my actions in this issue.

It is somewhat difficult to respond to Secretary Lehman's comments contained in his book since they are so off the mark and distant from the truth. Perhaps it is best to just factually address each one and let the reader draw his or her own conclusions.

Lehman states the Secretary of the Navy provides guidance for the percentage to be promoted from each community. This is not true. The Secretary provides a "precept letter" which addresses matters in general: consider more women, consider more minorities, Explosive Ordnance Disposal officers are needed, etc. Numbers are not used. This letter is provided to all members of the board and to the Bureau of Naval Personnel officers who manage the board proceedings. These officers track the selection numbers and work closely with the board president to fulfill the precept. Lehman did not provide me percentages.

Lehman states that the CNO, Admiral Trost, directed me to ignore the secretary's guidance. This is not true. Several times Lehman says that Trost was directing my actions. That is not true. While I kept him advised after the board reported out, he never told me what to do. I assumed he could see where this was headed and wanted to be impartial in what followed.

Lehman states that the two other senior members of the board, Rear Admirals Ramsey and Marriott, protested to me about my alleged percentage allocations. This is not true. While they had every opportunity they said nothing to me or to the three Bureau of Naval Personnel officers who were running the board.

Lehman discusses a letter written by Ramsey complaining about my percentages. I have not seen the letter but the Senior Inspector General investigator told me the date was erased and changed and they chose to ignore the letter.

Lehman states that rumor has it that Trost sent a secret message to each board member reminding them of their oath of silence—i.e., "cautioning them to close ranks, clam up". This is not true.

Lehman states that Trost fired Marryott from his post as Superintendent of the Naval Academy. This is not true.

Lehman was the Secretary for almost eight years. It defies credulity to think he didn't understand how the system has been developed to protect the integrity of the selection process. As I remarked earlier, my experience prompted the Senate Armed Services

Committee to review the Secretary's action in a Marine Corps Brigadier General board. The result was one officer was not promoted.

I believe the simple answer to this sad tale is Lehman's inability to explain Secretary of Defense Weinberger's actions to approve the IG investigation and forward the selection board report to the next Secretary of the Navy for approval.

Index to the Oral History of
Admiral Bruce DeMars, U.S. Navy (Retired)

Agronsky, Martin
  NBC correspondent who filmed a program on board the ballistic missile submarine *George Washington* (SSBN-598) in the early 1960s, 68-70

Air Force, U.S.
  Student officers at the Armed Forces Staff College in 1966-67, 114-116

Alcohol
  Drinking by officers of the nuclear submarine *Snook* (SSN-592) in the mid-1960s, 156
  In the late 1960s the nuclear submarine *Sturgeon* (SSN-637) carried wine on board until told to ditch it, 121
  Drinking by the crew of the *Sturgeon* in the late 1960s, 155-156

Amphibious Warfare
  Exercises in the late 1950s by South Korean Marines on board the attack transport *Okanogan* (APA-220), 33-35

Antisubmarine Warfare
  In the late 1960s-early 1970s, U.S. nuclear submarines provided target services for ASW forces, 161-162
  Role of sonar and SOSUS in submarine detection in the late 1970s, 179

Applied Mathematics, Inc.
  Company that did development work for the submarine force in the late 1970s, 177-178

Arctic
  In the mid-1980s nuclear submarines made a number of voyages that included surfacing in the Arctic, 209-211

Armed Forces Staff College, Norfolk, Virginia
  Multi-service student body in 1966-67, 113-117

Armistead, Reginald Gray
  In the mid-1980s advised OP-02 on selling the submarine program to Congress, 205-207
  In 1987 inquired about a disputed Navy selection board, 216-218
  In the 1990s was a friend of Admiral Jeremy Boorda, 245

Army, U.S.
  Student officers at the Armed Forces Staff College in 1966-67, 114-115

Babcock & Wilcox Company
  In the 1990s built nuclear reactor cores for the Navy, 234-235

Bagley, Rear Admiral David H., USN (USNA, 1944)
  In the early 1970s sought submariners' views on Admiral Hyman Rickover, 163

Bagley, Rear Admiral Worth H., USN (USNA, 1947)
  In the early 1970s sought submariners' views on Admiral Hyman Rickover, 163

Bainbridge, Maryland
  Site of the East Coast Nuclear Power School in the early 1960s, 79, 85

Barr, Lieutenant Jon Michael, USN (USNA, 1961)
  Served on board the nuclear submarine *Snook* (SSN-592) in the mid-1960s, 92, 255
  ComSubPac, 1993-96, 255

Barry, Commodore John, USN
  The first U.S. Navy officer is honored by a memorial at the Naval Academy, 22-23

Base Realignment and Closure
  The submarine Base at New London, Connecticut, was saved from possible closing in the early 2000s, 260

***Batfish*, USS (SSN-681)**
  Navigation problems on initial sea trials in 1972, 139

Bilyeu, Lieutenant Commander Roland C., USN (USNA, 1954)
  In the mid-1960s was executive officer of the submarine *Snook* (SSN-592), 110-111

***Blackfin*, USS (SS-322)**
  In the 1950s her commanding officer was relieved for surfacing in the harbor of Vladivostok in the Soviet Union, 32

Blair, Lieutenant Peter S., USN (USNA, 1955)
  Served on board the submarine *Raton* (SSR-270) in the late 1950s, 44-45

Boggs, Representative Corinne "Lindy"
  Congresswoman who addressed Admiral DeMars as "General" during his testimony, 221

Bohannon, Commander William L, USN
  Commanded the nuclear submarine *Sturgeon* (SSN-637) in the late 1960s, 119-120, 125-128, 147, 255

Bonz, Lieutenant Philip E., USN
  Trained on the prototype S3G reactor at West Milton, New York, in the early 1960s and later served in the submarine *Triton* (SSRN-586), 56-57, 77-78

Boorda, Admiral Jeremy M., USN
Relationship with the nuclear power program while serving as Chief of Naval Operations, 1994-96, 252
Committed suicide in May 1996, 245-247

Bowman, Admiral Frank, USN
Served as executive assistant to Admiral DeMars, later headed the Navy nuclear power program, 222, 230-231, 253

Browning, Dr. William J.
Development work for the submarine force in the late 1970s, 177-178

Budgetary Considerations/Issues
In the submarine directorate of OpNav in the late 1970s-early 1980s, 182-185, 201-205

Bureau of Naval Personnel (BuPers)
Role in DeMars's duty assignments over the years, 33, 58, 88, 113, 132-133, 174, 178
Controversy over Navy and Marine Corps selection boards in 1985-86, 213-219, 269-270

Burke, Lieutenant James G., USN
First chief engineer of the nuclear submarine *Cavalla* (SSN-684) in the early 1970s, 134-135, 141, 170

***Capitaine*, USS (SS-336)**
Operations in the Eastern Pacific in 1959-60 involved mostly training, 41-53
Enlisted personnel in 1959-60, 42
Sank a decommissioned ammunition ship for practice around 1960, 50-51

Caroline Islands
U.S. Navy association in the early 1980s, 192-194

Carter, President James E., Jr. (USNA, 1947)
Cost-saving measures inflicted on the Defense Department during his term as President, 1977-81, 186

***Cavalla*, USS (SS-244)**
World War II submarine later preserved as a museum in Texas, 148-149

***Cavalla*, USS (SSN-684)**
Built by the Electric Boat Division of General Dynamics in the early 1970s, 133-138
Launching in February 1972, 137-138
Initial sea trials in October 1972, 138-145
Special operations against the Soviet Navy, 1973-74, 145-148

Propulsion exam in the early 1970s, 170
Decommissioning in 1994, 255

Cheney, Richard B.
As a congressman in the mid-1980s, asked for a briefing on submarine intelligence operations, 212

Chicago, Illinois
DeMars's boyhood in the city in the 1940s and 1950s, 1-13
DeMars and his brother attended White Sox baseball games in the 1940s, 9

Chiles, Vice Admiral Henry G. Jr., USN (USNA, 1960)
As ComSubLant in the early 1990s, 244

Clark, Admiral Vernon E., USN
As Chief of Naval Operations, 2000-05, 260

Cochino, **USS (SS-345)**
Submarine lost off Norway in 1949 after an explosion and fire, 43-44

Collisions
Involving U.S. and Soviet warships in the late 1960s, 124-126, 129-130

Columbia, **USS (SSN-771)**
Last U.S. submarine to be launched by sliding down the ways, 1994, 137

Computers
Computerization of torpedo firing tables in the late 1970s, 177

Congress, U.S.
OP-02 selling of the submarine program to Congress in the mid-1980s, 205-207
In the mid-1980s Senator Albert Gore Jr. made submarine voyages to the Arctic, 210-211
Representative Richard Cheney asked for a briefing on submarine operations in the mid-1980s, 212
Concern in 1987 over a disputed selection board for Navy captains, 215-219
Testimony to Congress in the 1980s and 1990s on the nuclear submarine program, 219-221
In 1996 passed a proclamation honoring DeMars, 253

Cook Islands
U.S. Navy association in the early 1980s, 194-196

Cooke, Commander Edward W., USN (USNA, 1946)
In the early 1960s commanded the ballistic missile submarine *George Washington* (SSBN-598), 68-69

Dalton, John H. III
  Was Secretary of the Navy when CNO Jeremy Boorda committed suicide in 1996, 245-247

Danzig, Richard J.
  As Under Secretary of the Navy in the mid-1990s, 263

Daspit, Rear Admiral Lawrence R., USN (USNA, 1927)
  Served in the early 1960s as Deputy Commander Submarine Force Atlantic Fleet, 62-63

David Taylor Model Basin, Carderock, Maryland
  Did tests in the 1990s on nuclear submarine angle problems, 242

DeMars, Admiral Bruce, USN (Ret.) (USNA, 1957)
  Parents, 1-5, 8-9, 12, 28, 138
  Siblings, 1-2, 4, 6, 10
  Wife Margaret, 1, 10-11, 20, 24, 27-33, 50-51, 54, 59, 75, 80-81, 103, 112, 117, 124, 129, 138, 158-159, 167-168, 185, 192-195, 199, 267
  Children, 26, 33, 54, 59, 81, 112, 114, 118, 167-169, 266-267
  Grandchildren, 266-267
  Boyhood in Chicago in the 1940s and 1950s, 1-13, 162-163
  Appointment to the Naval Academy in 1953, 6-7, 162-163
  As a Naval Academy midshipman, 1953-57, 11, 13-29
  Served in the attack transport *Telfair* (APA-210) in 1957, 24, 29-31
  Served in 1957-58 in the attack transport *Okanogan* (APA-220), 31-36
  As a student at Submarine School in 1958-59, 36-40
  Served in 1959-60 in the submarine *Capitaine* (SS-336), 41-53, 117
  Interviewed for the Navy's nuclear power program in the late 1950s, 46-47
  Attended Nuclear Power School at Mare Island, 1960, 53-54
  Training on a prototype nuclear reactor in West Milton New York, in 1960-61, 55-59, 77-78
  Served in the ballistic missile submarine *George Washington* (SSBN-598) in 1961-62, 52, 58-60
  Taught at the Nuclear Power School at Mare Island, 1962-64, 78-88
  From 1964 to 1966 served in the nuclear submarine *Snook* (SSN-592), 88-112
  Attended Armed Forces Staff College in 1966-67, 75, 111-117
  Served 1967-69 as executive officer of the nuclear submarine *Sturgeon* (SSN-637), 117-128, 150-153, 164-165
  Taught at Submarine School, 1969-71, 129-130
  Student at prospective commanding officers' school, 1971, 131-132
  Commanded the nuclear submarine *Cavalla* (SSN-684) from 1973 to 1975, 127, 133-140, 163-164, 168-169
  For a few months in 1975 was Deputy Commander Submarine Squadron Ten, 153-154, 159-161, 165-170

In April 1975 DeMars suffered broken ribs while being lifted from the submarine *Greenling* (SSN-614) by helicopter, 166-167

Served 1975-78 on the Atlantic Fleet Nuclear Propulsion Examining Board, 170

Commanded Submarine Squadron 12 in 1978-79, 175-180

Served 1979-81 as OP-22B, Deputy Director of the Attack Submarine Division, on the OpNav staff, 181-185

From 1981 to 1983 held three simultaneous billets while serving in Guam, 185-190

Was Deputy OP-02, 1983-85, 201-208

From 1985 to 1988 was Deputy Chief of Naval Operations, Undersea Warfare (OP-02), 72, 208-218, 222, 255-257

Served 1988-96 as chief of Naval Reactors for the Navy, 138, 221-263

Activities since retirement from active duty, 21-23, 263-267

Disciplinary Problems
Minimal in most nuclear submarines in the 1960s and 1970s, 152-153

Doyle, Vice Admiral James H., Jr., USN (USNA, 1947)
Was a student at Nuclear Power School in the early 1960s before commanding a nuclear-powered frigate and becoming OP-03, 83-84

On the board of the Naval Historical Foundation in the 2010s, 84

Dunn, Vice Admiral Robert F., USN (Ret.) (USNA, 1951)
In the late 1980s was Deputy Chief of Naval Operations (Air Warfare), OP-05, 205, 255-256

As president of the Naval Historical Foundation in the 2010s, 256

Electric Boat Division, General Dynamics Corporation, Groton, Connecticut
Built the nuclear submarine *Sturgeon* (SSN-637) in the mid-1960s, 118

Built the nuclear submarine *Cavalla* (SSN-684) in the early 1970s, 133-140

Nuclear submarine construction in the 1980s-1990s, 137, 221, 235-236, 239-241, 254-258

Electronic Warfare
In the mid-1960s the nuclear submarine *Snook* (SSN-592) had the WLR-6 surveillance system, 88-89, 92-94

By the nuclear submarine *Sturgeon* (SSN-637) in the late 1960s, 126

Energy Department
Role in the Navy's nuclear power program, 1988-96, 223-226, 229, 252-253

Enlisted Personnel
On board the battleship *Missouri* (BB-63) in 1954, 17

In the crew of the attack transport *Telfair* (APA-210) in 1957, 30-31

On board the submarine *Capitaine* (SS-336) in 1959-60, 42, 52

On board the ballistic missile submarine *George Washington* (SSBN-598) in 1961-62, 52, 70-73

At Nuclear Power School in the early 1960s, 82
On board the nuclear submarine *Snook* (SSN-592) in the mid-1960s, 97, 101-102
In the crew of the nuclear submarine *Sturgeon* (SSN-637) in the late 1960s, 118, 121-124, 151-153, 155, 164
In the crew of the nuclear submarine *Cavalla* (SSN-684) in the early 1970s, 142-145
In the crew of the nuclear submarine *Greenling* (SSN-614) in early 1975, 154

Enterprise, USS (CVN-65)
Decision not to decommission the ship in the early 2000s, 261-262

F4U Corsair
Accident involving a carrier plane during a midshipman cruise in 1956, 18

Fagan, Commander John F. Jr., USN (USNA, 1946)
Commanded the Nuclear Power School at Mare Island in the early 1960s, 78-79

Foley, Admiral Sylvester R., Jr., USN (USNA, 1950)
Served as Commander in Chief Pacific Fleet, 1982-85, 196

Foster, Thomas L.
Worked in the Navy's nuclear power program from 1963 to 1994, 230-233, 253

Fulton, USS (AS-11)
Submarine tender based at New London, Connecticut, in the mid-1970s, 160-161, 165, 169-170

George Washington, USS (SSBN-598)
Forward deployed out of Holy Loch, Scotland, in the early 1960s, 58-75

Gore, Senator Albert A. Jr.
In the mid-1980s made submarine voyages to the Arctic, 210-211

Greenling, USS (SSN-614)
Faced problems while en route to the Mediterranean in 1975, 153-154, 165-166
In April 1975 DeMars suffered broken ribs while being lifted from the submarine by helicopter, 166-167

Griffith, Captain Dwaine O., USN
Student at prospective commanding officers' school, 1971, 131-132
In the 1980s ran the Navy's deep-submergence program, 256-257

Griffiths, Vice Admiral Charles H., USN (USNA, 1946)
Served in ballistic missile submarines in the 1960s and 1970s, 74
From 1977 to 1980 was Deputy Chief of Naval Operations (Submarine Warfare), OP-02, 72, 181-185

Guam, Mariana Islands
   Activities in the early 1980s concerning Guam, the Marianas, and Micronesia, 185-200
   Vestiges of World War II still evident in the early 1980s, 189, 200

Haggerty, Thomas
   Chief nuclear test engineer for Electric Boat during the construction of the nuclear submarine *Cavalla* (SSN-684) in the early 1970s, 134-135

Hall, Captain Donald P., USN (USNA, 1950)
   Commanded Submarine School in the early 1970s, 131

Hayward, Admiral Thomas B., USN (USNA, 1948)
   Issues in the early 1980s, when Hayward was CNO, on what type of attack submarine to build, 183-185

Hidalgo, Edward
   As Secretary of the Navy in the late 1970s, did not choose DeMars to be his executive assistant, 182-183

Hofford, Captain Robert F., USN (USNA, 1961)
   Individual who did a great deal over the years on behalf of the Naval Academy, 22-23

Holt, Captain Edward J. Jr., USMC
   Served in the mid-1950s as a company officer at the Naval Academy, 24-25

Holy Loch, Scotland
   Forward base for the ballistic missile submarine George Washington (SSBN-598) in the early 1960s, 60, 66

Honigman, Steven S.
   Served as general counsel of the Navy, 1993-98, 252, 262

Intelligence
   Special intelligence operations against the Soviet Navy in the mid-1960s by the nuclear submarine *Snook* (SSN-592), 92-110
   Special operations against the Soviet Navy in the late 1960s by the nuclear submarine *Sturgeon* (SSN-637), 119-128
   Special operations against the Soviet Navy, 1973-74, by the nuclear submarine *Cavalla* (SSN-684), 145-148

Ireland
   Irish-born John Barry, the first U.S. Navy officer, is honored by a memorial at the Naval Academy, 22-23

Japan
Sasebo was the site of the 1966 change of command for the nuclear submarine *Snook* (SSN-592), 108-109

Jenks, Lieutenant Commander Shepherd M., USN (USNA, 1949)
In the early 1960s served as engineer and executive officer of the ballistic missile submarine *George Washington* (SSBN-598), 64-67

Kelso, Admiral Frank B. II, USN (USNA, 1956)
Attended prospective commanding officers' school for submariners in 1971, 133
As a detailer in the Bureau of Naval Personnel in the late 1970s, 178
Chief of Naval Operations, 2000-04, 226-228, 236-237, 261-262

Korea, South
Amphibious exercises in the late 1950s by South Korean Marines on board the attack transport *Okanogan* (APA-220), 33-35

Kossler, Rear Admiral Herman J., USN (USNA, 1934)
Commanded the diesel submarine *Cavalla* (SS-244) in World War II and attended the commissioning of the nuclear submarine *Cavalla* (SSN-684) in 1973, 148-149

Laning, Captain Richard B., USN (USNA, 1940)
In the early 1960s commanded the forward-deployed submarine tender *Proteus* (AS-19), 73

Larson, Admiral Charles R., USN (Ret.) (USNA, 1958)
DeMars contemporary who rose to high rank, 27-28, 213

Leave and Liberty
In Annapolis for midshipmen in the mid 1950s, 19-20
In the mid-1960s crew members and their families from the nuclear submarine *Snook* (SSN-592) visited Mexico, 103-104, 159

Lehman, John F., Jr.
As Secretary of the Navy, was involved in a controversy over Navy and Marine Corps selection boards in 1985-86, 213-219, 231, 261, 269-270

Leisk, Lieutenant Commander William H. Jr., USN
In the early 1950s served in the submarine *Blackfin* (SS-322), 32
Commanded the submarine *Capitaine* (SS-336) in the late 1950s, 41-46, 50, 61-62

Loposer, Commander Avery Kenneth Jr., USN (USNA, 1952)
Commanded the nuclear submarine *Snook* (SSN-592), 1966-69, 108-112

Los Angeles (SSN-688)-Class Submarines
Role of the submarine directorate around 1980 in continuing with construction of the class, 183-185

SubACS (Submarine Advanced Combat System) developed for the class in the 1980s, 204

Mare Island Naval Shipyard, Vallejo, California
Site of Nuclear Power School in the 1960s, 53-54, 78-88

Mariana Islands
Activities in the early 1980s concerning the Marianas and other islands in Micronesia, 185-200

Vestiges of World War II were still evident in the early 1980s, 189

Marine Corps, U.S.
A Marine C-120 aircraft flew DeMars to Yap in the early 1980s, 193-194

Controversy over Navy and Marine Corps selection boards in 1985-87, 213-219, 269-270

McCoy, Jan Jenkins
In the 1980s was High Commissioner of the Trust Territory of the Pacific, 190

McHale, Yeoman William (Gannon), USNR
In a book published in 2008, wrote about his service as a crew member of the nuclear submarine *Sturgeon* (SSN-637) in the late 1960s, 122, 150-151, 155, 164

McKee, Admiral Kinnaird R., USN (USNA, 1951)
In the mid-1970s commanded Submarine Group Eight in the Mediterranean, 166-167

In the late 1970s-early 1980s served as Director, Naval Warfare, OP-095, 202-203

Served 1982-88 as director of the Navy's nuclear power program, 224-225, 230, 253

Medical Problems
In April 1975 DeMars suffered broken ribs while being lifted from the submarine *Greenling* (SSN-614) by helicopter, 166-167

Mexico
Visited in the mid-1960s by crew members and their families from the nuclear submarine Snook (SSN-592), 103-104, 159

Micronesia
U.S. Navy activities in the Marianas, Carolines, and Palau in the early 1980s, 189-200

Mies, Admiral Richard W., USN (USNA, 1967)
Served in the late 1970s on the Atlantic Fleet Nuclear Propulsion Examining Board, 170

Served as EA to DeMars, later was Commander in Chief Strategic Command, 222
Chairman of the Naval Submarine League, 264

Missiles
On board the Polaris submarine *George Washington* (SSBN-598) in the early 1960s, 61, 67-69
The nuclear submarine *Sturgeon* (SSN-637) fired a SubRoc in the late 1960s, 126-127
Tomahawk missiles on board U.S. submarines in the 1980s-2010s, 233-234

***Missouri*, USS (BB-63)**
Training cruise for midshipmen in the summer of 1954, 16-17

Mystic, Connecticut
Pleasant home life for the DeMars family in the 1960s and 1970s, 114, 117-118, 129, 132-133, 167-169

NR-1
Nuclear-powered Navy research vessel, 261

Naha, Okinawa
Port in which the nuclear submarine *Snook* (SSN-592) received logistic and intelligence support during special operations in the mid-1960s, 94, 99-100, 103, 107-108, 157

National Naval Medical Center, Bethesda, Maryland
In April 1975 DeMars suffered broken ribs while being lifted from the submarine *Greenling* (SSN-614) by helicopter and was treated at Bethesda, 166-167

Naval Academy, Annapolis, Maryland
Appointment process for DeMars in 1953, 6-7, 11
DeMars played lightweight football in the mid-1950s, 7-8
Relationships between officers and midshipmen in the mid-1950s, 13-14, 24-28
Athletics in the mid-1950s, 14-17
Academics in the mid-1950s, 15-16
Summer training cruises in the mid-1950s, 16-19
Liberty in Annapolis for midshipmen, mid-1950s, 19-20
Fundraising for the academy, 21
Memorials at the academy, 21-22

Naval Historical Foundation
Role in the early 21st century, 264-266

Naval Postgraduate School, Monterey, California
In the early 1960s some of the officer students were drafted involuntarily into the nuclear power program, 86-87

Naval Reserve, U.S.
　Seaman John Melvin, a reservist, served on board the ballistic missile submarine *George Washington* (SSBN-598) in the early 1960s, 70-73

Naval Underwater Systems Center, Newport, Rhode Island
　Role of in the late 1970s, 177

Navigation
　On board the nuclear submarine *Snook* (SSN-592) in the mid-1960s, 91, 101
　Navigation problems on the initial sea trials of the submarine *Batfish* (SSN-681) in 1972, 139
　On the initial sea trials of the nuclear submarine Cavalla (SSN-684) in 1973, 139-140
　The nuclear submarine *Seawolf* (SSN-575) ran aground during a training exercise in the Gulf of Maine in 1968, 150-151

New London, Connecticut
　Homeport for Submarine Squadron Ten in the mid-1970s, 153, 159-161, 165-166, 169-170

Newport News Shipbuilding and Dry Dock Company
　Nuclear submarine construction in the 1980s-1990s, 205-207, 221, 235, 242, 258

News Media
　NBC correspondent Martin Agronsky filmed a program on board the ballistic missile submarine *George Washington* (SSBN-598) in the early 1960s, 68-70
　In 1987 *The Washington Post* published a revealing article about a disputed selection board for Navy captains, 215-216, 269-270

New Zealand
　U.S. Navy association in the early 1980s, 194-196

Nichols, Lieutenant Commander Christopher O., USN (USNA, 1961)
　Commanded the nuclear submarine *Greenling* (SSN-614) in the mid-1970s, 153-154, 165-166

Nimitz, Fleet Admiral Chester W., USN (USNA, 1905)
　Based on Guam in 1945 while serving as Commander in Chief Pacific Fleet, 187, 197, 200

Nuclear Power Program
　Vice Admiral Hyman Rickover interviewed DeMars for the program in the late 1950s-early 1960s, 47-49
　Nuclear Power School at Mare Island in the 1960s, 53-55, 78-88
　Training on the S3G prototype reactor in West Milton New York, in 1960-61, 55-59, 77-78

In the early 1960s some of the officer students of the Naval Postgraduate School were drafted involuntarily into the nuclear power program, 86-87
Prospective commanding officers' school, 1971, 131-132
Construction of the nuclear submarine *Cavalla* (SSN-684) at Electric Boat in the early 1970s, 133-140
Role of the Atlantic Fleet Nuclear Propulsion Examining Board in the late 1970s, 170-175
During DeMars's tenure as director, 1988-96, 138, 221-263
When the Soviet Union collapsed in 1991, U.S. submarine construction dropped dramatically, 232-233
Initial sea trials for new submarines, 1980s-1990s, 240-243
Interviews with candidates for the program, 1988-96, 247-251
Decommissioning of nuclear-powered cruisers in the 1980s-90s, 258
Disposition of reactors from nuclear-powered warships, 258-259

Nuclear Weapons
On board the Polaris submarine *George Washington* (SSBN-598) in the early 1960s, 61, 67-69

Okanogan, USS (APA-220)
Ship's officers in 1957-58, 32-33
Operations in 1957-58 included a deployment to the Western Pacific, 31-36

O'Keefe, Sean
Brief tenure as Secretary of the Navy, 1992-93, 233, 261

Okinawa
The nuclear submarine *Snook* (SSN-592) received logistic and intelligence support at Naha during special operations in the mid-1960s, 94, 99-100, 103, 107-108, 157

O'Leary, Hazel R.
As Secretary of Energy, 1993-97, 225-226, 252

OP-02
Role of the submarine directorate around 1980 in continuing with construction of the *Los Angeles* (SSN-688) class, 183-185
As one of the three major warfare "barons" in the Navy in the early and mid-1980s, 201-208, 255-256
Selling of the submarine program to Congress in the mid-1980s, 205-208, 211-212, 219-221
Oversaw nuclear submarine voyages to the Arctic in the mid-1980s, 209-211

OP-095
Office of Director, Naval Warfare, on the OpNav staff in the 1980s, 202-203

Osborn, Captain James B., USN (USNA, 1942)
In the early 1960s commanded the ballistic missile submarine *George Washington* (SSBN-598), 61-63, 66-68, 72
In the mid-1960s was chief of staff to Commander Submarine Force Atlantic Fleet, 75, 117

Owens, Vice Admiral William A., USN (USNA, 1962)
In the early 1990s was DCNO for Resources, Warfare Requirements, and Assessments, 237

Paisley, Melvyn R.
In the 1980s shifted funds to pay for SubACS (Submarine Advanced Combat System, 203-205

Palau Islands
Vestiges of World War II were still evident in the early 1980s, 189
U.S. Navy involvement in the early 1980s, 197-198

Patton, Lieutenant Commander James H. Jr., USN (USNA, 1960)
In the early 1970s served as the first executive officer of the nuclear submarine *Cavalla* (SSN-684), 142-143

Pay and Allowances
For Naval Academy midshipmen in the mid-1950s, 27
DeMars was not able to qualify for extra pay for being in the nuclear program, 174

Photography
Through-the-periscope intelligence photos taken by the nuclear submarine *Snook* (SSN-592) in the mid-1960s, 98-99

Polaris Missiles
Rapid development program in the late 1950s, 63-64
On board the ballistic missile submarine *George Washington* (SSBN-598) in the early 1960s, 61, 67-69

Price, Representative Charles Melvin
Congressman whose wife christened the nuclear submarine *Cavalla* (SSN-684) in 1972, 137-138
Spoke at the *Cavalla*'s commissioning in 1973, 146

Proctor, Commander Erman O., USN
Served on the staff at Submarine School in the late 1950s, 38-39

Promotion of Officers
Controversy over Navy and Marine Corps selection boards in 1985-86, 213-219, 269-270

Propulsion Plants
    The prototype S3G reactor was used for training at West Milton, New York, in the early 1960s, 55-59, 77-78
    On board the ballistic missile submarine *George Washington* (SSBN-598) in the early 1960s, 65-66
    On board the nuclear submarine *Snook* (SSN-592) in the mid-1960s, 95
    On board the nuclear submarine *Cavalla* (SSN-684) in the early 1970s, 134-136, 142-145, 170
    Role of the Atlantic Fleet Nuclear Propulsion Examining Board in the late 1970s, 170-175
    Inspection visits during DeMars's tenure as director of the Navy's nuclear power program, 1988-96, 138, 221-222
    In *Virginia* (SSN-774)-class submarines, 237-239, 243
    Initial sea trials for new nuclear submarines, 1980s-1990s, 240-243
    Disposition of reactors from decommissioned nuclear-powered ships, 258-259

***Proteus*, USS (AS-19)**
    In the early 1960s was a forward-deployed tender in Holy Loch, Scotland, 73

Puget Sound Naval Shipyard, Bremerton, Washington
    Role in the disposition of reactors from decommissioned nuclear-powered ships, 258-259

Punaro, Arnold L.
    In 1987 was a Senate staffer at the time of a disputed Navy selection board, 216-217

Racial Issues
    Harmonious racial climate on board the nuclear submarine *Sturgeon* (SSN-637) in the late 1960s, 164-165

***Raton*, USS (SS-270)**
    Operations in the Southern California area in the late 1950s, 44

Religion
    In Guam shortly after World War II, 200
    In Micronesia in the early 1980s, 188, 191-192

Reynolds, Rear Admiral J. Guy, USN (USNA, 1959)
    In the mid-1980s, at NavSea, ran the program for SubACS (Submarine Advanced Combat System), 203-204

Rickover, Admiral Hyman G., USN (Ret.) (USNA, 1922)
    Proponent of education, 25
    In the late 1950s-early 1960s interviewed DeMars for the Navy nuclear power program, 47-49

Ran the nuclear power program in the 1950s-80s, 53, 64, 70, 79-80, 81, 84-85, 132-145, 163, 171-173, 183, 185, 220, 223, 225, 229-231, 242-243, 248, 252

Royal Navy
Housing in the early 1980s for British naval attachés serving in Washington, D.C., 185-186

***Sam Rayburn* (MTS-635)**
Serves at Charleston as a moored training ship for the Navy's nuclear power program, 259-260

Sasebo, Japan
Site of the 1966 change of command for the nuclear submarine *Snook* (SSN-592), 108-109

Scotland
Holy Loch was the forward base for the ballistic missile submarine *George Washington* (SSBN-598) in the early 1960s, 60, 66

Seabees
Projects in Micronesia in the early 1980s, 190-191, 198-199

Sealion, USS (LPSS-315)
Sinking of the decommissioned submarine in 1978, 176

***Seawolf*, USS (SSN-575)**
Ran aground during a training exercise in the Gulf of Maine in 1968, 150-151

***Seawolf* (SSN-21)-Class Submarines**
SubACS (Submarine Advanced Combat System) developed for the class in the 1980s, 204
When the Soviet Union collapsed in 1991, U.S. submarine construction dropped dramatically, 232-234

Selection Boards
Controversy over Navy and Marine Corps selection boards in 1985-87, 213-219, 269-270

Severance, Lieutenant (junior grade) Laverne Stanard Jr., USN (USNA, 1957)
Student at Nuclear Power School in 1960, 53-54

Shellman, Rear Admiral Curtis B. Jr., USN (Ret.)
In the late 1960s commanded the nuclear submarine *Sturgeon* (SSN-637), 118-120
In the mid-1970s commanded Submarine Squadron Ten, 146, 153-154, 159-161, 165, 169
Worked for Electric Boat after his retirement from active duty, 169, 254-255

Ship Handling
On board the nuclear submarine *Snook* (SSN-592) in the mid-1960s, 90-92, 96-97
Difficulties around State Pier in New London, Connecticut, in the mid-1970s because of currents in the Thames River, 160-161
Problems in handling nuclear submarines in the 1990s, 242-243

Siskin, Edward
Served as Admiral Hyman Rickover's representative at the Electric Boat shipyard in the early 1970s, 135-136, 140

Smith, Rear Admiral Dickinson M., USN (USNA, 1955)
Served in the late 1970s-early 1980s as OP-22, Director of the Attack Submarine Division, on the OpNav staff, 182

Smith, Captain William D., USN (USNA, 1955)
Served as a detailer in the Bureau of Naval Personnel in the late 1970s, 175

Snook, USS (SSN-592)
Built by Ingalls Shipbuilding, commissioned in 1961, 207
In the mid-1960s had the WLR-6 electronic surveillance system, 88-89
Ship handling in the mid-1960s, 90-92, 96-97
Special intelligence operations against the Soviet Navy in the mid-1960s, 92-110
Suicide attempt in the mid-1960s by one of the ship's officers, 106-107
Drinking by the boat's officers in the mid-1960s, 156

Sonar
On board the ballistic missile submarine *George Washington* (SSBN-598) in the early 1960s, 62-63
On board the nuclear submarine *Snook* (SSN-592) in the mid-1960s, 90-91, 96-97
In the nuclear submarine *Sturgeon* (SSN-637) in the late 1960s, 119, 124-125
Role in submarine detection in the late 1970s, 179-180

SOSUS (Sound Surveillance System)
Role in submarine detection in the late 1970s, 179-180

Soviet Navy
Submarine operations in the mid-1960s, 90-93
Special intelligence operations against the Soviet Navy in the mid-1960s by the nuclear submarine *Snook* (SSN-592), 92-100
Special intelligence operations against the Soviet Navy in the late 1960s by the nuclear submarine *Sturgeon* (SSN-637), 119-128
Collisions involving U.S. and Soviet warships in the late 1960s, 124-126, 129-130
Special operations against the Soviet Navy, 1973-74, by the nuclear submarine *Cavalla* (SSN-684), 145-148
Soviet submarines got more and more quiet as the 1970s and 1980s progressed, 162, 179, 212-213

Soviet Union
    In the 1950s the commanding officer of the submarine *Blackfin* (SS-322) was relieved after surfacing in the harbor at Vladivostok, 32
    Patrols in the vicinity by the nuclear submarine *Snook* (SSN-592) in the mid-1960s, 92-110
    When the Soviet Union collapsed in 1991, U.S. submarine construction dropped dramatically, 232

ptr*Sturgeon*, USS (SSN-637)
    Operations in the Atlantic in the late 1960s, 118-120, 150-152
    Special operations against the Soviet Navy in the late 1960s, 119-128
    Enlisted crew members in the late 1960s, 118, 121-124, 151-153, 164
    Harmonious racial climate in the late 1960s, 164-165
    Decommissioning in 1994, 255

SubACS (Submarine Advanced Combat System)
    Developed in the 1980s for the *Los Angeles* (SSN-688) and *Seawolf* (SSN-21) classes, 203-205

Submarine Base, New London, Connecticut
    Saved from possible closing in the early 2000s, 260

Submarine School, New London, Connecticut
    Training for prospective submarine officers in 1958-59, 36-41
    Revision of the curriculum in the late 1960s-early 1970s to reflect the increasing role of nuclear submarines, 129-131

Submarine Squadron Ten
    Home-ported in New London, Connecticut, in the mid-1970s, 153, 159-161, 165-166, 169-170

Submarine Squadron 12
    Role of in development issues in the late 1970s, 175-180
    Sinking of the former submarine *Sealion* (LPSS-315) in 1978, 176

Submarine Warfare
    Training at Submarine School in 1958-59, 36-41
    Training operations by the submarine *Capitaine* (SS-336) in the Eastern Pacific in 1959-60, 41-53
    Relationship between diesel submariners and nuclear submariners in the mid-1960s, 113
    Special intelligence operations against the Soviet Navy in the mid-1960s by the nuclear submarine *Snook* (SSN-592), 92-100
    Special intelligence operations against the Soviet Navy in the late 1960s by the nuclear submarine *Sturgeon* (SSN-637), 119-128

Revision of the Submarine School curriculum in the late 1960s-early 1970s to reflect the increasing role of nuclear submarines, 129-131
Role of Submarine Squadron 12 in development issues in the late 1970s, 175-180
Issues in the early 1980s on what type of attack submarine to build, 183-184

Subroc
Test firing by the nuclear submarine *Sturgeon* (SSN-637) in the late 1960s, 126-127

SubSafe Program
Implementation on board the nuclear submarine *Snook* (SSN-592) in the mid-1960s following the loss of the *Thresher* (SSN-593) in 1963, 95-96

Telfair, **USS (APA-210)**
Attack transport that was decommissioned soon after DeMars reported aboard in 1957, 29-31

Thunman, Vice Admiral Nils Ronald, USN (USNA, 1954)
As executive officer of the nuclear submarine *Snook* (SSN-592) in the mid-1960s, 91, 98, 102-103
Service in the Bureau of Naval Personnel in the late 1970s, 174
Served 1982-85 as Deputy Chief of Naval Operations (Submarine Warfare), OP-02, 201, 205-208

Tomahawk Missiles
On board U.S. submarines in the 1980s-2010s, 233-234

Torpedoes
On board the submarine *Capitaine* (SS-336) in 1959-60, 50-51
Sinking of the former submarine *Sealion* (LPSS-315) in 1978, 176
Computerization of torpedo firing tables in the late 1970s, 177

Total Quality Management/Leadership
Not embraced by the nuclear submarine community in the early 2000s, 228

Triton, **USS (SSRN-586)**
The prototype S3G reactor was used for training at West Milton, New York, in the early 1960s, 55-56

Trost, Admiral Carlisle A. H., USN (USNA, 1953)
Served 1986-90 as Chief of Naval Operations, 213, 216, 226

Turner, **USS (DD-834)**
Training cruise for midshipmen in the summer of 1956, 17-18

Virginia **(SSN-774)-Class Submarines**
Funding for in the early 1990s, 226-227, 235

Design characteristics, 237-239, 243

Vladivostok, Soviet Union
In the 1950s the commanding officer of the submarine *Blackfin* (SS-322) was relieved after surfacing in the harbor at Vladivostok, 32
Patrols in the vicinity by the nuclear submarine *Snook* (SSN-592) in the mid-1960s, 101, 105-106

Ward, Rear Admiral Norvell G., USN (USNA, 1935)
Served in the early 1960s as Commander Submarine Squadron 14, 71, 74

Washington Post, The
In 1987 published a revealing article about a disputed selection board for Navy captains, 215-216

Watkins, Captain George C., USN (USNA, 1944)
Older brother of future CNO James Watkins, he commanded the stores ship *Mars* (AFS-1) in 1965-66, 108-110

Watkins, Admiral James D., USN (USNA, 1949)
Commanded the nuclear submarine *Snook* (SSN-592), 1964-66, 91-110, 147, 156, 159
Served 1982-86 as Chief of Naval Operations, 201, 207-208, 252
As Secretary of Energy, 1989-93, 225-226

Webb, James H., Jr., Captain, USMC (Ret.) (USNA, 1968)
Served 1987-88 as Secretary of the Navy, 215

White, Captain Steven A., USN
In the early 1970s worked for Admiral Hyman Rickover in the Navy's nuclear power program, 133, 136, 182
In the late 1970s was in the submarine directorate of OpNav, 182, 185

Wilber, Ensign James R., USN (USNA, 1957)
DeMars roommate who was married in Idaho soon after graduating from the Naval Academy, 20, 29

Wilkinson, Rear Admiral Eugene P., USN
As Commander Submarine Flotilla Two in the late 1960s, banned wine on board his submarines, 121

Wood, Midshipman Noel T., USN (USNA, 1954)
Leadership style at the Naval Academy in the mid-1950s, 14
Served in the Bureau of Naval Personnel in the mid-1960s, 113

Wright, Captain Richard M., USN (USNA, 1941)
Was badly burned in 1949 during a fire on board the submarine *Cochino* (SS-345), 43
As Commander Submarine Division 51 in the late 1950s, administered the process by which DeMars qualified in submarines, 43-46

Yap, Caroline Islands
U.S. Navy association in the early 1980s, 192-194

Yates, Captain William K., USN (USNA, 1948)
Commanded the nuclear submarine *Snook* (SSN-592) in 1963-64, 89

Zumwalt, Admiral Elmo R., Jr., USN (USNA, 1943)
His Z-gram directives in the early 1970s had more impact on the surface Navy than on aviation or submarines, 163-164